DANCING IN THE RAIN

A JOURNEY OF FAITH

TINA ROSE COLEMAN

WESTBOW
PRESS®
A DIVISION OF THOMAS NELSON
& ZONDERVAN

WestBow Press books may be ordered through booksellers or by contacting:

WestBow Press
A Division of Thomas Nelson & Zondervan
1663 Liberty Drive
Bloomington, IN 47403
www.westbowpress.com
844-714-3454

wedding pictures by John A.Nelson

ISBN: 978-1-6642-8528-6 (sc)
ISBN: 978-1-6642-8527-9 (e)

Print information available on the last page.

WestBow Press rev. date: 12/19/2022

WHY I WROTE THE BOOK

I am not a swashbuckling daredevil. I am an ordinary woman that has been on a journey with my sovereign God who has done extraordinary things for me. His story must be told. It is a story of a personal relationship with me that required patience, encouragement, and love beyond measure on His part. Many have asked when my "book" would be written, and I felt compelled to begin the journey once I gained perspective of God's impact on my life. It's a story of a simple, human, woman that encounters a glorious God and lessons he had in store along the journey. I didn't choose to write the story; it chose me.

DEDICATED

To my Sovereign God, who did extraordinary
things for an ordinary woman.

To Gib, my gift from God, who always anchored me by holding
my hand. He has supported me through every step of life.

ACKNOWLEDGEMENTS

I could never acknowledge all the people God has used to support, inspire, and direct me in life. From Oklahoma to Minnesota; from my neighborhood to Europe, Asia, and Africa; and from my childhood to my senior years. The list is endless. However, a few made my life an adventure. I offer them my sincere thanks and admiration.

> To my life-long friends from all areas of our lives. From Oklahoma, Sydney Wilson and Judy McDowell. From our small church that trained and nurtured us; Pastor Richard Wohler, Joan and Bill Murphy, Mary and Ron Hall, Mary Ann and Tom Dahlquist, Sharon Dahl Hinz, Kathy and Brian Nelson, Norm and Debi Swanson, and John and Jan Petersen. From our church of 30 years: Pastor Galen Call, Vonnie Folsom, Tom and Leann LeBarr, Steve and Louise Wentworth, and countless others.
>
> To God's Army: Pastor Todd Olson, Berean Sunday School Class, Leon and Pauline Hass, Elizabeth Vonderharr, (a fantastic supporter of our mission work and getting this book published.) And undying gratitude for our prayer warriors that spent countless hours on their knees supporting us. I fear we wore out your knees.
>
> To Doctors that fought for our daughters especially Cich, Etzwiler, Thatcher, the African team, the Mayo Clinic Staff and all the attending doctors in Illinois.

To those that contributed to the book through music and pictures: Will Lopes, musician, John A. Nelson, wedding photographer, and even Blake Sheldon who unknowingly made an impact on Wendy.

To our childhood families that taught us how to love, live, stretch ourselves, and respect authority, especially God's. And to my siblings, Patricia Frost and Carl Rose.

Most of all to my family. They have always been there for me, but especially through writing this book. They have lost me to the computer, heard my frustration, encouraged me, proof-read and been patient. Gib, our kids, grandkids, siblings.

To God, my Father, Jesus, my Savior, and the Holy Spirit, my companion. Without these three, I would never have learned to Dance in the Rain.

DANCING IN THE RAIN

CHAPTER 1

Suddenly the sound of shots rang out. Pop, pop, pop! Oddly, they were only on the metal roof above me. Instead of cowering, the small children began to laugh and shout and run into the courtyard. Afraid they would be targets for the shooters, I ran after them. The bright Kenya sunlight blinded me as I ran into the courtyard. Before me was the most joyful celebration of dancing, shouting, hand raising, and singing I had ever seen. In spite of the bright sunlight, rain was falling. The children spun round and round as the rain danced on their heads. The noise I had heard had not been gun shots, but rain drops pounding on the metal roof. The joy of these children was exhilarating to see. Soon their delighted teachers joined them, and large circles formed as they danced and swung arms. We Americans stood in wonder with silly grins across our faces. Our first thoughts were to grab an umbrella, but instead, they began pulling these silly white people into their delighted circle. As clouds moved in the rain poured down, and we caught their exuberance and joy. I looked across the compound here in Nairobi, Kenya, to see my daughter, Teri, with her head tilted back with rain dancing on her face. How alive and happy she was. She was soaking in every moment, joy, and laughter her heart could absorb. At 42 she was a triumph of determination, inspiration, and endurance, and, as a mom, I could only pour out my thanks to God for allowing me to see her so happy. With a grateful heart I stood still, smiling at the picture of life-giving water, gratefulness, and happiness played out before me. Rain was not an imposition to these people. It was a gift of life to them. How privileged we were to be able to experience this with them. Pure gratefulness was the base of this celebration.

Content in my own world, I felt a tug on my arm and looked down to see a beautiful, black face staring up at me. I shook my head trying to clear my brain -fog and listened as this tiny girl spoke to me.

"Why aren't you dancing?" She asked innocently.

"I was just watching," I replied.

"No," she protested. "You need to dance with me!" She pulled me into the circle where we began praising and singing, swaying, and swirling. Teri looked across the heads of the students with delight in her eyes. We had spent so many hours, days and weeks preparing lessons to teach here and now the most teachable moment of all was for us, the Americans, to learn the gratefulness and reliance on God these people experience daily. Water was so valuable in this African nation, and God was pouring it out on us. Dancing in the rain was the only proper reaction. So, I danced and thought of an arduous journey I had traveled to reach this place where I understood this simple lesson.

It all began 35 years earlier. Thinking back to that day I remembered even then the rain was pelting the window. The big drops slammed into the pane, adhered, and began sliding down. Each drop looked like it was dancing against the glass until it was shattered and gave up to a power greater than itself. The sky was gloomy and dark. Tears slid down my cheeks much like the rain drops. There was no sun, no joy, no bursting of enthusiasm, only a heaviness that engulfed me.

I glanced over my shoulder to see my seven -year -old, Teri, lying in a bed with multiple tubes supporting her. What had the doctor said? Malignant? How could that be? She is so healthy and energetic. This can't be right.

I turned back to the rain and gloom that seemed to absorb my feelings. Why are the heavens opening up today? It seemed the angels were weeping with me. Can the angels really feel my pain? How long has this nightmare been going on? Had it really been only two days ago when Gib, my husband, noticed the odd swelling in her neck? So many doctor's appointments, tests, rush to surgery and then that word - MALIGNANT.

As we sat with the doctor after the surgery, his words ricocheted through me striking pain and burning themselves into the depth of my being. "Malignant, malignant, malignant," was all I heard. The walls swayed and the antiseptic smell of the hospital turned my stomach into a churning pit. He had said that word so calmly that there must be a mistake. He must not be talking about Teri. I withdrew my mind from his gentle words. Perhaps, if I refused to listen, it wouldn't be true. I could get up and run out the exit, and the nightmare would stop. Right? Why were there tears on my face when I didn't believe a word he was saying? Why was Gib pulling me into his chest if this was all wrong?

My anguish was so great I wasn't aware of anyone around me until I heard our pastor speak, and I looked up to see the surgeon was gone.

"Tina, he didn't remove all hope. He said many positive things. Do you hear me, Tina?" Pastor Wohler gently spoke.

"I don't want to hear any of it," I half shouted. "I don't want to hear any of it."

Mary, my dearest friend, slipped from her chair and walked down the hall to the restroom. I knew her own pain was too great to stay and watch mine. Gib, Pastor, and I just sat in silence. Deep Silence.

Finally, Gib said, "Honey, are you ready to go and see her?"

Unable to answer, I stood up. "I need to go to the restroom first," I muttered as I rushed down the hallway. Alone at last, I bent over the sink to wash my hands and looked up into the mirror. The person looking back was pale with mascara streaks down her cheeks. I washed away all the evidence of my earlier weakness and stood face to face with myself. I waited for the reflection to say something. Nothing, only silence prevailed. I just couldn't give in to my fears or grief. I knew I had to be brave for Teri. Suddenly, Mary stood beside me. Without a word, she slid her arm around my waist, squeezed and we turned to leave the restroom.

I briskly headed back to Gib but didn't look at his face for fear the anguish in his eyes would destroy what little control I had. We walked silently through the doors of the Intensive Care Recovery Unit. The walls were lined with beds holding "sick" children. I spotted one child sitting up at the far end of the room and headed toward her. Thank heavens my child wasn't "sick" like the others.

But Gib stopped by the side of a different bed with a child connected to multiple tubes, a heart monitor beeping, and an oxygen mask. He gently called my name, and I turned to see him stroking her hair. Suddenly, I knew it was Teri, my Teri. "Oh God, why have You let this happen to her? She is only seven years old. This is too great a burden to place on her." I silently shouted those words to God.

I quickly reached her bed and became painfully aware of the strain the four-hour surgery had been on her tiny body. Her light brown hair hung limp on the white pillow. Her skin appeared white even though she had a beautiful summer tan. I needed to touch her, and, as I laid my hand on her cheek, I realized how cold it must be to her. She opened her eyes and tried to speak but closed them again quickly and drifted into sleep. Slowly, I leaned forward to kiss her, and wiping my tears from her face, I felt the overwhelming need to ask her to forgive me. This was all my fault! But I will have to deal with that later. I heard her stir and looked to see her staring at me.

"Mommy, is it over?"

"Yes, dear. Just rest now and get strong."

Determined to give her all my strength, I zipped a protective armor over my heart and decided I had to deal with my own guilt when I was alone. For now, she would not see me cry. Gib had gone out and was returning with Pastor and Mary. She was delighted to see these special people. He whispered to Teri until she opened her eyes to see them. Gib's eyes met mine, and I was surprised at how blue they shone. His outward control was stemming from an inward peace. He led me from the room telling the nurses where we would be.

We slipped into a conference room and began calling relatives. Although my mind was in turmoil, I recited what I knew like a mechanical toy that had a recording installed. I repeated results of the surgery and the preliminary diagnosis and prognosis. I heard an occasional question, answered them, and was relieved no one cried or gasped. Quickly I hung up before anyone could cry or express their dismay. We called Shane, our oldest child, and his mature 12-year-old voice asked immediately how Teri was. We told him the surgery was over, she was in recovery and the final results would come tomorrow. He handed the phone to Wendy, his little sister, as her tiny, exuberant, 4-year-old voice bubbled with excitement. She told me how Shane had picked her up from the neighbor's and brought her home to cookies and even milk. I closed my eyes and listened to her giggle. Her world was completely normal. Mary took the phone from me and asked Wendy if she wanted to spend the night at her house. Wendy squealed with delight, and Mary arranged with Shane to pick both of them up. Now I only had Teri to think about.

Relieved the phone calls were over, we checked in on our sleeping girl and then went outside to walk Pastor and Mary to their cars. We had been inside so long I wondered when the rain had stopped and changed to the hot summer day. How odd the day had passed normally outside without turmoil. Once inside again, we passed the front door of the hospital, and I recognized the gold truck pulling up in front. Encouragement flooded over me as I saw our friends, Bill and Joan climb out. Bill was always a stabilizing force in everything he did. Surely, Bill would come in and make everything normal again. I knew I could count on Bill!

Following our greetings, we settled in a small alcove to talk. They listened intently as we told them about the surgery and prognosis. When we mentioned cancer, Joan stiffened, and her eyes clouded over.

Joan said, "Mary called us and told us that Teri had Hodgkin's, but I didn't know that was cancer."

I explained that Hodgkin's, a type of lymphatic cancer, was predictable. We had been told they had great success and expected Teri to do well. That's all we knew so far. To my relief she didn't start to cry. I was becoming obsessed with not crying. I didn't want anyone to see what was eating me up on the inside, and I certainly didn't want to see fear in them.

Still, because I trusted Bill and Joan so much, I relaxed in their presence. They wanted to see Teri, so we warned them of her appearance. We described the tubes running in and out of her, as well as her paleness, and the huge bandage on her neck that was hard like a cast so she couldn't move her head. We warned them that she drifted in and out of sleep but would probably know them. With that, we took them in to see Teri.

Teri was awake staring at the ceiling. The moment she spotted them her tiny smile grew into a genuine burst of joy. Bill and Joan were like Uncle and Aunt to her and Teri loved them deeply. I backed away to give them room beside her bed. Joan held Teri's hand, and they expressed their love, concern, and relief at seeing her. She soon closed her eyes to rest. I was aware of everyone around me, but I no longer made the effort to converse. I sensed thoughts were flying around in my brain, but I was unable to catch hold of them and form questions or sentences. This sensation was strange and foreboding. I envisioned I was floating into the corner of the room near the ceiling and watching everyone, including myself, function. I wondered if I stayed up there in the corner if my body would leave the room without me. Fatigue became oppressive, and I wanted to be silent and just stare.

Soon, Bill broke the silence saying it was time to get dinner, and Teri immediately clutched Joan's hand. "You'll stay here with me, won't you?" Without any more conversation, Joan pulled a chair beside the bed, took Teri's hand in hers and announced, "They will have to chase me out! I'm staying right here!"

Gib, Bill, and I went to a nearby restaurant and had a quiet dinner. Bill sensed the need for distraction, and we talked about frivolous things. When we returned to the hospital, I heard a nurse ask Gib if I was going to spend the night at the hospital. He didn't hesitate or even look at me when he answered. "No, I think she needs to get some sleep and I am sure she wouldn't get it here."

Bill and Joan turned to leave but I was confused. I wondered why Bill wasn't making all things right? I had counted on him "fixing" things. Why was he letting me down? Why was there still all this weird reality around me?

As they left, Gib bent over Teri and said, "We're going home to sleep, Honey. We will see you in the morning. Sleep well."

"Bye, Daddy. Night, night Mommy." I touched her cheek, and she closed her eyes already breathing evenly. The nurses reminded us they were there all night so we could call anytime, and we started our trek home.

At first, we rode in silence. Gib reached across the seat and took my hand and still we remained silent. Abruptly, I inquired. "What are you thinking about?"

"Everything and nothing in particular," he responded. "How about yourself?"

"I was wondering why we ride along in silence."

"I guess we don't need to talk. Just knowing the other one is there is enough for the moment."

I continued, "We have said very little about Teri."

"Perhaps we feel the pain but don't want to talk about it. That would only make it more real. I don't have to ask you how you are feeling because

I am feeling the same way. Why all the questions? Are you uncomfortable with my silence?" he inquired.

"Not really. I was just wanting reassurance that you understood my silence." I enjoyed the trust that existed between us, and I was aware I had not laid out my pain in front of God all day. Quick appeals, yes, but nothing deep. I feared if I approached Him, I would lose all control. Yet, I sensed God wasn't demanding that of me right now. He knew, like Gib, that I trusted Him, and I didn't need to use words. So, even with God, I sat in silence.

Long past midnight I fell into bed desiring a long-awaited rest. Gib quickly drifted into sleep, but I continued to toss and turn unable to relax. I slipped out of bed and went into another room. There, I relived the day in my mind and was surprised when no tears came. I demanded, "Where are you, God? Why don't you draw near to me? No one else can help, why don't you?"

He seemed to say to me, "I am right here, Tina, where I have always been. I have been waiting for you to notice my presence. You need to open the armor around your heart so I can minister to you."

I grabbed my Bible and it fell open to the story of Abraham and Isaac. I read it again and wondered about Abraham. How could he trust God so much? He didn't yell at Him like I wanted to. He didn't question God like I was doing silently. Abraham had such a deep, genuine, and complete faith, and his actions spoke of that faith. I began appraising my own faith. I really did believe that God loved Teri even more than I did. I was sure He was in ultimate control. Suddenly, I realized I didn't mistrust God, I was mistrusting myself. I wasn't sure I was strong enough to meet the days ahead. Instead of focusing on my faith, I was focusing on my weaknesses. I needed to change my focus to the strength of my Savior. I knew I didn't believe God because others told me to. I believed God because I trusted Him myself. I rested in his arms while tears escaped my closed eyes. They weren't tears of desperation but tears of joy when I realized that my faith was truly genuine. I rejoiced I had a God strong enough to focus that faith on. I renewed my promise to God, gave Him back the complete control of my children, and slipped back into bed. I was confident now that tomorrow I could face whatever life had to deal to me because God had my greatest treasures in His hands. Finally at peace I fell asleep.

Suddenly, the ringing alarm clock jarred me from a deep sleep. Turning it off, I snuggled into the curve of Gib's arm and closed my eyes. The birds outside the window chattered to each other in their morning ritual. I couldn't remember what day of the week it was but my contentment in Gib's arms convinced me it wasn't important. I sat up in bed and a sudden pain struck me in the stomach. Falling back on my pillow, I wondered what could be causing this tightening around my middle. There was no sound in the house, no laughter, not even arguing. Then, I remembered why it was empty. Shane and Wendy were at Mary's and Teri – oh Teri!

I grabbed the phone and dialed the number of the ICU. The nurse reassured me Teri was fine and had a restful night, and all her tubes had been removed. Relieved, we dressed between phone calls and hurried down to see her. Soon, they moved and settled her in a regular room and Mary brought the other kids.

Teri was sitting up in bed when they arrived, and Wendy proudly presented her with a homemade card. Shane had helped Wendy make it, and it was covered in stickers and glitter. Teri loved it, but tired easily and was ready to sleep. We went to the playroom where Wendy busied herself with new toys.

Sitting opposite Shane I inquired if he knew what cancer was. He shrugged and said he knew the word. I explained that we have all kinds of cells in our body and cancer is just an uncontrolled growth of cells. In Teri's cancer, that group joined together in a mass. That mass is called a tumor and made a swelling like the large lump we saw on Teri's neck. They cut her tumor out. They would continue checking to be sure there weren't more bad cells anywhere else. Then, she would have to have some radiation treatments, kind of like x rays, to be sure it is all gone.

He simply asked if she would be okay, and I related the doctor's assurance and he simply nodded and stood to go back to her room. Staring at him as he walked away from me, I realized he had faith in what I said, and in the doctors. I wondered if his faith was as simple as that or if he was keeping doubts to himself. We had never lied to him, so he didn't expect it now. He believed if we said she would be okay that she would be. Suddenly, I realized I was the one doubting. God had never lied to me. Was my faith as trusting as Shane's?

Wendy spotted I was free, and as I stood up, she ran full force at me with her arms extended. This was a drill we often did, and I held out my hands as she grasped them, climbed her feet up the front of me, arched her back and flipped her legs over her head landing on her feet. Giggling, she said, "Does Teri have to stay here until her owie gets all better?"

"Yes, but you can come see her every day."

"Can I ride up and down in her bed?" she inquired.

"When she is feeling a little better," I laughed. I picked her up and clutched her tightly to me. She tried to wiggle free, but I clung to her. I wanted her energy and vitality to pass to me. She began kicking, trying to free herself.

I whispered, "Wendy, please give Mommy a hug."

She sensed the change in my voice and stilled. First, she put her tiny hands on each side of my cheeks and smiled. Then, she wrapped those tiny arms around my neck and squeezed as hard as she could. Giving me exactly what I needed, she was done, wiggled loose, and dropped to the floor as I wiped my tears from the top of her head.

We turned to see Shane walking toward us, and he reported Teri was sleeping. Wendy slipped her hand into Shane's showing she was ready to go home, and Gib asked Mary to drop them off at our house as we would return there soon.

Mary said, "I have to do something first," and she quickly turned and walked toward Teri's room. Behind her back she carried a Raggedy Ann doll she had made for Teri. Soon she returned empty handed and smiling.

Gib returned to Teri's room, and I walked the kids and Mary, my life saver, to the elevator and then watched them head to the parking ramp. Once out of sight, I turned and found my way to the tiny chapel. The lights were low and gave a feeling of calm as I sat alone in the room. Not really knowing why I was here, I began first praising God and rejoicing in who He was. Quickly I switched and began telling Him I didn't want to learn endurance, faith, and trust. I wanted Him to wave a magic wand over me and give me all the traits of the saints. Afterall, I was too hardheaded, and it would take forever for me to learn those lessons. Only God knew this was all my fault because of that naive agreement I had made with Him. Now, I wanted out of our agreement. "Release me," I verbalized. Fearing tears would escape and show my weakness in my faith, I jumped to my feet and hurried out of the chapel. I rationalized that God would understand. He knew I didn't want to talk anymore.

As I started down the hallway, I saw a team of doctors outside Teri's room. Fearful, I quickened my step. In the center of them all was Dr. Cich, the oncologist I had met before the surgery. He introduced other specialists, pediatricians, and residents and said they would make up her team. As they filed into a room a resident stopped me.

"Mrs. Coleman, I should warn you that you should expect marital problems. Very few families withstand the stress of a child with cancer without major marital problems."

Stunned, I could only reply," Thanks for the warning."

As I turned to enter her room, I pondered what he had just said to me. Surely God wouldn't allow something to happen to my marriage as well as my child. My God would never allow that.

I heard Teri ask Dr. Cich what was wrong with her. I watched as he laid his folders on the end of her bed, sat down in no apparent hurry, and began quietly talking to her. His tan coat hung loosely from his shoulders, and his limp, brown hair fell carelessly across his forehead. At that moment, there was no other person alive to him. He explained to her she had cancer, explained cancer in terms she could understand, and then he told her she would be in the hospital for a few days undergoing tests. She asked if the tests would hurt, and he honestly told her most would not but two would.

Accepting all he said she asked, "Then, will I get to go home?"

"Yes," he smiled. "When the tests are all over you get to go home." Satisfied, she shifted her attention to her new Raggedy Ann that Mary had made for her, and the doctors left.

Later that day, Pastor returned, and Gib and I went with him on a walk outside the hospital. As the sun beat down on me, I knew it was time. I had to own up to this being all my fault. So, I began by relating an experience I had with God a few months before. I explained that after reading the Bible verse about laying up treasure in heaven, I realized my greatest treasures were my children. God wanted me to give them to Him without reservation. I knew I could sacrifice my belongings, my money, my things, and myself, but was I willing to sacrifice my children? Would He take them to the other side of the world as missionaries where I wouldn't see them? What would He do with them? What would He demand of me? For 45 agonizing minutes I had fought God. Then, tearfully, I had relinquished each child to Him. Now, because of that, He was 'calling in the chips' so to speak. He was demanding I make good on my promise that Teri belonged to Him. If I had never agreed, she wouldn't be in that bed right now. It was all my fault, you see?"

Gib remained silent and Pastor looked at me with compassion.

"I don't think you are understanding God right now." he said. "Tina, God knew what was coming. He prepared you for this by having you give Him your children. He is not vengeful. He is not 'calling in the chips.' He is walking with you through this and only wants you to realize He loves Teri even more than you do. This is not in any way your fault. Your promises to God allow Him to shower your kids with love, protection, and angels. You have been given a beautiful example of how He prepares us for battle. He has girded you up with His armor. He has prepared you for battle."

I was astonished and comforted by his words. Of course, he was right. God had prepared me, and I could rely on His strength and not mine. Relieved, I nodded and slipped my hand into Gib's. It was a relief to not carry this guilt any longer.

Although weary, I was battle ready. Never had two days taken so long to live.

Our Three Kids

THE FAITH OF A CHILD

CHAPTER 2

The week that followed was filled with cards, gifts, and greetings that poured in at home and at the hospital. The last time I had counted there were 85 cards the nurses had put on the wall as well as a pile still on her table. There were so many stuffed animals there was hardly room for her in the bed. Every day there were tests to determine where the cancer had taken hold in her body. Teri faced each test with complete trust and faith in what the doctor had told her and even trusted the resident to hypnotize her during the bone marrow extraction and only managed a small moan. We were allowed to take her home for a day mid-week and she was thrilled to be outside and on the way to her home. She hadn't asked many questions and I wondered if she really grasped it all when, on the ride home, she quietly asked, "Why did all this happen to me, Mommy?"

I slid my arm around her and pulled her to me quickly. Unsure if I held her tightly for her confidence or mine, I prayed silently as I went ahead. "I honestly don't know why, Teri. Maybe God will let us know someday, but maybe we will have to wait until we are in Heaven before we know. There are reasons why God allows things. It might be for you to grow up into a compassionate person, or a person that cares about other people and their problems. It might be for your Daddy and me to trust God more. It might be for one of us to share Jesus with someone in the hospital. It might be for reasons we never find out. The main thing is that we believe that God knows more than we do and will give us strength to make it through all of this. I guess He knows the reason and He will take care of it. What do you think?

"Oh, I was just wondering if you knew why. I have already told all the nurses about Jesus and the doctor too. I think I might want to grow up and be a doctor. I'd know what it feels like to be sick, and some doctors don't know that. But I don't know why Pastor prays for me every time he visits."

Confused, I replied, "What do you mean?"

"Well, God already knows I am there. We asked Him once to take care of me so why do we have to keep asking Him over and over?"

Staring into her huge blue eyes I could only answer, "I guess because we adults don't always have as strong a faith as you do, Dear." I turned to look out the window at the blue sky and thought "and a little child shall lead them."

Teri loved the attention she was receiving from all our friends, but she really soaked up the attention from the doctors and nurses. She made friends with every staff member and her bubbly personality won over even the grumps. Often, I would return to her room to find a nurse watching Gilligan's Island with her and both laughing aloud. I learned that she had promised not to cry when they gave her a shot if they promised to watch TV with her. She was like an invading worm that enters you and wraps itself around your heart and won't let go. One nurse got too close to Teri and couldn't give her a shot as she didn't want to hurt her. These people became an intricate part of our lives at a critical time in our daughter's life and we felt so secure leaving her in their protection when we went home each night. Dr. Cich came daily to see her and explained more each day as we began to understand this monster that had invaded her body. There was no way of knowing where this cancer came from, but this disease was predictable. They had to pinpoint exactly how far down her body it had progressed. Then, they would radiate that area. Next, we would have a second radiation series that would hit the next area the cancer would attack. That should prevent it from going any further. The percentages of beating this were higher than most any other cancer. The prognosis was really good.

As I shared this with my parents, they only patronized me. Their dealings with cancer had always ended with terminal results so they listened but didn't really hear anything I was saying. I had already run into others that seemed to scoff at my positive attitude. I repeatedly questioned

Dr. Cich to clarify until one day I explained my problem to him and asked if he was being completely honest with me.

He appeared unoffended by my questions. Completely at ease he responded, "Tina, most people think of cancer as a death sentence. However, we are making great strides in many types. This cancer is one of the few that is predictable. I can gather medical journal articles for your parents if you think that would help. Most importantly, you must understand that for me to give you false hope would be a very cruel game for me to play. I have nothing to gain by losing your trust. I am now and always will be completely honest with you."

I stared deep into his soul through most caring eyes I'd ever seen and responded. "I have watched you with Teri. Your compassion and care for her won me over early. I have felt I could trust you completely, but I keep getting undermined by their bland voices and attitude. Forget about the articles. I think only time will convince them and other doubters."

Smiling, he said, "Just be sure to let me know whenever something is bothering you. Teri is my patient, yes, but her family is important to her well-being. If something is bothering you, it will filter down to her. I need you to promise me you will alert me to any problems. We are all in the same boat together. I will always be honest."

"Thank you for your understanding. I promise to be honest with you too."

Teri's last "test" was to be a second surgery to "stage" her cancer. They would remove her spleen, pull lymph nodes from throughout her body. From that they would know exactly where the cancer was. That morning came and it began to rain. Why did it always rain on days like this? I was annoyed at having to carry an umbrella and the gloomy sky hung over me and I couldn't smile. Again, rain was interrupting and making everything inconvenient. Were the angels crying with me?

I was even more nervous than the first surgery. Afterall, the first time she had something awful they needed to remove, but now she seemed fine. As we waited, I felt like the floor was on fire so I jerked my feet up with each step. I paced as we waited for them to come take her away. Could I refuse to let her go? Could I not release her to the doctors and tell them they couldn't cut on her? As they wheeled her away through the big doors, I felt desperate and a failure that I hadn't even fought them off.

The hours drug on as we waited. Gib's parents were driving the 13 hours from Oklahoma. Although the surgery was only four hours, I felt like we had spent at least 13 hours waiting. Time seemed to tick by in tiny increments before the surgeon finally entered to say all was well and Teri was in recovery. After seeing her and knowing she was fine, my tension level didn't ease. The adrenaline in my system seemed to grow and I was so antsy I couldn't sit down. Later, I was happy to see Gib's parents truck pull up in front so we could go outside to greet them. We brought them up to date and went inside to take them to Teri. Bill and Joan arrived at the same time, and I grew more desperate to escape. After showing the Colemans in to see Teri, then the nurses' station, and finally the waiting room I announced, "I am going out to eat."

Gib was visibly shocked by my statement. "Honey, my parents just got here."

"Fine, they can go out to eat with us."

Gib's mom quietly said, "We already ate in the car. We could stay here."

I jumped on that and replied, "Okay, that's great. I am leaving. Who is going with me?"

Usure of what to do, Bill and Joan started out with me and after a quick conversation with his parents Gib joined us. "Tina, that wasn't exactly nice. My parents just arrived."

"I know. I will apologize later, but I just had to escape. I want a nice meal and no talk about Teri for a couple of hours. I'm sorry I need that, but I do."

Two hours later, refueled by laughter, a good meal and no crisis, we returned to the hospital to find Gib's parents relaxing in the waiting room. After checking again on Teri, we all went home. I apologized to Gib's parents and his mom was quick to put me at ease declaring that no apology was needed. She added she felt I was doing fantastic; I wasn't convinced I was doing so great. The next few days Teri loved having her grandparents visit every day, and they also spent time with Shane and Wendy before leaving a few days later.

The doctors never gave us a number for the stage of Teri's cancer, instead, they showed us the level of known involvement and the area that would be covered by the first round of treatment. There was no involvement in the lymph nodes below the abdomen so that was good news. She would have two rounds of radiation but no chemo.

Finally, the day came to take Teri home and I felt strange. I had come to depend on these capable people. What if something went wrong at home? I felt frightened and unsure of myself. Teri sat down on the side of the bed and began crying. She kept repeating that she didn't want to go home. Was she afraid? I told her I would bring her back to see her new friends next week. That relaxed her and she got up and began making rounds hugging all the nurses. Many of them had tears in their eyes as they said goodbye to her. They had tended to her every need, watched TV with her, made her laugh, and she had brought sunshine into their lives. They would miss her, and we all experienced a bitter-sweet parting. Once home we taped all the cards to her bedroom door overflowing onto the walls. She climbed into her double bed surrounded by so many stuffed toys and clutching the Raggedy Ann doll Mary had made for her, she fell asleep content to be home.

A week later Gib, Teri and I went to the University of Minnesota's Medical Center. It was a massive complex of buildings, and we parked in a huge lot and took a shuttle to the main entrance. I grasped Teri's hand; afraid I would lose her in this maze laid out before us. They gave us directions and we followed arrows and colored lines down stairways and through crowded hallways until we saw the sign for the radiation department. Once we entered, we were greeted by efficient personnel that was knowledgeable and expecting us. Still, I searched for the familiar face of Dr. Cich even though I knew he wouldn't be there.

After they examined Teri and took x-rays, they took us on a guided tour. The huge radiation machine hung from the ceiling above a small table. Teri would lie on the table and a plexiglass shelf would be lowered over her chest. They would place thick blocks on the shelf that would block areas they wanted to protect like her heart, lungs and reproductive system. Whatever wasn't blocked would be radiated. It would only take a few minutes and we would be on our way each day. The first round would take 6 weeks. She would have a month off and there would be a second precautionary round. We should complete the first round by November and the holidays would be our month off. They told us of a closer parking area near a backdoor we could enter, and we were set.

As we left Gib asked if I thought I could find my way around the next day. I was good with directions and thought I would have no problem but said I would start early tomorrow just in case.

"Come on, you two," Teri shouted. She ducked into a staircase and took off. For the next five minutes we followed her through the maze leading back to the front entry with her never missing a turn. I turned to Gib laughing and said, "If I get lost, I will just follow Teri."

I decided to drop Wendy off at the neighbor's the next morning as Kathy had volunteered to keep Wendy each day as we went to treatments. Her daughter, Charie, was Wendy's best friend and they would play together. This was a gift of love that would allow Wendy to avoid daily trips to the radiation center. Shane would be building a fort with his neighborhood buddies but would have Kathy to check in with as needed. Relieved the kids were taken care of, Teri and I headed to treatments.

Even though we parked in a new place and entered a different door, Teri confidently led me to the radiation department. She had an Xray and returned to sit down on the floor and played with a toy while we waited to be called. I soon became aware of someone standing near me and looked up into the blank eyes of the radiation doctor.

"Mrs. Coleman, there is a large spot on the x-ray of Teri's lung, and we fear the cancer has spread to her lungs. We need you to take her upstairs for a more in-depth test."

I politely got directions and started out the door with Teri. Inside I was rebelling at the cold presentation of this fact that just shattered my world. This may be an everyday event to them, but my daughter had a monster inside her, and it was alive and moving. Discouraged, I wondered if maybe, just maybe, we really wouldn't be able to beat this thing after all. I couldn't protect her from this, and I was helpless. Once the test was completed, we went back downstairs and waited. Finally, the doctor appeared again and quickly stated the spot was cancer and they would be removing the blocks over her lungs. They were ready for her treatment, and they took Teri away. I sat stunned and unable to figure out what I should be doing. So, I just sat and waited. I remember nothing else the rest of the day.

The next day I found myself functioning like a robot. Determined not to allow myself to "feel" anything so I couldn't be hurt again, I did just what was needed and continued to the next task. We walked along the tree-lined walkway from the parking lot to the backdoor of the building and Teri skipped and twirled in front of me. Her energy was bursting and so far, there was no visible side effect of her treatments. The walkway was picturesque and should be captured in a painting or on a postcard. At the end of the path, near the door, was a stone bench. Teri raced to reach it and seated herself like a queen on her throne. As I neared, she patted the space beside her declaring I should sit too. Once I was settled, she announced she wanted to pray.

"God," she respectfully spoke. "I want You to do me a favor. Would You not let it snow until my treatments are over? I want to walk this path every day and I don't want snow in the way. Since I know You can do anything, I ask You to stop any snow from coming. Thank You, God. Amen."

"Okay, Mommy, we can go on now." She jumped up and ran to the door. Stunned, I said nothing.

Numbly I followed. Would God be able to honor her prayer? She had complete faith He would, but we did live in Minnesota, and this seemed an unreasonable request. However, we were supposed to be done with treatments by early November, so maybe, just maybe, we could make it. I whispered a prayer that He would honor the faith of a little seven-year-old.

As usual, Teri made friends in every department we went to. Her energy penetrated the hospital, the other patients, and their families, and they looked forward to seeing her each day. Her favorite fellow- patient was a small girl about her age named Susie. The two of them spent hours together playing on the floor and waiting their turn at radiation.

Teri continued to spread her joy everywhere. Each morning the school bus driver stopped at the end of our driveway to pick Teri up so she wouldn't be jostled by the other kids. She had made friends with the driver, a college boy, and he watched over her with great care. She invited him to attend church with us and he came for the Fall Kickoff Sunday when we had a potluck meal. Ben was good looking and personable and the single girls at church rushed to grab a seat at our table. Ben only had eyes for Teri, and she basked in his attention.

Teri would attend half days of second grade and after dropping Wendy off at Kathy's, I would pick Teri up from school. She would eat her lunch in the car, and we would go for treatment. She had no trouble keeping up at school and did well in her studies.

One day my dad called to say that Daddy, Mother, my Granny and Granddad were coming to Minnesota from Oklahoma. Our family was thrilled. We prepared for company and then my sister called announcing her family was coming from Chicago area too. This frightened me. It was too many people to have quality time with anyone. Yet, I busied myself with preparations in spite of my hesitations. I envisioned my Granny stretched out on a bed with me sitting on the floor next to her. She would talk to me and share her great wisdom and I would share my fears and forebodings. I knew I could absorb strength from this great woman of God. Sadly, it didn't happen like that. As I feared, there were so many people in the house and so much hubbub that deep conversations didn't happen. Everyone avoided asking how we were really doing. Mom did go to one radiation treatment with Teri and I, but she seemed removed from the situation and was careful not to become involved. I had worn this mask of strength for so long I couldn't remove it. I knew they all felt this would be the last time they would ever see Teri, yet I had no strength to try to try to tell them she had a good prognosis. I hid my pain in my heart. As their car drove away taking my dreams of meaningful times with them, I knew that once again I had depended on people to meet my dreams. Once again, my dreams were shattered.

Home became an escape for me as things seemed almost normal there. Shane and Wendy still needed my attention. Shane had become quiet and kept his thoughts to himself. I knew he had more "knowledge" of cancer than Teri or Wendy and wondered what friends might have said, but we never discussed it. He talked about the fort he and his friends were building and the neat bike path they had set up. His schoolwork never suffered, and he appeared to be taking it all in stride. He had asked Jesus into his heart a couple of years before. It happened one Sunday night on my sister, Patricia's birthday. He had been in his room after church and came out to tell us he had asked Jesus to be his Savior. Since it was Patricia's birthday, we called and told her. She was excited. Shane already shared his biological birthday with her husband, Newell, and now he shared his spiritual birthday with her. Since I knew he was a believer, I felt he would survive this chaos fine. Also, he thought of Teri as a little kid and that separated him from her a bit. However, he seemed to be gradually changing from an outgoing personality to a quiet and reserved guy. The question was if this was just a natural evolution of his personality or caused by the crisis around him. Years would pass before he connected the change in himself with Teri's cancer.

Wendy loved to cuddle in my lap with a favorite book for me to read to her. I loved this "normal" time and knowing she was healthy. She seemed to be totally obedient until one day I was putting away laundry and moved the hanging clothes in her closet. The entire back wall was covered in crayon. I had stopped her from coloring on the walls, or so I thought, and she had quietly retreated to her closet, moved her clothes to cover her evidence, and colored to her heart's content. Sneaky, sneaky, Wendy!

She had always been deathly afraid of doctors and shots and when at the hospital she would often scream when a white coat approached. She began to see that doctors were not always doing things that hurt Teri and one day Dr. Cich approached us as we sat in hallway. She jumped up on the seat behind me and peeked out at him. Slowly, he extended his hand and asked her if she would shake hands with him. Reluctantly she slowly extended her leg to him. Grinning, he took her leg and shook it. Laughing, I said, "I guess you have made great in-roads. At least she isn't yelling"

Beautiful fall days passed as treatment after treatment happened. Teri had very few side effects. She lost hair along the neckline in back, she lost a bit of her appetite and was a little less energetic than before. Overall, she was doing great. A nice gentle fall rain fell on us as we exited the car. About half-way to the door, Teri doubled over in intense pain. Stomach cramps gripped her, and she hung onto me to keep walking. As we stumbled into the backdoor of the radiation unit, Teri vomited all over the doctor. He rushed her into a back room as I tried to apologize and followed as quickly as possible. He turned and asked me to wait in a side room as he picked her up and placed her on a gurney. A few minutes later he stood before me and asked what had happened. I told him she had said she wasn't hungry, but I had made her eat her sandwich. I just didn't want her to lose strength.

Slowly he shook his head. "Never, never force her to eat. Her body tells her what it needs. We will have to reduce the amount of radiation given in half and that means the treatments will continue to late December to get all the amount she needs. There will be no treatment today."

I only nodded. Once she was rested, we started to the car. The rain, wretched rain, fell and I couldn't open an umbrella to protect us because

I was trying to hold her upright. She was too big for me to carry and too weak to walk of her own accord. So, we clumsily lurched our way to the car. She quickly fell asleep as I drove home.

"Oh, God, I am so sorry I made her eat. Now, how can You honor her prayer if we will continue treatments until late December? Oh, Father, what an inhumane mom I am to force her. Yet, she has such faith that You will do this. What do I say to her? How do I help her understand reality? Help me handle this." The rain became a trickle and did nothing to ease my pain.

Rattled, scared, confused, and disappointed I drove home through rush hour traffic. Finally, I allowed tears to slip out of my eyes. I felt defeated. "God, help me," I cried. My faith isn't as pure and strong as Teri's." The rain had stopped, and I continued crying as I came up over a rise in the road to see God in front of me.

The sky was aflame with the most magnificent sunset I had ever seen. Pinks, blues, oranges, whites, and even colors I had no name for burst across the sky. Oddly the colors contrasted yet flowed into each other. The hues seemed to change as I looked at them. The beauty was hypnotizing. I struggled to keep my focus on the cars around me as I looked at this masterpiece God had painted for me. Of course, others were getting the benefit from it, but He had painted it for ME! I was overwhelmed with gratefulness. God had shown up for me. I wished I was able to capture the picture on canvas, but I am not an artist. Besides. God's work was beyond any painting I had ever seen. He was speaking to me. Somehow this would all be okay. He had shown me the faith of a child and the power of my Father. I was reminded to put my trust in Him not in people. He would never disappoint me. My confidence was renewed and although I didn't know how, I was confident He would somehow honor the prayers of a little girl with complete trust in Him.

It wasn't long for the Adversary to attempt to crush my trust. A few days later, in early November, I awoke to a full-blown Minnesota blizzard. Apprehensively, I entered Teri's bedroom to tell her and before I could say anything she whispered, "Mommy, it hurts to breath." I rushed to call the doctor and after a quick trip to the local pediatrician, Teri was diagnosed with pneumonia. Now there would be no treatments for 5 days. During those days, the sun came out and melted the snow, and the first day back to treatments we found our backdoor path clear all the way. Feeling good again, Teri skipped along in front of me.

"Isn't it great, Mommy? God only let it snow when we couldn't come for treatments. I told you He would keep the snow away." Was she naïve or too trusting? I couldn't shatter her dream, so I said nothing. Still, I wondered how honest I was really being with her. After all, honesty isn't just answering questions. Sometimes it meant you had to bring up the unspoken things. On the other hand, was her faith just that much stronger than mine?

Teri's 8th birthday was quickly approaching. She had been showered with so many gifts and since she appeared so mature, I suggested we have a "Santa Anonymous" birthday party. I explained that each girl would being a gift for a child that wouldn't get a Christmas gift. We could all go together to turn the gifts in. We would still have a party, cake, games, etc., and she would still get family gifts.

She sat pondering and staring at the ceiling. Finally, she said, "I guess that would be good. I have lots of stuff and I wouldn't want a kid to not have a Christmas present to open. Would I be able to buy a gift too?" Assured, she seemed excited.

The party was a huge success. Each girl explained her gift and the age of the kid that would enjoy it. We played games, did a craft, ate cake and ice cream, and piled into cars to take our precious gifts to the drop-off site. Each girl giggled as she put her gift in the bin. Teri slipped hers in last and they all cheered.

I went to bed that night thinking how mature and unselfish my daughter was. Years later she told me she had felt cheated that day that no gifts were for her. I realized I had expected a lot from an eight-year-old.

Instead, I had seen maturity in Teri in other ways. Teri had spent so much time in hospitals and with medical personnel I wondered how she was relating with her friends. Gib and I had agreed that we would rather her hear all things from us first, so we tried to be completely open with her. I knew I had to talk to her about the possibility of death. So, the next day as we came to her stone bench, I asked her to sit and rest with me.

Trying to keep apprehension from my voice I began, "Have your friends at school asked about what is happening to you?" She nodded. "Have you been able to explain it to them?"

"Sure, Mom. I just told them I had two operations and I have cancer."

"Do they know what that is?"

"I don't know."

I continued, "Some of them may have a relative or friend that has had cancer and they will know about it."

"That will make it easier then," she replied.

"No, that could make it harder."

Her eyes showed surprise and she asked, "Why?"

Taking a deep breath and praying constantly, I dove in.

"Many people have cancer. It can grow anywhere in your body. Since it just means any uncontrolled growth of cells, the word cancer really takes in all sorts of diseases. It can grow slowly or quickly and there are all sorts of treatments. Some have operations, radiation, pills, and medicines. All of these are to stop it from growing. Most people win the fight and get well. But some cancer can't be stopped, and that person will die. Some of your friends may have had a relative or friend die from cancer. Some of them may think you will die too."

"Does it hurt to die?"

"I don't know. Sometimes it does. What do you think happens to you after you die?"

She thought a moment before answering. "Well, I would go to Heaven to be with Jesus."

"Right." I agreed. "That doesn't sound like a terrible thing to happen, does it?"

"Am I going to die, Mommy?"

"I don't know for sure. I can't tell you what will happen tomorrow or the next day. But I do know that Doctor Cich feels we can beat this thing and he is sure these treatments will work and that you won't die."

"Why did you tell me all this?"

"I wanted to be sure that you understood everything. Someone might ask you if you are going to die and I wanted you to think about it before they asked."

We sat holding hands for a long time until she raised her head to look me in the eye. She smiled as she spoke.

"Mommy, the doctor is a lot smarter than my friends. If he thinks that I am going to be okay, then so do I. The funny thing is that friends might think they know more than my doctor. I'll just tell them to wait and see who knows more, them or my doctor."

With a nod of her head that showed she was finished; she stood up and began pulling me along. I stared at my grown up eight-year-old. She didn't listen to the world around her, but to the people that should know. My little girl with cancer would be reassuring others instead of having them reassure her. She had a tiny body but a mature spirit. I learned I couldn't protect her from the pain of maturity, but instead in many ways, maturity already had a hold on her.

JOURNEY TO THE MOUNTAINTOP
CHAPTER 3

Christmas was quickly approaching, and the heavy snow had held off since the November snow. Our final day of round- one treatments was cold and blustery but following the treatment, Teri and I stopped on our stone seat again to rest. We had sat here so many times. We had discussed death, love, fears, God, and we had listened to the silence. I would miss this special time with Teri. We both knew after weeks of rest; we would return for another round of radiation. By then snow would have covered our path and we would be forced to go through the front of the building instead of the back door. Smiling at each other, we automatically bowed our heads to pray. I prayed first thanking God for all the ways He had met our needs. Then, Teri prayed and specifically thanked "her Father" for not letting it snow on treatment days even though we took a lot longer than expected. I still had my head bowed when she began tugging on my coat.

"Look, Mommy. It's starting to snow."

I raised my face to feel the snowflakes touch my cheeks. Warmth flooded through me. "Thank you, God, for honoring the prayer of a little girl. Her faith is so complete."

We drove home through the snow and the true beginning of winter that year. We didn't see our yard again until spring. God let nature loose and it changed seasons that day.

A month passed quickly, and we welcomed a new year by returning to our daily trips to the University. I continued to drop Wendy at her friend

Charie's house and off we went. This second round of radiation treatments were a preventive measure, and they were directed at her abdomen. Destruction of any possible loose cancer cells was the purpose, and Teri had gained strength and vitality over the break. She was physically ready, and the first few treatments went well. The third day Teri was excited to see her friend Susie again. We had rejoiced with Susie when she had finished her treatments before Christmas, and it was fun to see her again. The girls sat on the floor playing and the two mothers sat to talk.

Delighted to see them, I started the conversation, "I am really glad we have run into each other again. Is this your first recheck?"

Her eyes clouded over, and she looked over my shoulder as she responded, "This is not a recheck. We are here for treatments. They have discovered cancer in Susie's liver."

I struggled to control my response. My emotions were whirling around inside me, and I asked her gentle questions while wondering if I could focus enough to hear her answers. While she spoke, words were screaming in my brain. "This tiny precious child has a recurrence. That could only mean . . . What could it mean for us? Susie finished all her treatments and now she must start over. Will we? Will Susie die? Will this happen to Teri? Oh, this poor family." Although unspoken, the words burned into my being. I hoped my responses to her were okay as my mind was certainly not in the conversation.

Silence fell between us with nothing to say. I certainly couldn't voice all the thoughts in my head. Soon, Teri had her turn at treatment, and afterwards we escaped to home. That night, when I told Gib, I saw in his eyes all the same thoughts ricocheting around his brain that had occupied mine earlier. Again, there seemed there was nothing to say.

For the next two weeks Teri and Susie saw each other daily. Susie's dad began coming more often, usually carrying her to and from appointments. Then, suddenly, Susie didn't come anymore. Disappointed, Teri turned her attention to her doctor.

She asked if she could make brownies for him as he always seemed sad. I agreed and she was convinced that would be the right weapon to make him smile. She took her precious gift to him the next day. After treatment, he asked to see me alone.

"Mrs. Coleman, I don't think you and Teri realize the seriousness of what we are doing here?"

"Excuse me. I don't understand your statement."

"Well, Mrs. Coleman, you and Teri are always happy and now bringing me brownies, and I think you don't realize we are in a battle for Teri's life against cancer."

I took a deep breath before answering in a quiet but controlled voice. "Doctor, we are very aware of the monster inside Teri. We are just choosing to be positive."

He shook his head and sent me on my way. Later, as I walked in our house, the phone was ringing, and it was Dr. Cich. He was laughing when he said, "Tina, would you please keep that 'Baptist' optimism under control. You are upsetting my radiologist."

I burst into laughter. "I guess he called you to tattle on me."

"I tried telling him you understand, and it is your faith. I'm afraid he didn't buy it. Yes, he says you smile too much."

"He should try it once in a while." I replied.

"Okay, "he continued. "I promised him I would call you and make sure you knew what cancer was. So, consider yourself called." We both laughed and hung up. It was delightful to have something to laugh about with all the darkness around us.

One problem that continued to gnaw at me was how to discipline a child with cancer. I tried to ignore my dilemma and hoped Teri wouldn't do anything "big" where I would be forced to react. I had sent her to her bedroom for minor infractions of the rules, but I pondered what I was going to do if something more substantial reared its head. I remembered when Teri was in the hospital a nurse had approached me.

She began with, "I am sorry if I am overstepping my boundaries, but I feel compelled to give you some advice. Teri is so sweet that you will be tempted to let her get away with behaviors you wouldn't allow if she were healthy. Don't do that. Discipline her like she was healthy. The doctors expect her to make a full recovery and grow into an adult. You don't want her to grow into a selfish 'prima donna' that no one can stand. I know from experience. They didn't expect my son to make it so I gave him free reign and he grew into a person the world can't stand. The world is paying for my mistake. I just wanted to share that with you." Then, she slipped away.

So far, there hadn't been a problem. One morning I entered her bedroom to find her playing with some of Shane's most precious belongings. He was gone so I knew she hadn't gotten permission and he would never have allowed it even if he were home.

I gathered up the things, said a couple of curt remarks and started out of the room.

"Aren't you going to spank me?" she asked.

I paused with my back to her. The showdown had arrived.

As I turned to face her, she continued. "You used to always spank me for getting into Shane's things before I was sick."

Realization flooded over me. Remembering what the nurse had said about discipline, I stared into the eyes of my now eight-year-old woman in a child's body and said, "Yes, that was always the rule." I sat on the bed, pulled her over my lap and swatted her a few times. She sat up with tears in her eyes and her response astonished me. "I guess I'm all better now, eh?"

"Yes, I think things are back to normal." I left the room whispering a prayer of thanksgiving and prayed He would keep things "normal" for a while and keep her from growing into a self-centered and selfish adult. I asked Him to give me strength to do my job. I hoped whenever I doubted my job of a parent, He would remind me of that day.

On one of the trips to Dr. Cich's office for blood tests, the rain was again pouring down in sheets of water all over us. I muttered to myself, "God, one of these days you are going to have to explain to me why you always have it raining on me at inopportune times." We were running late so we hurried down the hallway to the lab. I heard someone call Teri's name and turned to see a man holding a tiny, bald child in his arms. Instantly, I recognized the man as Susie's dad, but the tiny bundle didn't resemble Susie at all. I spoke to her, but she buried her head in her dad's neck. I was repelled by what I saw. She was only a shell of the vivacious child I had seen at the University just a couple of weeks before. Teri said nothing, just nodded to her parents.

After a short conversation, I knelt down to try to help Teri navigate this difficult social situation. "Teri, remember Susie?" I asked. "You used to play with her every day at treatments."

All Teri could manage was to nod her head and tug on me to move on. I made excuses as to our need to hurry and off we went to the lab. I had trouble breathing and wondered why I was able to have a child that was healthy and running down the hallway while beautiful Susie was . . .

Once around the corner, Teri abruptly stopped. "Was that really Susie?"

"Yes, I am afraid it was."

"Why does she look like that?" I closed my eyes but all I saw was Susie's big black eyes staring at me.

As calmly as I could I explained that the radiation had not stopped her cancer, so Susie had taken chemo or pills to try to stop the cancer. That is why her hair had fallen out. This was something else to try. Her voice sounded more like a statement than a question.

"It's not working is it, Mommy?"

"I don't think so," was all I could muster.

Once back in Dr. Cich's exam room she blurted out, "We just saw Susie, Dr. Cich. She's not getting well, is she?"

His eyes never left hers. He squatted down in front of her and placed his hands on her shoulders. "No, Teri. Nothing is working with Susie. I am afraid we have done all we can. She just isn't getting better."

"Oh," she replied and fell silent.

He continued his examination of Teri and kept quietly reassuring her that she was looking better than the last time he saw her. Finally, Teri spoke. "I know I am getting better; I am just sad Susie is not."

"Me too," was his reply.

After he examined her and pronounced her in great shape, Teri went out to visit with the nurse and I turned to him and asked, "Are you telling me everything?"

"I thought we settled that in the hospital. Don't you trust me?"

"Yes, I do. But after seeing Susie today I just don't know what to worry about."

"Do you have to worry about something? Why not let me do the worrying?"

I stared at him again. Could this man carry the worry for me? Did he carry the worry of all his patients? His steadfast personality gave me the answer. He already was.

"Okay," I said. "If you will promise to tell me when to worry, I won't worry until you tell me to."

"I think that sounds like a good plan. I promise I will not keep things from you and when it is time for you to worry, I will alert you. Until then, let me carry the burden."

Relieved, I smiled and let go of my concerns. This small man sure had mighty shoulders.

Two weeks later Teri's second round of treatments came to an end and our trips to the University stopped. We celebrated with a special dinner and now the waiting game began. We would have monthly trips to see Dr. Cich, but life would generally get back to normal. Teri started to attend school full time and soon discovered she didn't have friends. Their lives had continued without her. It was worse than the first day of school in the fall when all kids were anxious to make new friends in their class. Teri was now the outsider, and it would be an uphill struggle for her to make new friends. We were so thankful for her neighbor childhood friend, Julie, that never left her side.

The first couple of months Dr. Cich examined her from head to toe and announced she was doing fine. Slowly apprehension begin to drain from me. If Teri complained about an ache or pain, I was more relaxed, and my calls to Dr. Cich became fewer and fewer.

On the third monthly visit, Dr. Cich entered the room and appeared exhausted and pale. When I commented on his appearance, he didn't look at me when he said, almost under his breath, "I have been up most of the night the last few days. Susie is no longer with us."

"Since when?" I asked.

"Night before last."

I knew he was trying to protect Teri, but he looked so vulnerable himself. Finally, I asked, "How do you do it? How do you keep your objectivity when something like this happens?"

He saw Teri was reading a book, so he sat down and turned his chair to face me.

"Honestly, sometimes I don't. Some patients you get closer to than others. If I know from the beginning my chances aren't good to beat it, I keep my distance. But Susie had a tumor we almost always beat. I was as shocked as her parents when treatments didn't work. I didn't want to give up, but nothing changed. And then, she was gone." I had seen the compassion of this man. This father of seven loved children and wanted to give them a fighting chance. This was breaking his heart.

Teri must have been listening because she got down off the exam table and walked over to him, took hold of his arms, and spread them and walked into his inner circle. She put her arms around his neck and said quietly, "We can be sad together," as she hugged him tightly. Tears flowed freely from all three of us until he leaned back and said, "Well, Sunshine, we need to look you over."

"Okay," she replied, "but I am doing just fine!"

As he examined her, I was again overwhelmed with guilt. Why was I allowed to have a daughter doing fine while they are burying Susie? I wasn't a good person, and they weren't bad people. This didn't make sense. I felt so undeserving and so guilty to be rejoicing in the health of Teri. Somehow, everything was all confused. Later when I learned this was survivor's guilt, and others felt the same way, but I still didn't like the feelings it created in me. It lingered for a long time. That night, Teri reminded us to pray for Susie's parents, and she remembered for many days and weeks ahead.

Life was returning to normal and that meant it was speeding up. We had lived so many months agonizing over each hour of every day that now a 24-hour day passed at a speed capable of breaking the sound barrier. Positive things were happening all around us and we rarely kept up with everything. In this new and rapid lifestyle, our dear friends, Norm and Debi, got married and all the family rejoiced in the event. Joy was our new partner in life.

One day Teri came into the living room and said, "Mommy, I asked Jesus into my heart." There were lots of questions followed by joyous hugs and congratulations for making such an important decision and she closed the discussion with, "Now, I want to be baptized."

Two weeks later, Pastor Wohler had the privilege of baptizing Teri while our friends and family watched and rejoiced together. Lots of tears of joy were shed that day and much celebration and rejoicing.

A year later when summer came, we traveled to Nebraska to spend some time with Norm and Debi and to meet their newborn baby Most of us went to a rodeo for a few hours leaving Deb at home alone with their new baby and our cocker spaniel. She tied her to a stake in front of the house and she began to bark as Deb went back inside. The cocker spotted a monster in the corral, and she constantly barked at it. The monster, a prize bull, got madder and madder as this annoying creature kept barking.

Finally, the bull broke through the corral and prepared to attack the dog. Pawing the ground as it bellowed forced Deb to look out the widow curious at the racket. At that moment Deb panicked. She ran full- force toward the dog yelling at the bull, "No, no, no! Stay where you are."

She got between the bull and the dog, pulled the stake out, and drug the dog toward the door. The bull continued pawing the ground, snorting, and lowering its head as Deb kept running and yelling, "No, no, no!" Once safely inside the house she began to realize the ludicrous stunt she had just pulled. She had taken on a bull. Frightened, she called Norm's uncle to tell him the bull was out free and in a matter of minutes men arrived to corral the bull and rebuild the fence. When we returned from the rodeo Deb told her story. We were all stunned she had taken on that bull. Our dog and Deb were safe, but the result could have been so different. For years ahead we laughed about the brave and foolhardy behavior she showed that day.

Gib's parents had bought a camper and invited us to go east with them that summer. It was quite a feat to pile a family of five with a cocker spaniel in with Gib's parents and Aunt in such close quarters. We all quicky adapted and found a place to ride in comfort and the fun began. There were only three beds, so the two older children and the dog slept on the floor. Wendy cuddled with Aunt Jinkers, her soulmate, and we set out on our adventure. We headed to New Jersey to Gib's brother's family. Shane sat up each night with Gib's parents and us and we played cards while Jinkers, Wendy and Teri slept. It was a wonderful, bonding time with the grandparents and was so successful it became an annual summer event from then on. The trips across the United States gave us the opportunity to show the kids the mighty and beautiful country we called home.

Fall was a new school year with Shane starting 7th grade, Teri starting 2nd grade (Attending school full days), and Wendy starting pre-school. I got a job teaching at the pre-school so I could spend the day with her. Next, we started a new ministry at church – a puppet ministry. Gib, Shane, and I were all puppeteers while my dear friend, Kathy, (I call her my little sister) ran the audio, planned, timed the programs, and prepared the props as the performance went on. Teri and Wendy usually sat on the first row and laughed and enjoyed the performances as we traveled to other churches. Others joined us and we all stretched ourselves in new ways.

One weekend Kathy gave us a beautiful gift by volunteering to watch the kids so Gib and I could take a much-needed escape weekend. Our trip up north to Duluth was one long date and we savored the time alone with no crisis on the horizon.

The school year passed with only minor problems, and we looked forward to the summer ahead. Soon, we started our second adventure in the camper. We set off to the West and the granite edifice, Mt. Rushmore. The older kids were impressed at the size of the heads on the mountain. Wendy was more interested in chipmunks running around.

The heat that traveled with us brought the opportunity for the first tradition established for camper trips. Each afternoon, the kids gathered around Aunt Jinkers and chanted "ice cream, ice cream, we all scream for ice cream." Jinkers loved ice cream and thought a proper day would include it. She, in turn, would convince her brother (Grandpa, the driver) to find the nearest DQ or equivalent. It was always a great time of the day.

The nights were spent in campgrounds. The days were driving, stopping, touring, and driving more. Wendy was usually in the back beside Jinkers, Teri near Grandma at the table. Grandpa was driving, Gib in the passenger seat, and Shane in the middle perched on an ice chest between them. There was lots of testosterones in the front! I traveled between groups listening to old family stories recited by Grandma and Jinkers.

At last, we reached Yellowstone. With beauty all around us, we watched geysers, saw deep pools, and animals. We saw a moose and evidence of bears but no encounter. Wendy repeatedly asked who set Old Faithful to go off when we were there to see it, and how they made it shoot up into the sky. No explanation satisfied her. It was just too complicated for her brain.

Other highlights of the trip included seeing bison running freely, Custer's last stand battle ground and the delightful stop at a prairie dog town that frustrated our cocker who couldn't catch them. The Rocky Mountains kept us craning our necks so not to miss any beautiful sight. We checked out the huge bones at the Dinosaur National Monument, and the kids' imaginations ran wild. They roared at each other and pretended to be Tyrannosaurus Rex for hours. A quick turn south and we were soon floating in the Great Salt Lake. After making so many memories, we were ready for the long trip home and our own beds.

Since Teri no longer had a spleen, she took penicillin daily. Her recurring strep throat stopped with the prophylactic penicillin and her overall health improved. I was still fighting being overprotective, and she even had a mild bout of shingles. Even the lingering financial strain seemed so small a price to pay for Teri getting stronger each day. Our friends started coming over again and all the kids filled the house with joy and delightful noises of their friends. Finally, finally, life was full, busy, happy, and we had a joyful household again. The daily annoyances seemed insignificant as they paled in the light of cancer.

At a regular follow-up appointment Dr. Cich asked, "How long has it been?"

"Over three years," I responded.

"Well, I am no longer concerned with the possibility of recurrence. I think we only must watch for secondary problems that might arise from the radiation treatments. Bring her back in a year unless a problem arises."

Thrilled I asked, "Are you saying she is cured?"

"Now don't put words in my mouth. I told you from the beginning I never use that word unless I can tell you where the cancer came from in the first place."

I retorted with a smile on my face, "I just think you are overly cautious. However, I'll accept it that way if you can't bring yourself to say that word."

A warm laugh erupted from deep within him. "You know I am only a phone call away. See you in a year."

"You seem awful happy, Mom'" Teri said as she redressed.

"I certainly am, and we are going to Dad's work and make him take us out for lunch and celebrate!"

We had made it up the mountain to the top. Throughout the Bible God had so many important things happen on a mountaintop. From Noah's ark settling on top of a mountain, to Abraham preparing to sacrifice Isaac, to Moses' meeting God on Mt. Sinai receiving the law, to even Jesus giving a Sermon on the Mount. These and many other events throughout the Bible took place on mountains and now I found myself on the mountaintop with Him. Here, so close to Him, nothing seems mundane. The mountain seemed motionless up there and it was easy to rise above circumstances and view His majesty. Although not physically on a mountain, I closed my eyes and thanked God for leading us out of the valley and keeping us moving upward. He had revealed Himself throughout the climb, prepared us for each step, and made each step easier. Now, we'd made it! Wow! I loved the view from up here.

LIGHTNING STRIKES TWICE

CHAPTER 4

Another Summer burst onto the scene with enthusiasm and freedom we hadn't felt in years. Free! Free from Cancer! Free from worry! Free to run, dance and jump. There were no signs of the dreaded big "C" and we graduated to bi-yearly appointments. Shane was fifteen and working on getting his driving permit. Wendy was seven and busy with her friend Charie. Teri was free from treatments and busy with her friend, Julie, and we all wanted to turn loose and take a summer vacation; and like all families, money was short. So, we planned a garage sale.

Teri was looking forward to "playing store" with real money and customers. Our family had worked so long and hard choosing things we could part with. Shane and Wendy had sorted through all the toys and games, and we had an abundance of things to attract people. Teri's only disappointment was her best friend, Julie, from down the street, was sick and on bedrest and wouldn't be at her side to sell, sell, sell.

The moment we raised the garage door people poured in and the fun began. Seven-year-old Wendy was a little sad to see her "baby" toys taken away, but she was smiling when Teri kept her up to date with how much money she was making. About mid-morning Teri began to fade. Before long she began dragging herself inside to rest a bit and then drag herself outside to sit in a lawn chair and watch the people come and go. The garage sale was quickly losing its excitement for her. Shane took over her position and the day slowly wound down.

The second day of the garage sale, Norm and Debi, who had recently moved to St. Louis, called and invited us for the 4th of July. We quickly held a family meeting, and we decided the money for the garage sale would be well- spent and equally enjoyed by all if we took off for St. Louis. We had less than a week to finish the garage sale, pack up, donate the leftovers, pack our bags and head out.

The day before we were to leave, I took the girls swimming. Teri swam a few minutes and then climbed up and stretched out in the sun along the edge of the pool.

"What's the matter?" I inquired.

"I'm only tired, too tired to continue swimming," she answered.

"Well, our trip to St. Louis will be a great time for you to catch up on your rest." I shrugged it off and went about preparations for our trip.

Early the next morning we loaded the car and started out. Teri quickly fell asleep and slept most of the morning. Occasionally, she woke asking for a pop or bathroom stop but quickly fell asleep again. Before long, the bathroom stops got overly frequent and we cut her off drinking anything. I wondered if she had a bladder infection. Since I had never had one, I had no idea if that was a symptom. We tried distracting, chastising, and encouraging. Still, she would cry and beg to stop every 15 minutes. We were relieved to reach St. Louis and have Teri near a bathroom. The next day she was tired, had a sweet- smelling breathe like a strong orange, and we only allowed her to drink milk or water. How I wished I had asked Julie's mom more questions about the virus she had.

The next day we all piled into the car and went downtown St. Louis to see the Arch. Teri walked slowly and said she wanted to see the Arch but just could not walk there. Quickly, Gib hoisted her onto his back, and we covered the block to the Arch. He sat her down on a stone wall. She stayed there while we walked away to an incline overlooking the Mississippi River. The sun felt warm and gentle, there was little noise, and all was well. Gib and I both turned back toward Teri. Fear engulfed me as I saw a child that looked like she had just escaped a concentration camp. Pale, so white she seemed to disappear, clothes that fit fine a week ago were hanging from boney shoulders and she appeared to be fighting to hold her head up. Panicked, I turned to Gib for reassurance only to see the same fright in his eyes. Neither of us said a word as we raced down the incline and grabbed her demanding, "Honey, where do you hurt?"

"No, Daddy, I don't hurt. I just want to go home and sleep." He scooped her up in his arms as I gathered the other kids and we raced to the car. What could be wrong with her? Back at Norm and Deb's house, we settled her in bed, found she had no fever, and she fell asleep.

When I went downstairs Deb finally asked, "Are you afraid that her cancer is back?"

"Oddly, no." I replied. "At her last exam just a couple of weeks ago, the doctor had said she was cancer free. He shied away from using the word cured since he can't prove where it came from in the first place. However, we were promoted to bi-yearly check-ups. and we are just to watch for side effects. Perhaps she has the same virus her friend has. We will leave first thing in the morning and head for the doctor's."

Two days later I sat in the doctor's office with Teri sleeping in the chair beside me. Soon, we followed the nurse back to the exam room passing Dr. Cich in the hallway. He looked up smiled at me and then glanced down at Teri. He couldn't conceal the shock on his face. He turned away as we passed. A few minutes later I could hear him pacing outside our exam room. I remembered the agreement we had made earlier. I had promised not to worry until he told me to, but now I could hear him pacing. Finally, I yanked opened our door to see him standing, staring at me. He stepped into the room trying to act like he had just been coming, greeted me without looking at me, and went directly to Teri's side. Throughout his examination of her he never turned back to look at me.

"She has no fever?" he asked. "Do you remember if she had a fever with her original diagnosis?"

My heart skipped a beat as I said, "No, she didn't."

Still not looking at me, he continued saying, "take her over to the lab and have some tests run and bring her back here to rest until we get the results."

With that, he turned, muttered "It's time to worry," and was gone before I could ask any questions. A strange sensation swept over me. I felt as if I was occupying a space here and now, but I was reliving events three years earlier. I remembered back then I had tried to convince him she only had a virus. However, this wasn't the same. Only two weeks ago he had said he wasn't worried about the cancer any longer. "No, God, please! Don't let it be that. I know the chances are terrible if the cancer returns. Please, God, don't let it be that. You won't let this happen will you, God?"

Teri spoke barely above a whisper. "Does he know what's wrong with me yet Mommy?"

"Not yet, Honey. We need to get blood tests and come back here and wait until we do know."

Okay with my answer she slipped back into that deep, deep sleep and as I stroked her hair, I smelled that strange, sweet breath again. How long will we have to wait? What will the answer be?

We didn't wait long. He had put a rush on the results and suddenly he threw open the door and had a huge grin on his face. "It is not Hodgkin's!" he proclaimed as he collapsed into the chair. "You have no idea how long I stood outside the door waiting to come in. How I feared it was active again."

"I know, I heard you out there," I laughed. "But I never really thought it was Hodgkin's again."

He sat up straight. "Why?"

"Because a couple of weeks ago you said it was fine."

The joy in his eyes turned to concern as he carefully chose his words. "Don't you realize that could all change in a month?"

Below my breath I muttered, "I guess I should have been more afraid."

Instead, I looked at him and said, "You have told what it isn't, but what IS it?"

"I think I know, but I want a specialist to look at her first. Take her over to the hospital and I will have him see her there."

"Wait," I said. "What do you think it is?"

"Diabetes," he stared at me waiting for a reaction. I didn't know enough to react. "Take her over to the hospital and I will meet you and Gib there."

He turned and walked to Teri's side and gently called her name. She woke and smiled at the man she trusted so much. "Teri, I want you to go to the hospital and I will run more tests there. You don't have cancer."

A pitiful cry began deep inside her. Too weak to protest much, she cried from deep within and the sound stabbed my heart. The cry continued all the way to Joan's house where I would drop Wendy. As Wendy listened to her sister sob her little heart was breaking to see the big sister, she idolized reduced to sobbing. Wendy crawled across the front seat and sat as close to me as possible. "Mommy, make her stop crying."

"I wish I could, but I can't. She will stop when we get to Joan's. I called Daddy and he will be there. We will take her to the hospital to get well and you will stay with Joan for the afternoon."

We rode on in silence, holding onto each other and listening to the one we loved crying pitifully in the backseat. All the while I was asking myself if I should be afraid.

Gib was sitting on the deck drinking a coke when the girls and I arrived. Joan hadn't seen us in two weeks and the change in Teri was reflected in her eyes as she struggled to greet us. Teri settled into a chair as Gib followed me inside.

"What is it?" he asked.

"Dr. Cich thinks she has diabetes," I began to cry as I answered.

"I don't know anything about diabetes, but I am relieved it isn't cancer," he replied "Why are you crying? Surely nothing is worse than us having to fight cancer again."

I sputtered, "I am just so afraid. I don't really know what I am afraid of. I am so confused. I just know I don't think I can fight anything again."

Gib placed his hands on my shoulders, turned my face up to his and said "Oh, come on now! You are and always have been a fighter. This won't beat you anymore than cancer did. Let's go and take her to the hospital, Dr. Cich is expecting us."

A few hours later the pediatric endocrinologist, Dr. Etzwiler, came by and assured us the diagnosis of diabetes was correct. When he asked if we had any questions, we realized we didn't know enough to ask any. He promised to spend time with us tomorrow explaining everything and left.

Teri looked so pale, fragile, and small for a 10-year-old. The tears began to slide down my face.

"Why? Just plain and simple, why? Why does so much have to happen to such a little girl?" I wasn't sure if I had said that out loud or not. No one answered. There was no answer.

"Why can't it happen to me instead?" The tears flowed harder, so I walked to the end of her bed so I would not disturb her.

Finally, Gib spoke barely above a whisper. "Tina, you know as well as I do that you will never find the answer to the question why. For a reason we don't understand, God has allowed it to happen to her instead of you or me. Our job is not to ask why but to accept it and help her live with it."

"That sounds too simple," I brushed him off. "I already did that once. I accepted her cancer, I lived with it, I fought it, I taught her to live with it. Why do I have to do it all over again? Didn't I get it right the first time? I don't want to teach my daughter to give herself shots, to eat just certain things, to learn all about diets and stuff like that. I can't! I just can't! Maybe I am too dumb to learn it all. But I just can't do it."

I fled from the room into the hall ashamed of my own weakness. I stopped in front of a window. I was relieved when I saw it wasn't raining like crisis time before. That must be a good sign. Rain had always intruded when things got bad. I cried without restraint until I sensed Gib standing beside me. He wasn't touching me, he didn't say anything, he just stood there. Looking out at the people bustling here and there didn't stop my feeling of bewilderment. Then, I knew. This feeling of bewilderment would never leave me again. After all, just a few hours ago hadn't Dr. Cich revealed that having faith she was cured was a "false hope?" In desperation I turned to God.

"Please, God. You are the only absolute I have. Help me!" I pleaded.

"Let me climb back up into your arms and rest. You've let me rest before, let me rest now." I stood perfectly still waiting, absorbing His love and remembering the scripture that seemed to be challenging me. In Psalm 46 He says, "Be still, and know that I am God." Slowly, very slowly I felt His strength become mine. He would give Teri the strength she needed through me. He was in control. He would take care of it all He would fight whatever battle she needed if I would just let Him. Positive I had God on my side, I opened my eyes to see Gib leaning against the window staring at me.

"Are you okay?"

"I think so. I just needed a little perspective. I'll be fine" I assured him.

He smiled, looked relieved, and half laughed, "You were making me nervous."

We both laughed, grasped hands, and walked back to Teri's room to face the battle ahead.

The next day we were to begin the training and the explanations. The knowledge that was second nature to all these people was foreign and overwhelming for me. We went home for a good night's sleep, and it rained all night. We were shocked at the amount of water flowing in the streets as we turned into Bill and Joan's neighborhood to drop off Wendy and Shane for the day. The water was over the curb as we turned into their driveway. Once again, the rain interrupted my life at a time of crisis. Why didn't I ever get to see the rainbow afterwards?

Gib and I met with the doctor in the morning and then he left for work. By lunchtime it was raining again, and I chose to ignore it. I went to the hospital cafeteria, sat down with my food, and drew an invisible circle around myself. At least none of this world of hurt would touch me for a while.

"Well, Tina, tell me how you are doing?" I looked up to see Dr. Cich pulling a chair into my private circle.

"Honestly? Terrible. I have never felt so lost and confused in all my life. I don't have enough knowledge to ask any questions. I don't know if I need to be afraid. They keep throwing medical terms at me and I just want to crawl into bed and cover my head. Is that honest enough?"

He patted me on the back and smiled. "You are not unintelligent, and you will eventually get it all. I know how overwhelming it is to you right now. When I first knew it wasn't Hodgkin's, I was relieved. Later, as I thought about it, I wished it were. You see, I could fight and win against cancer. Now, you have a long road ahead of you with a totally different set of emotional problems with diabetes. Adolescence with a diabetic can be a nightmare. Teri's combination is rare. You have an acute disease and now a chronic one. You don't have immediate danger anymore, but diabetes is a life changing disease of habits and schedules, diets and shots."

"That's what everyone keeps saying. What really scares me is with cancer the responsibility was yours with me just hanging on for direction. Now, it will rest with me and Teri, and that is scary."

"True. However, remember you are never more than a phone call away. Dr. Etzwiler and I will be sharing Teri's care. One of us will always be available."

"You've already proven that to me. Thank you. Don't worry about us, we will make it."

"I never had a doubt." he replied as he rose. "Teri said to tell you to hurry back upstairs. She wants to show you how to test her urine. She has it all down pat now."

"Oh, I am sure she does. I think she will learn all this faster than I will."

Laughing he said, "Knowing Teri I have no doubt that is how it will be. I will be by tomorrow. If I miss you, call anytime."

Once back upstairs I entered the room to find Gib along with Teri and her new doctor, Dr. Etzwiler. Teri was interrogating him.

"Are you the one that made them wake me up every two hours to take my blood?"

"Yes, I am."

"Well, I didn't like that a bit. I didn't get good sleep."

A smile spread across his face, "Neither did I. They called me every two hours after they woke you and gave me your blood sugar readings. Then, I told them how much insulin to give you. So, I didn't get good sleep either."

A mischievous grin spread across her face as she relented, "Well, I guess that's okay if you had to get up too." Immediately I saw a bond form between doctor and patient. Teri could win them over in an instant.

The rain continued throughout the day and when we called Joan to see how the kids were doing, she said Shane and her son were in their canoe out in the street just paddling along and loving the fun. She hoped the water would go down so we would be able to get into their driveway by evening.

Over the next hours we learned more about diabetes than our mind could absorb. We came to realize how close to a coma Teri had come before diagnosis and how extremely sick she had been. Finally, totally exhausted, we fell into the car and headed to Joan's. The waters had receded back to the curb as we turned into her drive. She had a warm meal prepared and Bill and Gib settled in the living room. While Joan got the meal on the table, I called Mary to update her on everything and when I hung up Joan surprised me by saying, "I think you should spend the night. It is supposed to keep raining and you need to be close to the hospital. Isn't tomorrow when the kids have to be there too?"

"Yes, but are you afraid we wouldn't make it back? We are half an hour away but is it supposed to rain that much?"

"They are predicting it will rain all night. I just thought it would be safer."

Evidently Bill and Gib were having the same conversation as Gib came into the kitchen and announced we would be spending the night. The kids cheered and for once the rain seemed to bring happiness. However, in the middle of the night water began seeping into the basement where we slept. We alerted Bill and Joan, and the four adults and older kids began pulling up carpet and trying to keep the water from ruining everything. All night we worked together and as the sun came up, the water stopped. Relieved, we all fell exhausted into chairs, and I wondered how much more could rain screw up my life.

We had an early appointment with the dietician, and as she rambled on, I was unable to focus on her words. I looked at Gib to see if he was getting what she said, and he just shrugged his shoulders. We endured the meeting, took the pamphlets, and were relieved to see her go. Joan brought Shane and Wendy up for the next training session.

We began practicing giving a shot into an orange. We drew saline into the syringe and then were to shoot the orange. Each of us tried it and the orange wasn't intimidating, and we did well. Then, came the decisive moment. We were all frightened when they said we were ready to stop giving an orange the shot and do it to a real person. The nurse offered her arm and asked which of us would go first. We were all cowards.

I looked up to see everyone looking at me and I realized I had been elected without a ballot.

"Are you sure we have to do this?" I cautiously asked.

"You can't shoot an orange at home all the time. Now is the time," she smiled and extended her arm. With her coaxing, I finally did it and her voice never changed when I "stabbed" her. Gib went next and did fine. I offered my arm for Shane and he, too, did fine. Teri was next. "I want to do it to my Daddy!" She announced. He reluctantly held out his arm and she proceeded. When she was about to penetrate his skin, she became very nervous. She pushed the needle in very, very slowly. The nurse pointed out that a sudden jab hurts so much less, and Gib testified to that.

We all turned to look at Wendy sitting in the corner. She continued shooting her orange, stabbing, pushing, stabbing, pushing. Teri shouted, "No way is SHE giving me a shot." Just then as Wendy pushed down the plunger and the sterile water passed into the orange; the juice began squirting from all the tiny holes of the orange. The orange was at full capacity. The juice shot high into the room from all directions and Wendy announced," I am not going to do this to anything but an orange."

43

"You can say that again!" Teri added, and we all laughed.

From that moment on, Teri began giving herself shots, and by the next day the staff announced we were ready to go home. I protested, feeling totally inadequate, but they insisted we would do fine. The nurse handed me a slip of paper with the phone number of the nurse's station advising us to call any time day or night. Fear crept up my throat with a bitter acid taste. How could I do this?

Politely we thanked them for everything, and we drove away fearful and wondering if we knew all the new rules. I wondered if I could study the food exchanges, plan menus, and learn what to do if she had an insulin reaction. Thank heavens, Mary was waiting when we arrived home. She brought a meal and gave lots of hugs and encouragement. Although I still had deep anxiety, Mary's confident voice and love raised my spirits.

Our family was scheduled to attend the Diabetes Education Center training in a week, and we had so much to learn in a short time. We had always been a flexible family. We ate when and what we wanted without much planning or schedules. Now, they were telling us this was all going to change. Dr. Cich had been right, this was a life changing disease.

But I didn't want to change. Everyone and everything kept telling me I had to, but I just didn't want to. I questioned myself as to what lesson had I not learned the first time around. What did I not get right so that God had to have a rerun? I thought about how Abraham had questioned God for clarity in Genesis 15. God hadn't gotten mad at him. So, can I ask God to clarify why I must do this? Dare I ask Him to explain? God seemed so far away.

I often relied on Joshua 1:9 where it says. "Have I not commanded you? Be strong and courageous. Do not be frightened, and do not be dismayed, for the Lord your God is with you wherever you go."

Yet, why couldn't I feel or sense God within me now? Hadn't I been strong enough? I was struggling. *Needed a sign.* I needed a rainbow. I needed a promise that things would get better. I was free- falling.

The rain had stopped, and the sunset was full of vibrant colors. Still, I saw no rainbow.

WHO'S IN CONTROL?

CHAPTER 5

For the first two weeks of managing Teri's diabetes, we tried to follow every rule they laid down. All five of us attended the Diabetes Education Center for a week of training. Our minds tried to store all the information about food exchanges, planning menus, insulin reactions, adjusting insulin, testing blood and urine, calculating school lunch programs, and even practicing ordering in a restaurant. Teri caught on quickly and I often found myself saying I would learn it later. When home, Teri would proudly show her friends and family how to test blood, draw up insulin and even give herself shots. Everything was beginning to be sorted out when school began. Shane was starting 10th grade, Teri 5th grade and Wendy 2nd grade. I had a new job working in the school library where the girls attended grade school.

Before school started, I met with Teri's teacher and saw the panic on this young, inexperienced woman's face as I explained the basics to her. It didn't surprise me as even I was still reeling from it all. I assured her Teri could take care of herself and since I was now working in the school library, I would be close by. We weren't many days into the school year when Teri started begging to stay home each day. She revealed that when she was having an insulin reaction, the teacher thought she was faking it to get out of class. Teri had gone to the nurse's office more than once and drank multiple cups of orange juice to calm things down. On top of that, since Teri needed a mid-morning snack the teacher made her sit in the hall to eat it and the classmates were starting to tease her and during lunch would dangle food in front of her that she couldn't have. Even with multiple meetings with everyone involved, the teasing continued. Teri's self-assurance disappeared and pride in her accomplishments was buried. There seemed to be no support anywhere. Again, her friends pulled away and Teri was miserable. She quietly endured the year.

Toward the end of the school year the class was going up north for a week of outdoor education. I was to go as a parent chaperone. The students were to pack together with a friend, two in one suitcase. Two days before we were to leave, Teri stomped into my bedroom and announced, "I'm not going!" She explained that her best friend was no longer going to pack with her, and she wasn't even in a cabin with any of her friends. She threw a paper on the bed and ran out. Sure enough, the names on the list of her cabin were unfamiliar.

I went to her and said, "Teri, you can pack with me. No one is in my room with me. You can be my buddy."

"Aren't you a little too big to be my friend?" she giggled.

"Maybe a little old but not too big. Many of your friends are taller than me." We both laughed, she agreed, and we went as planned.

The trip was a disaster. She lagged behind everyone and rarely took part in classes. She cried herself to sleep every night. However, when we returned to the city, she told everyone what a great time she had, and I kept quiet.

The school year was finally over, and we prepared for another trip in the camper. This time we were traveling to California. All three of the kids were to be in their cousin, Diane's, wedding. As we rode along the highway, I often found myself thanking God and Gib's parents for sharing their belongings with us, showing our kids America, and making wonderful memories.

One night on this trip we stopped at a campground that had an amusement park next door. The grandparents and Jinkers stayed in the camper while the 5 of us went to ride the rides. We were unsure if Wendy would try all the rides or not. Finally, as we stood in line for the last one, and as we rounded the last turn, she realized it was a roller coaster. Protests began at once. She pushed away from me and said, "Oh, no! I'm not going on that." I suggested when we got to the top she could step through the car and wait for us on the other side of the tracks. She was more afraid of being left alone than the ride, so she climbed into the car with me. By the end of the ride, my face and neck were bleeding from her scrapping her fingernails down my face in fear. We exited and she ran all the way back to the camper and threw herself into Aunt Jinkers's arms. When we arrived, I saw anger in Jinkers eyes I had never seen before. "I should turn you over my knee and spank you for frightening this little thing to death."

"But Jinkers, look what she did to me," I replied.

"You deserved it all," she responded, and that closed the discussion! So, Wendy always had an advocate in her corner.

Shane's high school years were speeding by while all this chaos was going on. He was now entering 11th grade. What a joy he had been. We loved his high school years as he included us in everything. We attended sports events from football, to tennis, to downhill ski meets. He was in plays and choir. He was active in church, worked in the bus ministry (to pick up neighborhood kids and bring them to church), and summer camps. He was well-rounded, and an excellent student.

Of course, girls were a big part of his life. He was always dating one or maybe two girls at a time. One Sunday morning I had great difficulty keeping from bursting into laughter when I filed into the choir loft to see him sitting on the second row of church between two girls he was dating at the same time. He had a look of desperation on his face. Each girl held a hymnal in their hand with it stretched out toward him. Having no idea what to do he held one hymnal in his right hand and another hymnal in his left, stared straight ahead, and tried to sing.

On his 16th birthday, Shane was working at a fast -food restaurant. Gib's parents were up for a visit, so we all slipped into the restaurant, and (with the manager's permission) we began singing happy birthday. He looked up, saw us, and tried to act like he didn't know us. We just sang louder. When we reached his name the rest of the crew burst into laughter, and we exited quickly. He hated and loved it all at the same time.

Shane was easily one of my favorite people to be around and we teased each other a lot. If he forgot a chore, I would say "Uh oh. You forgot to take the garbage out." With a gleam in my eye, he would come to full alert, and we would race each other to his bedroom. I would try to strip the sheets off his bed, and he would try to stop me. We would fall in gales of laughter onto his bed and wait for another day, another forgotten chore, and another race. In two years, he would be going off to college and I knew I would miss our daily fun.

Wendy was entering 3rd grade. She was becoming quite a little gymnast and it was always nerve racking to watch her tiny legs quiver on the balance beam. She was an average student, but a perfectionist. Still unwilling to try new things, she wouldn't play board games or cards since it would take a learning process, and she wanted to be excellent the first time. She was shy, had a few awfully close friends and was content to spend time with family.

Teri was entering 6th grade which meant middle school and a new building. Hopeful things would go better for her in the future, we bought our back-to-school clothes and supplies, and everyone was ready for the new year.

A few days before school was to start, screams rebounded off the tile walls of the bathroom. I held Wendy, now 9, in the tub while Gib continually sponged her. Her fever was above 102 and she was hallucinating. She would bury her head in my neck trying hard not to see the monsters. She screamed they were coming out of the ceiling light, and she feared they would carry her away. The screams were filled with terror and panic and slowly she would peek to see if they were gone, only to clutch and tear at me trying to hide.

Shane ran into the bathroom to see what was wrong with his little sister. Grasping at a teachable moment, I told him this was like a bad drug experience, and he should never take drugs. I have no idea if that lesson had any effect on him but, he stayed and watched, and I knew he was praying for his sister. We kept sponging her off, over and over until the fever began to come down. As she cooled to my touch, the monsters disappeared, and she quieted. All three of us were exhausted by the time we put her back in her bed. In the adjoining bedroom Teri's fever was nearly as high yet she seemed to tolerate it much better. We sponged her in her bed until hers came down also. Finally, we collapsed into bed at 5AM wondering how early we could wake up to call the doctor.

Morning came with both girls still sick and a quick call to the clinic proved neither of our specialists were in town. We made an appointment with the doctor on call. He diagnosed Wendy with an ear infection and

Teri with a virus. Two days on antibiotics and Wendy was bouncing around like a freed bunny. Teri's fever started down, but she didn't really recover. School started and Shane too, had spent one night throwing up. However, he was determined to earn a perfect attendance at school that year, so he went to school that first week even though he felt a little queasy. A couple of attempts to send Teri to school that week only led to a call from the school nurse and my having to bring her home. She was just too weak. Then, the vomiting started. More doctors' appointments and finally they put Teri in the hospital. Thus, began the cycle. A few days in the hospital, a few days home. Then repeat. Finally, the associate diabetes doctor admitted he didn't know what was making her sick. Dr. Etzwiler was the top diabetes specialist, but because of that he was often gone for conventions, meetings, and training others. We had to rely on the associate.

"This has gone on too long," the associate doctor said. "It appears to be a virus but, on the other hand, I get concerned when something lingers this long." He sent us to Dr. Cich for a complete work-up.

I needed answers so we headed to Dr. Cich's office. Once there I relaxed as we passed him in the hallway. Afterall, he would find the underlying cause of this. Looking at Teri, his eyes seemed to sink as he saw her condition. "Tina, I have been called to the hospital on an emergency. I will call another specialist to examine her and have him call me at the hospital as soon as he is done, and we will decide what to do. I am so sorry I have to go." I only nodded as he disappeared out the door. Gib was gone on a work trip, Dr. Etzwiler was out of town, and now Dr. Cich was leaving. I felt let down and abandoned.

"Where is he going?" Teri protested.

"To the hospital to take care of someone," I responded.

"Are they sicker than me?"

"I guess so," I muttered and thought to myself this would be the third doctor in ten days and none of them her regular specialist. An hour later, we left with pills and a diagnosis of pneumonia. Later that night she was admitted to the hospital with uncontrolled vomiting. The pattern repeated itself, three days in the hospital, three days home. Twenty-one days after the onset of this illness, she vomited for four hours straight. Gib was traveling again so I called Dr. Cich and when I heard his voice, I began to cry.

"Tina, what is the matter?" he asked.

'I just can't stand it any longer. Teri's been vomiting for 4 hours, and I haven't slept through the night in 3 months. I need to know what is wrong with her. I am at the end of my rope."

"Then leave right now and I will meet you at the emergency room. I want to see her tonight."

I slipped on my shoes and looked up to see Gib walking into the bedroom after arriving home from his trip. Together we entered the emergency room, and I was so relieved to see both Dr. Cich and Dr. Etzwiler waiting for us. While Dr. Etzwiler started examining her, Dr. Cich turned to me.

"Tina, how are you?"

"I'm sorry if I overreacted."

He gently took my arm. "In all the time I have known you and all we have been through; this is the first time I have known you to really cry." He spoke so softly it was barely above a whisper.

"I only cry when I am desperate," I whispered back.

"As soon as he gets the diabetes under control, I will start a complete work-up. I will try everything I know to get to the bottom of this. But, Tina," he paused. "You need to be aware that if the cancer is active, we will have a really rough go of it. She would have to have chemo and the diabetes will go wild."

"I can manage anything but uncertainty. I realize that our chances will be low, but the unknown is harder than reality. I must know what is making her sick all the time. Just find out."

"I will leave no stone unturned and that means I also want her to be seen by a psychiatrist."

"That's fine with me but you better advise him not to tell her his specialty. Even for a twelve-year- old, she will play all sorts of games with him if she knows."

With humor in his voice, he continued, "I've already warned him that she is one smart cookie and will have him wrapped around her little finger if he is not careful."

I laughed, "Is he as easy a mark as you?"

Feigning insults, he stumbled back with his hand on his heart, "Just what do you mean by that?"

"Just that you are a sucker for kids. You can't deny that."

Smiling he turned to walk away, waved and said, "And I thought I hid it so well."

The next day the psychiatrist entered the room with a bounce in his step. He took us to a conference room and allowed me to stay as long as I wouldn't say a single thing. I sat behind Teri so she wouldn't see my reactions as he began. He made light conversation with her for a few minutes when she suddenly looked him in the eye and asked, "Exactly what kind of a doctor did you say you were?"

"I didn't say," he quietly responded.

"Oh," she smiled as she continued. "Don't you want me to know you are a psychiatrist?"

I nearly broke into laughter watching his face. I didn't even know she knew that word, and he seemed to have no answer for her. He only nodded and her body language spoke volumes. She pushed herself back into her chair, crossed her legs, took on an air of sophistication and answered his questions with a vocabulary advanced for her age.

When she finally left the room, he turned to me and said, "She is certainly an articulate young lady."

"I'm sorry. I am sure it is impossible to get a valid interview with someone that takes control like that. She really put on a dog and pony show for you."

"She can really converse with adults. Is she that good with her peers?"

I explained her world was made up of adults, mostly those in the medical field, and that school had become a nightmare. She had no friends as they had moved on without her and usually just ignored her. She had only attended five days out of 16.

"She appears to be in complete control of herself now and certainly not in a depression. Let's wait and see what they find in the physical work-up." Thus, he gave her a glowing report. Once again, she had manipulated the situation. Afterall, she was again with adults.

Days passed, the blood sugars were under control, we went home and two days later she was sick again. Once again, Gib was traveling, and all reports had come back negative, and we still had no clue as to what was making her sick. We considered taking her to Mayo Clinic, but her doctors were Mayo- trained and were in conversations with them and four other major medical centers throughout the states. There were no answers anywhere.

No one knew what to do next. No one took control.

This continued for months. Sometimes she would last five or ten days before it hit again. One thing was sure, it would come back. We crept up to four shots per day. Gib and I would give her two to relieve her some, and she would manage the other two.

I tried to put my faith in doctors. I tried to trust God to come and change things. No matter how much I prayed, pleaded, or tried logic, nothing was working. I tried blaming the doctors, blaming myself, blaming Teri, blaming anything I could come up with. All I found was chaos. There was no control in my life or Teri's.

As I sat in the hospital room one day, Pastor came in carrying a small package for Teri. Her eyes lit up at him and his treasure when he dropped it on her bed, and she grinned up at him with immense pleasure. She ripped into it and pulled out a tiny bunny. Delighted, she started bouncing it around the bed and he tried to smile, but it disappeared into the darkness of his eyes. Turning to me he asked, "How are you, Tina?"

"Fine," I lied.

He appeared frustrated and blurted out, "I don't get it. Why does she get sick all the time?"

"Her diabetes is out of control. They call it brittle diabetes," I explained. "Her blood sugar goes way up, and she starts burning muscle tissue for energy and then vomiting. Next, she gets dehydrated, and we have to bring her in to get everything leveled off again."

"She looks fine now."

"Yeah, but you should have seen her last night when we got here. She was near comatose."

"I still don't understand. She's been here three times in the last four weeks. She's never been like this before."

I sighed. "No one understands it. I guess it all started with that virus she had Labor Day weekend." We both looked at her. She was so beautiful. Her complexion had always been so perfectly clear that it reminded me of a porcelain doll. Her thin brown hair curled softly around her chin and her long eyelashes seemed to flutter as she played.

"Where's Gib?"

"Out of town on business," I said.

"He sure seems to travel a lot."

Too quickly, I defended him. "It's not too bad most of the time. A little rough right now since he is finishing his master's degree. When in town, he is gone two nights a week to class and two nights he studies, writes papers, or gets ready for tests. But he doesn't usually travel on the weekends so that helps. We are both committed to him completing his degree."

"Everything is okay, isn't it?" His voice sounded like he was pleading with me. "I mean, you don't need anything do you?"

I sensed his need for me to be fine, so I replied, "Oh, everything is okay." I sat staring at him across Teri. Instead of speaking I allowed my thoughts to rumble around in my head. Can't you see I'm in terrible shape? Can't you see I am lying? Can't you see I am sick of hospitals, emergency rooms, needles, I V's, vomit, and doctors? Can't you hear it in my voice or see it in my eyes? He gazed out the window as my frustration began to turn to anger. Can't you sense I am quiet? Why are you so insensitive now?

Suddenly, he turned from the window and announced, "I have to be going now, Tina. Do you want to walk me to the parking lot?"

"Sure," I responded, positive he wanted to talk out of Teri's earshot. The ride down the elevator was spent in discussion of the weather, and as we stepped off, he headed to the chapel. Relieved, I followed him inside and he stopped at the desk and asked the woman to stamp his parking ticket as he was a visiting pastor. Then, to my surprise, he pulled the door open and stepped into the bustling hallway. As we reached the main door, he remarked, "You really shouldn't go outside with me, it is too cold. I'll be back tomorrow. Call if you need anything." And he was gone. I needed something NOW and he was gone. Again, NO one was in control. My last hope walked briskly away and disappeared into the parking garage.

"Well, God, it's just You and me. No one else understands or cares. I was a fool to get my hopes up. I won't do it again," I muttered as I turned to go back to Teri's room. As I walked past the coffee shop, I spotted the associate diabetes specialist sitting at the bar eating lunch. I walked in and sat down beside him and ordered lunch. Politely, he asked how I was doing, and we conversed a little.

Abruptly he said, "Are you absolutely sure Teri is giving herself all her shots?"

"What?" I almost yelled!

"We find that many of our diabetics don't give their shots and start bouncing like this. Does she give them all in front of you?"

How dare he question the integrity of me or my daughter. "Certainly! She gets four shots per day. We give her two and she does the other two. We try to share her burden without taking it completely away from her."

Hearing my defensive voice, he quickly continued, "I'm not questioning whether you are good parents or if she can be trusted. I am just saying that we have found in the past that many young diabetics bounce like this when they are skipping shots. Just be sure she gives them in front of you."

"She does," I answered curtly.

Having finished his lunch, he paid and left. I attacked my sandwich with vengeance. How dare he think Teri could do something like that. Why can't they just find the simple culprit that is causing all that? Isn't anyone in control of their senses? Isn't anyone in control of this?

Back upstairs in her room, I found Teri napping, so I quietly sat down and began rehashing my day. Gib was traveling for business so I couldn't talk to him, Pastor had been insensitive so I couldn't talk to him, and now the Associate Diabetes Specialist had unjustly accused me of being a careless mother. I couldn't decide whether to be angry or wallow in my self-pity.

"God," I whispered. "I don't have any answers. I was so sure we had made it when we beat the cancer. Now, I just don't know. I have fought to adjust to diabetes, diets, blood testing, shots, and all these hospital stays. It's just too much, God. Gib needs me to hold down the home while he works and finishes school, Teri needs me at her bedside, Shane needs me to be the mother of a teenager, and Wendy needs me to have enough energy to be involved in a 9 -year -old's life. And, God, no one not even Pastor sees my needs. Not one single person! No one. No one. No one."

I shut down. The questions were so big and the answers so small. I didn't want to talk even to God. I picked up my Bible and started looking through the book of Psalms. Surely, there was an answer in all of David's problems. I came to Psalm 91:1-2. "He who dwells in the shelter of the Most High will abide in the shadow of the Almighty. I will say to the Lord, 'My refuge and my fortress, my God, in whom I trust. '"

Was this my relationship with God? Was I abiding in Him? Was He giving me permission to just rest and abide? If so, then I could stay here with Him without talking. He was holding me like a father tenderly hold a tiny baby. He was giving me nourishment and shelter. I was protected, and I could relax. He was allowing the Holy Spirit to talk for me. The Spirit was interceding for me. He could tell God my needs. Together they would minister to me. I closed my eyes and thanked God for being my father, my Abba.

Comfortable in Him I drifted off into a troubled sleep. I dreamed I was running down an endless dirt road totally alone. Yet, I knew I wasn't really alone. I ran and ran and ran until I suddenly felt a cold hand reach out and touch my arm. Gently a nurse brought me back to reality.

"Mrs. Coleman, we have moved Teri to another room. You were sleeping and I didn't want to wake you. I am going off duty now and didn't want you to wake to an empty room."

"Thank you," I said as I gathered my belongings and followed her to Teri's new room.

"So, you decided to wake up?" Teri giggled.

"How long have you been in here?" I asked.

"Only about twenty minutes. I tried to call Pastor to tell him I was in a new room, but no one answered."

"After I go to the restroom, I will try to call him again." I stopped by the conference room and used that phone. Pastor's oldest daughter answered. She recognized my voice and at once asked if I had seen him today. Confused, I replied he had been here earlier. There was silence on the other end.

"Is something wrong?" I inquired.

Finally, she mumbled, "I thought he would tell you."

She went ahead to relate a frightening story about her younger sister in a crisis hundreds of miles away and how he was really hurting. I told her I had no idea and for him to call me once he got home.

Sitting in the quiet of that conference room, I recalled the darkness in his eyes, the distracted attention, and the silence that had surrounded him. In my own self-pity I had not recognized his agony. He had been unable to see my pain because his was so immense. We had played the silly game and waited for the other one to make the first move. We had failed each other.

"Oh, Abba, forgive me. I was looking at the splinter in his eye when I had a beam in mine. Forgive me for judging his actions and allowing anger to control me. Please, God, give him assurance that his daughter will be okay. Please comfort him and give him wisdom on how to handle this crisis."

The next morning at church I waited until the crowds had moved away and I drew him aside.

"Would you forgive me?" I asked.

"What on earth for?"" he responded.

"For judging you and being angry you didn't minister to me yesterday. I was very selfish, and I am truly sorry. Will you forgive me?"

"Of course, but is there anything I can do for you now?"

"You already have," I smiled.

His face wrinkled in confusion. "How?"

"By being human. Yesterday, your oldest told me about the crisis in your life. I had expected you to be my 'fix-it' man. Whenever tragedy or trials hit, I have always called you to 'fix-it'. When you left the hospital yesterday, I was angry you left without fixing anything. It never entered my mind that you could have problems as big or bigger than mine. I only thought you were supposed to fix mine, not need some of your own fixed."

He gazed over my shoulder. looking at nothing but space and replied "Tina, the only 'fix-it' man either of us needs is God. We must learn to completely rely on Him. Afterall, everyone else will let us down. Our only job is to just care for each other."

"I promise to do just that. I will no longer assume my problem is the only one. We will be praying for you as I know you pray for us."

A tiny smile crept across his face, and he nodded as he walked away. I noticed his gait was slower than usual and his shoulders sagged as if he had a huge weight stretched across his shoulders.

I could only pray, "God please take care of him. He takes care of so many others and now he needs to be taken care of. Give him strength and insight. Help us both to dwell in the shelter of You, the Most High. Help us to trust you to be our refuge."

As we left church that day, it was gently raining. For the first time, instead of being angry at its inconvenience, I leaned my head back and let the rain hit my face. It felt good and cleansing. It washed away so many tangled thoughts and frustration. I didn't have control of my life, but I knew Who did and I knew He would never leave me. The rain was warm and refreshing. God was washing me. I discovered the rain finally had a point in my life.

AFRAID OF TOMORROW

CHAPTER 6

The next few weeks proved to be a deep valley for both Pastor's and our family. After weeks of anguish and action, prayer and love Pastor's daughter's problem was resolved, and healing took place. Gib and I had thought Teri's uncontrolled diabetes was temporary but, we soon accepted it was a long-term problem. Our neighbor, Kathy, had been wonderful occupying and babysitting Wendy, and letting her spend hours playing with Charie, but it became a rare event when all five of us were able to sit down and have a dinner together. In six months, Teri had been hospitalized more than nine times. I would stop by her school and pick up assignments and force her to do homework even in the hospital. She saw me as a prison guard.

By mid-January, *in* desperation to stop the bouncing, Dr. Etzwiler decided to put Teri on an experimental insulin pump. It was about the size of a cell phone but at least 4 times as thick. It was black and was connected to a small tube that carried insulin to a needle implanted in her abdomen. It would deliver insulin to her body every two minutes. We would have to remove the needle every couple of days and replace it with a new one. She had to be careful setting it up to insure she didn't get too much insulin.

At first, Teri was curious. She enjoyed the attention and liked the idea that she was the first pediatric patient to try one out. They took her picture to run in a medical journal and she thought she was a star. That lasted until her first day at school. There, she felt like a freak. The kids made fun of her new contraption, and she began to openly rebel. She became irrational and screamed and cried at every suggestion anyone made. She would bury her head in the pillow and scream that she didn't want to be a freak with a "thing" hanging on her. It was big, black, very noticeable, and she had to have a belt to hang it on that created a problem as she usually wore dresses. She complained the needle hurt, the tape irritated her skin, and she cried so much her eyes were nearly swollen closed. Most mornings Gib would put her in the car screaming and drove her to school as she cried all the way. It was getting unbearable. Shane was accusing us of letting her capitalize on her illness. Wendy's academic level dropped immensely, and we were all living under the toll of tension.

One night, Gib and I decided we needed to escape. We left the girls at home with Shane and drove across town to Bill and Joan's house. The four of us decided to go to a movie we had been wanting to see at the theater near them.

As we walked through the door to buy our tickets, I was laughing at something when the usher touched my shoulder and said, "Are you Mrs. Coleman?"

"Yes, but I don't know you," I said.

"There is a phone call for you."

'What? No one knows I am here.' Leaving Gib and our friends I headed to the phone.

Once I answered I cringed as I heard Teri's voice. It was incredulous that she could find us clear across town when we were trying to escape.

She explained, "I knew you were going to Bill and Joan's, and I knew you wanted to see that movie, so I looked in the paper and found a theater near them and called. You were laughing as you came in and I heard it on the phone and told the guy that was you."

"So why are you calling?" I demanded.

"The needle fell out of my stomach, and I don't know what to do."

Angry, I retorted, "Put Shane on the phone."

I quickly gave him instructions to put Teri in the car and drive her to another friends' house. Jan was a nurse and could reinsert it. I called Jan to warn her they were coming and returned to Gib. I related all that had gone on and announced, "She is not ruining this night out for us. We are going to the movie and liking it! It wouldn't surprise me if she pulled that needle out herself just to get us home."

They all three stared at me in shock and we finally turned to buy tickets. Later, when we returned home, we saw that Teri appeared to shrink deep inside herself. She stared at the ceiling and refused to talk to us. Neither of us slept that night and when the doctor heard the entire story the next morning, he removed the pump. With the hope of the pump gone, would this be the way out of this pit?

Time marched by with little change until one day I stood by the window watching the rain leak out of the sky as if it seemed to overflow a huge bowl. The grey of the sky crept like fingers into my bedroom and engulfed me and wrapped me in gloom. Once again, nature understood me when no one else did. Early morning lights were on in the houses on the street as neighbors hurried to prepare for their day. A car passed now and then with its headlights breaking the grey and then there was emptiness. That was it - emptiness. That word described me. The world continued its daily pattern, but I was empty. I was grey like the sky. My emotions leaked from me like the rain. I didn't want to feel anything; not anger, not happiness, not frustration, certainly not gratefulness, just nothing. That's what I wanted to feel – nothing.

Those weeks and months of the roller coaster ride of hospital-home-hospital-home had taken their toll. I was choking on loss of hope. In my mind, Gib and Shane seemed affected the least by everything. They both had activities and responsibilities that allowed them to escape this chaos some. I felt a twinge of jealousy since I had no escape. Wendy had become a silent sufferer. Her self-esteem was low, and I had no idea why. I had begun to see her anger directed at Teri. She no longer wanted to compete with Teri or spend time with her. She saw Teri as too smart, too talented, too mature, and too sick to be a companion. She threw herself into her love for gymnastics and it became her world.

This grey gloom didn't appear to penetrate them. They were all doing okay. It was only me. I had taken a parttime teaching job at a local elementary and struggled to keep our family together while still doing good at my new job. Everyone asked how Teri was doing. They all spoke about Teri and how proud I should be of her. They all thought she was such a little "angel." If they only knew how her illness was destroying everything around her. She tried to manipulate everyone; family, doctors, friends, and she was becoming an expert at making others think they had chosen her way. How much was her fault and how much was the fault of the disease was unclear. I was a mess. I had begun to seethe and allow bitterness to replace any joy in my life. Guilt wedged its way deep into my emotions as I feared my anger at Teri would cripple her recovery. Pride had puffed me up as I was determined to grit my teeth and go on. I had felt justified in my anger toward others and especially Gib. Afterall, he could remove himself from the problem. So, I had allowed the spontaneity to slowly drain from our relationship. I had withdrawn from Gib, and I had withdrawn from God. I knew God was supposed to be in control, but I could see no evidence of it. I now relied on the past relationships with both God and Gib, and I had built no new bridges with either of them. I had reasoned if I dropped all expectations, then I couldn't be hurt more. So, now I felt like the greyness that surrounded me and wallowed in self-pity. God was nowhere. I felt like David when he called out to God, in Psalm 13 demanding, "How long O Lord? Will you forget me forever?"

I was a failure. I was a terrible parent. Teri had been through so much, Wendy had low self-esteem, Shane was going on without me. I was a worse wife. I was in open rebellion against my husband, and he didn't even know it. Without ever saying a word to him, I ate away at our relationship. I had begun disappearing when the kids were at school and not telling him where I was. Finally, I had started looking for an apartment and contemplating moving out on my own. I had told no one and only wondered why no one could see my desperation. My church was in deep turmoil so I could get no spiritual help from there. Slowly, I had begun to crack. Whether my disappointments were real or imagined, they were controlling me. I had felt I was made of glass and if Gib or anyone touched me, I would shatter into tiny pieces on the floor. I became determined not to let anyone see it all. No one would know too much. No matter what, I was too stubborn to ask for help. If they couldn't see on their own what was happening to me. I wasn't about to tell them! So, here I stood looking out the window with grey inside and wondering once again why rain always seemed to dance around me and rarely cleanse me. I had forgotten the lessons God had taught me.

I saw no escape, so I continued on the path I had created. Deeper I slid into the mire, and I would occasionally send out a tiny flag for help, but no one responded. They were all involved in their own struggles and didn't see mine. Months crept by, and I refused to humble myself before God. I felt even He let me down.

I began to feel a strange power within me. I dreamed of shocking everyone around me. I fantasized getting in my car and just driving hundreds of miles away and them never knowing where I had gone. Maybe then they would see what they had missed in me. Maybe then they would appreciate me. I felt God had given up on me. I couldn't see Him allowing me to stomp, scream and even pity myself. My circumstances were controlling me, and I only kept doing all that was expected of me as if by rote. For over a year, I rebelled in my heart. For over a year, Gib and God waited. They endured my demands, accusations of their failures, and my tantrums. Although he didn't understand me, Gib waited. At first, that just angered me more. I felt since he didn't do anything, he didn't care. In the middle of my anger, I sensed the Holy Spirit reminding me that Gib was waiting just like God was waiting. I ignored the nudging. However, every time I came close to making a drastic decision something I didn't understand stopped me.

I looked around for someone, anyone, to help me. Instead, I soon realized that every close family to us was undergoing some major crisis of their own. Some marriages were on the brink of breaking up, teenagers were in rebellion, jobs were lost, and with everyone hurting, I had no one I could ask for help. I began to question if God even knew me. Did He care? Did He even see or hear me? Why was there no help? Teri's illness was not the reason for my rebellion, it just showed the kinks in my armor. Was my faith founded on sand or rock? I was deep in mire and slush. Slowly, very slowly, the days drug by and trips to the hospital became less frequent. I was giving Teri shots more often than she was and she began attending school a little more often. As circumstances got better the gloom seemed to lift a little until one morning the April sun flooded into our bedroom and washed me with confidence. I snuggled into the curve of Gib's arm and smiled. He lifted his head off the pillow and stared at me and said, "Well, somebody is feeling great this morning."

"You can say that again," I responded.

"And to what do we owe this giddiness?"

"I'm just so relieved Teri is a 'normal' kid again. I know she must take shots and stay on a special diet, but I think she has broken the cycle of being sick all the time. The pump stopped the up and down bouncing, but she downright hated it. So, now it's gone. It just feels good to deal with 'normal' problems again."

"Well, the first 'normal' thing you must deal with is getting up. We better hurry or Teri will be late for school."

As we bustled around with morning chores, Gib gave her a shot and volunteered to drive her to school. His parents were coming for a visit today and we were all busy with last minute preparations. The day was comfortable. No crisis arose.

Grandma and Grandpa Coleman arrived by the time the girls got home from school. The girls bubbled with excitement as they visited with their grandparents. I got dinner in the oven and drew Teri's insulin into the syringe and told her to come to her bedroom to take her shot.

"You give it to me, Mom," she requested.

"No, Teri. You must do it yourself."

"Then you go out of here. You know it makes me nervous to have someone watch me." Her voice quivered as she spoke.

"Teri, this summer you will go to Camp Needlepoint and the counselors will watch. You just must get used to that. The nurses watch at the hospital. It is okay."

"I can't do it if you watch me," she demanded.

Shushing her so the grandparents wouldn't hear I continued. "Teri, I will sit here at the desk while you give your shot and I won't look. That way you will get used to me being here again, but I won't stare at you."

Realizing I wasn't going anywhere, she nodded in agreement. She sat on the edge of her bed, and I sat at her desk nearby. I stared at her pictures on the wall until I thought she was finished. As I turned toward her, I saw the syringe was tilted at a strange angle on the far side of her leg. I leaned forward to see what was wrong and saw the needle stuck in her bed as she pushed the plunger down releasing the insulin into her mattress. Stunned, I fell back in the chair, sucking in air and gasping like a drowning victim

"God," I cried out just above a whisper. "What are you doing?"

She jerked her head around to face me and shouted, "You promised not to watch."

"Oh, God help me," I pleaded in desperation.

Again, she protested, "You promised not to watch."

Numb and in shock, I stood up and walked out of her room unable to respond. I checked on the food in the oven, refilled another syringe and returned to her room. Without a word, I gave her a shot in her arm. Tears were rolling down her cheeks and she protested, "I didn't want to give it in front of you; I was going to give myself another shot later, I promise. You do believe me, don't you?"

I was incapable of responding to anything she said. I closed my eyes, shook my head trying to turn back time and pretend none of this had happened. I opened my eyes to see her staring at me. Her tears didn't cover the fear I saw in her eyes as she asked, "You won't tell Grandma, will you?"

All I could do was shake my head. I turned to leave her room and said, "Teri, I am going to my bedroom until Daddy comes home."

"Don't tell Daddy either," she pleaded.

"Teri, there is no way I would keep this from him. You just stay here until one of us comes to get you." I left her room closing the door behind me. I said nothing to anyone in the house but went straight to my room and closed the door behind me. I stretched out on my bed as thoughts boomeranged around my head. I closed my eyes in hopes the room would stop spinning.

"Teri, why would you do such a thing?" I asked myself. "I even fought the doctors when they suggested such a thing. I just don't understand. I trusted you. I feel like I just saw you shooting heroin and trying to kill yourself. Why, Teri?"

A deep, dark cloud closed in around me, and I could see no light, no hope, nothing. I began to shake all over. I was determined not to cry because I knew I bordered on hysteria. Into this darkness stepped Gib. I opened my eyes to see him standing beside the bed, but I couldn't understand that he was in my blackness with me.

Finally, his words penetrated. "Tina, I asked what we were having for supper."

I stared, unable to make my thoughts connect with my mouth to form words. He sat down on the edge of the bed as he asked what was wrong.

"We missed something –somewhere. She doesn't know how much we love her. Maybe we expected too much. Maybe we didn't really convey what we really thought."

Confused, he responded," Tina, you aren't making any sense. What are you talking about?"

"Gib, Teri gave her shot into her mattress," I managed to blurt out.

Stunned, his eyes reflected panic as he fell back on his pillow and tried to suck in air like I had done a few minutes earlier. I closed my eyes so I wouldn't have to see the hurt and anguish he was going through. After a while he spoke, "Tell me exactly what happened."

I related the series of events as best I could without editorializing. Once finished, we both lay perfectly still without moving.

"Gib, we can't stay here all night. Your parents are in the living room, and I am sure they are wondering what is going on."

"Are you up to getting dinner on the table?"

"If I stop thinking," I muttered.

"Okay. You take care of that, and I will go see Teri."

We had a plan yet neither of us moved.

"What are you going to say to her?"

He looked completely lost as he said, "I have no idea. I don't understand any of it. I guess I will just ask her why."

"I don't think she knows why. Do you think she has been doing it all year? Have we all been through this turbulence because she has been skipping shots?"

Although he tried to keep his face neutral, I saw the realization as it flooded over him. "Right now, all that doesn't matter. But I will say that from this moment on we will have to watch everything she does."

I turned my face into my pillow and began to sob.

"Stop, Tina!" I heard him groan in desperation. "You know if you start, if you give in, there is no way we can keep this from my parents tonight and we aren't ready for that. For now, we have to protect Teri at all costs until we know how to move forward."

I forced myself to sit up on the side of the bed and shut off my thinking. I rose and turned to face him, "Be careful, Gib. Don't injure her spirit."

A gentleness showed in his eyes, and he whispered, "See you at supper in a few minutes."

I busied myself in the kitchen and kept my mind occupied with small talk with grandparents. When dinner was ready, I sent Wendy down the hallway to call Shane and Teri for dinner. Teri and I avoided looking at each other for fear we would both collapse. Gib appeared tired but sat down and began conversing with his father immediately. As soon as dinner was finished, Teri excused herself and went to her room to do homework. We spent the evening visiting with the grandparents until bedtime when Gib had the girls come say goodnight. Shane and the girls slipped off to their rooms and I smiled at what great actors we were.

Around 11 it was time for bed, and we all said goodnight. His parents went to the basement, and we were at last alone in our bedroom. We spoke quietly so our voices wouldn't carry through the heating vents. Gib told me how she had repeated to him everything she had said to me and that she had asked him over and over if he believed her that she was planning to give her shot later. I questioned him on his response.

"I said I believed her, but I really have no idea what I believe. When I asked her why she did it, why she made herself sick over and over, she only tried to convince me it was the first time."

"You don't think that is true, do you?"

"At this point, I just don't want to think. I told her we would put all this on hold until Grandma and Grandpa leave in three days." So, we waited.

Gib drifted into a fitful sleep, tossing, and turning, waking suddenly and then going right back to sleep. I lay as still as possible next to him reliving the day. A progression of emotions flooded over me.

First was anger. Anger that we had been through so much for no medical reason. Anger at Teri for all she had done to this family.

Next came shame. Shame and guilt that I had been so naïve and had been angry at the doctors and couldn't see what was right in front of me.

Then fear hit. Fear that my child was trying to kill herself and I had no clue what to do about it.

Finally, overwhelming helplessness. This was too big a problem for me. I felt the same way I felt when she was first diagnosed with cancer. I was helpless, needed to pray, but even afraid to talk to God.

Quietly, I whispered "Please, God, let me crawl up into the palm of Your hand and rest. I know I don't deserve You; I've ignored You for so long. Yet, I need You, oh how very much I need You." I closed my eyes and pictured a huge hand open and waiting. I crawled into His protective, mighty hand and felt His Spirit touch mine and I mumbled, "I'm afraid, God. I am so afraid of tomorrow."

In His presence, I realized He had always been there. His steadfast love and peace had always been available to me. I had been in such turmoil and allowed my circumstances to control my emotions and spirit, that I had squelched the appeals of His Holy Spirit. I had slipped completely out of control. As I returned to Him in desperation, He reminded me the Holy Spirit had been with me through it all. The Spirit had earlier born witness of who Jesus was and now He was bearing witness that I belonged to Christ. He not only witnessed to God that I was one of His children, but He also witnessed to my spirit, mind, and intellect. All that time I had been ignoring Him, the Spirit had held me before the throne and interceded when I couldn't pray and lifted me before God. In turn, God had sustained me and now, at last, I understood what had stopped me from doing drastic and devastating things with my life. I had never been alone at all. I had refused to give Him control, yet He never left me unguarded. Now, I was ready for Him to help me in my weakness. I was ready to give up trying to control it all myself. I took my pain, problems, and fears and placed them in His hand. "Now, God, I know I can't do this. You take control. You be in charge and don't let me forget it again. Help me not to let circumstances block my path to You. Keep me in Your shadow daily. Help me to become steadfast like You." Completely drained and at peace, I drifted into an exhausted sleep, safe in His palm. My last thought was the desire that this same peace would hold me tomorrow.

A TINY STRAND

CHAPTER 7

Reality raised its ugly head within an hour of our getting up. Teri tried to stay home from school saying her blood sugars were too high and that she had a fever of 102 degrees. Touching her cool forehead, I called her bluff saying, "I don't know how you got this one to go so high without hot water." I said as I shook it down. Proud that she knew something I didn't, she took it, turned it upside down and the mercury slowly moved upward as she handed it triumphantly back to me. Suddenly I realized Teri's thinking and deceptive behavior was way beyond me. Stiffening I said, "Teri, we both know you don't have a fever. We both know you are going to school so you might as well stop stalling and get dressed. We told you last night we would wait until Grandma and Grandpa leave, but if you continue pushing, we can have it out right now. So, you choose. Either get dressed or let's have a show down."

Anger and hatred boiled in her eyes as she glared at me through tiny slits in her eyelids. She locked her teeth and spit out. "Okay, I'll go to school, but I won't get anything out of it." She jumped up and began throwing clothes around and dressing, so I left her room, and she slammed the door behind me.

She went to school the rest of the week without arguing. The only person she talked to on the phone was her diabetic friend from the hospital, Tim. Whenever I entered a room, she would either whisper into the phone or stop talking abruptly and remain silent until I left. How did he play into this scenario?

At the end of the week Gib's parents left and fear penetrated the house. The other two kids were aware of something brewing and were unsure if it involved them or not. Everyone was quiet, waiting for unspoken direction. I policed everything Teri did and watched her constantly. Wendy walked around in a daze like she was sleepwalking, and Shane just observed and waited.

Years later Teri wrote her memory of that time period. Here are her words:

> *I had faded away from everyone and I knew I was smarter than all of them. I hated most people but needed them so I could show my power. I shot my insulin down the sink, into my bed, or into an alcohol swab so my mom thought I was giving my shot. My friend, Tim, taught me all sorts of tricks. I even took money out of mom's purse to buy ice cream sandwiches at school. I got in so deep that I began to wish I was dead. I began complaining about going to the hospital. I felt if I stayed home maybe I would just die and no one would have to worry about me anymore.*

> *The day my mother caught me skipping my shot I had very mixed emotions. I hated her for catching, me but deep down I had hoped she would. I didn't really want to die but the depression had too much control to let me admit it.*

> *I wanted to be like everyone else. I felt if I just didn't take shots, I would be like everyone else. Then, as I got away with it, the power of controlling others made me feel triumphant and in charge. I thought I was smarter than anyone else. Mom became my enemy. I thought of her as "the woman."*

> *"That woman" was trying to destroy my power, me. I controlled Wendy because she saw me eat donuts and skip my shots and I felt powerful by threatening her. I was careful*

for Shane to never see anything because I knew he would tell and ruin it all.

I still pray that God will forgive me for all the deceitful things I did. I tore people and lives apart and I didn't care. I knew what I was doing, in a way, I became someone else, and I am so thankful that evil someone is gone. I was finally able to find myself again and that day I was caught, I found the ladder back out of the hole, and it gave me a chance to make it.

The weekend came and the "show-down" was imminent. Teri had revealed to me that Wendy had known she was skipping shots for quite a while. My heart was heavy for Wendy as I thought of the burden she had carried in silence. I found her in her bedroom and sat down for a long-needed conversation.

"Wendy, I want you to know that Daddy and I know that Teri has been skipping her shots and eating off her diet. We know that this has caused her to go to the hospital many times in the past months. Teri is sick. She doesn't want to be a diabetic. We all must help her through this. She must take shots to stay alive. I know you have seen her do things she shouldn't be doing."

Wendy dropped her gaze from my face to her folded hands in her lap. Her arms were shaking, and she clasped her hands in a tight grip. "She'll hate me if I . . ." her voice trailed off to nothing.

"Wendy," I continued quietly. "Teri needs us to help her, all of us. You must have known for a long time that she has been doing dangerous things. Sweetheart, you are not telling on her now. We already know. We want to help you, too. You have had a hard time keeping secrets that you really wanted discovered. I caught Teri last week giving her shot into her mattress. We know she has been doing it for a long time."

Her composure crumbled in front of me. Tears streamed down her face, and she could hardly talk fast enough to keep up with her thoughts. She related one incident after another of Teri's secrets and her crying never stopped. I pulled her into my arms and stroked her hair as she poured out all the ugly things. Her small frame shook as she sobbed, and my tears mixed with hers and they ran down her cheeks.

"Mom, I love Teri so much and I don't want her to die. Every time she gets sick and goes to the hospital, I miss her so much. I wanted you to help her, but I couldn't tell you. She told me she would hate me if I told you." I finally understood the problems Wendy was having in school.

We held on to each other for a long time before either of us was willing to let go. What a heavy burden my baby had carried. Finally, the eyes of a nine- year -old cleared, and she looked up at me and said so simply, "Can I go ride my bike now?"

"Only if you promise to be careful," I answered.

She giggled and said as she left, "Maybe I will." Then, she was gone.

The next days were filled with so many words – gentle, harsh, cutting, and even encouraging words of love and sadly, words of disappointment. Emotions ran deep as each of us vented the feelings we had gone through during the past months. We slowly cut out the scars we bore.

A few days later I got a phone call from the nurse's office at school. It was just an hour before school was to be over and Teri was telling the nurse she had been vomiting. The nurse didn't believe her. She put Teri on the phone. She pleaded for me to come get her, but I was determined to be tough, so I refused. I told her she had to ride the bus home as usual. Angrily she slammed the phone down, and a short while later I heard her stomp into the house, down the hall and slam her bedroom door in protest.

Again, I entered her room and she lay on her bed staring at the ceiling.

"Teri, we have to talk. I mean really talk. You need to tell me what is going on in your mind. What is bothering you?

"I don't know," she said nastily

"Why do you want to leave school? Did someone say something mean to you?"

Silence

"Are you lonely at school? Are your friends mean?"

"What friends?" she spat.

"Teri, I can't force you to talk to me. You must decide right now whether you will open up and talk to me."

Silence

"I am done then," I said as I turned to leave her room.

"What do you mean by 'you are done?" she demanded.

Keeping my back to her I continued, "There is nothing more I can do if you will not talk to me. I know there are a lot of things you think are secrets from me, but we can't talk about them because you won't let me in that shell, so I am done." I reached for the doorknob.

"Like what do you know?" She couldn't hide her curiosity,

Careful not to turn around so she would see the uncertainty on my face, I continued speaking with my back to her.

"Things like neighbors calling to tattle on you seeing you eating donuts at the grocery store. Things like your teddy bear being full of insulin. Things like the ideas Tim gives you to get away with all this. But none of that matters since I can't wait any longer." I turned the knob and began pulling the door open. I heard her start to cry but I kept looking forward and took one step through the open door when she shouted.

"But I'm afraid."

Gradually, I turned to face her, letting go of the door. "Afraid of what?"

"Everything," she cried out. "Just everything! I'm scared Dr Etzwiler will find out."

I closed the door and sat down on her bed. "Don't let that bother you, he already knows."

"How?" she demanded.

"He's been suggesting it for weeks. Besides I talked to him the day I caught you. I have talked to him every day this week."

"I hate being a diabetic." She screamed as loud as she could. "I hate shots, diets, testing, well, just everything! I HATE IT! I HATE IT! I HATE IT!"

At last, she curled up in a ball and began to sob. Finally, she was letting go. I climbed into her bed and wrapped my arms around her and let her cry. I began whispering after a while. She continued to cry and cry, shout, sob, and scream in anger and frustration. She vented her frustrations for many minutes until, exhausted she shivered into silence. Then, and only then we began to talk.

"Teri, it is obvious you have never come to grips with the fact that you are a diabetic. The first step is you accepting that. You can't deny it. It won't go away."

"Please, please let me have a pancreas transplant. Then I could eat what I want and not take shots and be normal."

"That is another thing you have to accept. Dr. Etzwiler has explained that the possibility of that would be far into the future. It is not a reality for you now. What is reality is that you need shots to live. Teri, were you afraid you would die this past year?"

"I don't know. I never really thought about dying. Sometimes I thought I wanted to die because I only wanted to be normal. The temptations were too great, and I just didn't want to be different. I don't know why I did what I did."

We stayed there on the bed for another hour or two talking about the past months. We discussed Wendy, school, self-worth, attention she got from illness, and relationships with each family member.

Realizing it was enough for one day I said, "Teri, these problems didn't arise in just one day and they won't go away in just one day. We must take each day like a step up a ladder. We may fall back a few times but together we can keep moving up. I'll have to work harder at listening and so will you. I won't always understand, but I will promise to try my very best. You will get angry at some of the rules we will have to make. I will listen to all your complaints as long as you try to control your anger. Will you do that?"

"I don't know if I can," she admitted.

"You won't always be able to, but will you try?"

She agreed and I promised to try. As I stood to leave, she confessed, "Mom, I am so afraid of tomorrow."

I smiled at her with complete understanding. "I know because I have been too. But I am not afraid anymore. Remember, Teri, God tells us not to be afraid. He is with you and me. He has given you a piece of His heart-His Holy Spirit. Christ left Him behind as a glimpse into His magnificence that awaits us in heaven. Ever since you asked Jesus into your heart, the Holy Spirit has lived inside you. We have nothing to fear. He will be our strength. He provides and sustains. He will hold you and me both up. I've failed at this too. I haven't depended on the Spirit to guide and strengthen me. That is when I become afraid. But the Holy Spirit will help us both if we just ask and wait on Him. Teri, we have a long way to go. We will take tiny steps each day. The cool thing is that we will take the steps together. Slowly the tomorrows will add up. Best of all, we don't need to be afraid of tomorrow. We have an army of angels to help us."

Confident we had made the first step; I left her room. Once I closed her door, I leaned against the wall and asked God to guide us. I knew that Satan would fight to discourage us.

It wasn't long till I felt like a speeding bullet struck me to destroy my hope. Like a bullet Satan churned and turned me upside down faster than I could see what was coming. Teri declared she was trying, but I was miserable observing what little effort I saw. She was returning to her old tricks. Suddenly, I was second guessing every statement or action she made and quickly becoming a jail keeper. Every day she shot down my hope.

A few days later Gib interrupted my thoughts and his voice sounded irritated when he said, "Are you listening to me?"

"It's no use," I responded. "Teri hates me. You should have seen her eyes. Our mother-daughter relationship can't be rebuilt- it has unraveled. Everything's unravelling, even this pillow my granny crocheted for me." Tears were streaming down my face as I tried to focus on the end of yarn on the pillow in my lap.

"Tina, forget that unraveled pillow and let's talk."

I jumped to my feet and threw Granny's pillow into the corner of my closet. I couldn't fix it and I couldn't fix Teri.

"What good is talking? I have talked and talked for the last seven months. But our 12- year- old daughter doesn't listen to anything we say. She hates school, she has no friends, she can't stand the sight of me, and all you want to do is talk."

I listened to the rhythmic sound of his pacing. One, two, three, four, turn. One, two, three, four, turn. Repeat, repeat, repeat. His shoulders sagged and his wrinkled face made him look weary. We had been through so much together. The toll on our family had been enormous.

He was speaking again. "We can talk this out."

"You simplify it too much. You didn't see her eyes. There was no remorse, fear, or guilt - only hatred for me catching her skipping shots, for enforcing rules now to protect her, and for watching her give herself shots. Her eyes burned holes in me. She said she would try, but I don't see that. It's all a lie. It was all for nothing."

Stopping beside me he remarked, "Tina, we can't give up. We have to plan what to do next."

Bewildered at his lack of understanding, I began to spew.

"Plan? Plan? What are you going to do? Outline a step-by-step, three-month wonder cure? Well, you are on your own! After all, she likes you better anyway. I just can't try anymore. There is nothing left inside me." I collapsed on the side of the bed and sagged below the weight of hopelessness.

Taking my hands in his, Gib called my name. As I looked up into his eyes, I saw such immense pain. "What you are really saying is that you **won't** try again, not that you can't."

"What do you mean?" I demanded.

"I mean that she has rejected you so many times that you're pulling back in self-protection. You are unwilling to take another chance for fear she'll reject you again."

I pulled away and walked to the window. Oddly, the rain outside was silent. My first thought was to ignore Gib and ask God why it rained every time I was in a crisis. Why? I could see the rain fall but there was no sound. It was just as silent in here. Gib was right. I was determined not to be hurt again. She had knocked me down so many times in the past months. She had called me a warden and worse. The pain was an open sore. My silence confirmed his statement.

Sarcastically I said, "So what's your great plan to make all right in heaven and earth?"

Ignoring my sarcasm, his voice droned on as he analyzed different scenarios. His optimism really annoyed me. Finally, I realized he had to see failure of his idea for himself. So, I decided the easiest solution was to humor him. He pointed out that Teri desperately wanted a 10-speed bike, and we should capitalize on that desire. He outlined a reward system that would allow her to earn the bike. We'd use colorful poker chips and for each day she stayed in school, she could put one chip in the bowl. Five full days of school and she could add a bonus chip. This was not to have anything to do with her shot, as that was a different problem. Once she reached 50 chips, she would get the bike. Although I never believed it would do any good, I agreed to his plan.

He left the room to tell Teri and I walked to the window only to see it was still raining. "Okay God, I think you are trying to tell me something with it raining every time there is a crisis. I guess I am too stubborn, slow, or dense to get your message. I struggle over and over; the sun comes out a few days and then the rain returns. What am I doing wrong?" Without waiting for God to answer, I busied myself with chores and tucked away my feelings for later.

Three weeks after we implemented the plan, Teri came into the kitchen to put her seventh chip in the bowl. She seemed to enjoy watching the chips grow but she commented that she knew I thought she'd never get enough.

I shrugged, "I guess that decision is up to you."

"Then you better start watching for ads because I am going to get my bike," she spat out as she stomped out of the kitchen.

Ten days later, she beamed with pride as she counted out 18 chips on the table. Gib was encouraged and I remained guarded and cautious. He turned and smiled at me as she left the room. I warned him not to get his hopes up as even earning the bike might not keep her going to school.

He actually laughed. "Don't be so negative. Look how rarely you get a call from the nurse's office. By the time she earns the bike, going to school will be a habit."

"Perhaps," was my only response. I wondered if Teri's anger at me would create enough motivation to keep her going.

As Teri's attendance at school became stable, her lack of friends became more evident. Her old circle of friends had moved on without her since she had been gone so often. Therefore, she found anyone who would befriend her and the parade of girls in tight clothes, heavy eye make-up and filthy mouths was another thing for us to argue about. One afternoon we had a heated discussion about these so-called friends.

She shouted, "The whole problem is that you want to live my life for me. You have to watch me give myself shots, watch me eat, make me go to school, tell me what time to go to bed and now even you want to choose my friends. You can't live my life for me you know."

"That's not the problem. You have destroyed my trust." I retorted.

"What trust?"

I paused, trying to regain control of myself. After all, I was the adult here and I needed to act like it.

"Teri, up until a few months ago I had complete faith in you. You assured me you were giving yourself shots, staying on your diet, and doing everything necessary to live within the boundaries of your disease. But, when I realized the truth, all that was destroyed. I don't know what to believe anymore."

"And I'll never get a second chance, will I?" She slammed the door as she ran from the room.

I stared at the spot where she had stood. Was she manipulating me again or was I being unreasonable? All self-assurance as a parent had long drained out of me and I had nothing to take its place. Logic, instinct, and wisdom were all foreign to me. I was sure of nothing in my life. "What am I to do, God? Am I too careful? Is she just trying to control me to get her way? What do I do?"

Abruptly the challenge came a few days later when she asked to attend a party with her new friends. Immediately, I bristled. I tried to thwart it, but Gib was insistent that she could go. After our show-down a few days earlier I questioned if my grounds were truly founded. Bowing to Gib's thoughts, I agreed to let her go.

As Friday night came, I tried to hide my own misgivings as I sent her off with a smile. In less than an hour she called asking if Gib would come pick her up. Once home, Gib asked her if the party was a bore.

"No, I just decided they aren't really my type - we don't like the same things. So, I just came home." That was the only explanation and the last we heard of those friends.

Eleven weeks after starting Gib's chip project, Teri finally had her 50 chips. We went to the store to purchase the bike she had chosen. While Gib left us to pay, she stood holding the handlebars and beaming with joy. How utterly beautiful she looked as her eyes devoured each part of "her" bike. Unaware of any other customers in the store, she giggled and wrinkled her nose in excitement. She was still grinning as Gib returned and they started wheeling the bike out the door. "Oh, by the way," she said still beaming, "Julie asked me to spend the night Friday night. Can I ride my bike over there?"

Panic flooded over me. She had not asked to sleep over since I discovered she wasn't giving herself shots.

"I don't know, Teri. What would you do about your injection in the morning?"

"I could just have her mom watch me." Her matter-of-fact voice took me by surprise.

"Dad and I will talk after supper, and we will let you know."

After dinner she ran outside to ride her bike and I told Gib what she wanted to do. I was surprised with the ease he gave his approval. When I objected, he reminded me that she hadn't missed a day of school in 2 ½ months and seemed to have dropped her questionable friends. I remained skeptical.

"You trusted her before. You let her go to the party with those friends." Gib calmly stated.

"No," I confessed. "I never trusted her. I just let her go because I was too tired to fight anymore."

"Whatever the reason, the result was positive. What are you afraid of now?" he queried.

"I don't know. I guess I see she has made progress in areas that are surface things. We still don't laugh, enjoy each other, or even desire to be together. Are there any really deep changes? Is she just biding her time?"

Quickly he responded, "Well, we're going to have to let her go sometime. Evidently, she thinks she can do it and she did volunteer to let Kathy watch her give her shot."

"I have nothing left to fall back on. She always seems to be trying to prove something to me."

"Then let her prove to you she can be trusted again. Put her on her honor to give her shot without you being there," He sounded so convincing.

I felt like I had been suddenly thrown into an ice-cold pool and I was struggling to tread water while the current was pulling me under. "But it's too soon," I barely whispered.

"It will always be too soon." He turned as she entered the front door and asked her to join us at the table. I reached out and laid my hand on her shoulder and she recoiled. I didn't release her. She shrugged her shoulder trying to loosen my grip, but I was determined she would let me touch her. Once she relaxed, I removed my hand. She looked up at me with questioning eyes. I smiled in return.

Gib spoke first and laid down a few ground rules for the overnight. "We believe you can be trusted to give your shot even if we aren't there to watch."

Slowly, her eyes shifted to me, and she asked, "But, you don't, do you?"

"I honestly don't know what I believe anymore," I added.

"But you'll let me go anyway?" She sounded unconvinced.

"Yes, I will let you go, and you can ride your new bike over there."

Saturday morning, I was cleaning the closet in my bedroom when she waltzed in. She related the great time she had and how they stayed up late and watched a movie. Her voice was vibrant and full, yet she shifted from foot to foot and avoided my eyes.

"What's the matter?"

"I want to tell you something, but I don't know how."

"Just spit it out," I encouraged and stiffened at the same time.

"It's about my shot. I gave it this morning without Kathy watching me. I just pretended you were there, and I just gave it. It wasn't hard at all. I guess I just needed a little time."

I stared into her eyes. They weren't filled with rage or anger. Instead, there was something new and vital. I saw pride and joy dancing. There was a gentleness that reminded me of a vulnerable little girl dressed in frills. I reached out and brushed the hair out of her face and she didn't pull away.

Before I could say anymore, she bent over and picked up my Granny's crocheted pillow I had thrown there months before.

"Hadn't you better fix that loose strand and reweave this before it all comes apart?" she asked. Our hands touched as she handed me the pillow and I felt suspended in time as memories of the last months flooded over me. Just as the deterioration of our relationship had been gradual, the rebuilding was going to take time, but I suddenly knew we had begun.

"Yes," I laughed nervously. "I think I should. I threw it there when I didn't think I had the patience to reweave it. I'm ready now to try it."

She turned to leave, and I called after her. "Teri, I'm very proud of you. I guess we both just needed some time."

"Thanks for trusting me."

Did I trust her? What was trust? Oh, I knew Abraham had shown his trust when he started to follow-through on sacrificing Isaac. I knew Moses showed his trust as he held his arms high as God parted the waters of the Red Sea. I knew David had shown his trust when he went into battle with Goliath with only a sling shot. But they were exceptional. I was just an average person. If I was struggling to always trust God, how could I trust Teri? Was I only willing to trust when it was simple or easy?

There in my closet with my unraveled pillow, I thought of my Godly grandmother. Her example had always been to allow the Spirit to lead, control and guide her. As I tugged at the loose strains of yarn, I could almost hear her speak. "Let go," she cried. "Let go and trust Him and Teri. It is time."

Was I ready? Was I once again letting circumstances control me? I was afraid and discontented. Peace and joy had escaped me. Suddenly I understood I was making a choice and I was choosing to be miserable. Granny was reminding me all she had taught me. I couldn't control my circumstances, but I could allow the Holy Spirit to control my reactions. My God was greater than everything I would face. Staring at the pillow, I continued thinking of Granny. I remembered a day she said to me, "Always remember YOU ARE THE DAUGHTER OF THE KING!"

Suddenly, a bolt of joy passed through me. All my baby steps of faith had led to this moment. All the ups and downs of life that had defeated me fell like broken dishes at my feet. I would no longer allow the world, situations, and people to steal my peace. I WAS THE DAUGHTER OF **THE** KING AND I WOULD START ACTING LIKE IT. In that moment my entire outlook on life changed. **Nothing, nothing,** could stop my spirit now from rejoicing - not death, not trial, not anger or frustration. No opinions, betrayals or disappointments would control me. I had what God had always wanted me to have. I had assurance, peace, joy, and a new outlook on life. Sure, I would have sorrow, but I would have joy in the midst of it. I would have pain and trials, but I would have contentment inside. People would disappoint me, but nothing could separate me from the love of God.

I rose from the closet, pillow in hand with a new attitude. I could not only repair Granny's unraveled pillow, but I also knew my life would never again unravel. Whenever I might have a hic-up in faith, I would think of Granny's pillow and remember, "I AM THE DAUGHTER OF **THE** KING!" Joy will surely flood my heart and soul. Yes, I was ready! Ready to Trust!

FOR EVERYTHING THERE IS A SEASON
CHAPTER 8

Roller coasters have always been a joy to me. The anticipation as the car climbs the first peak, the sudden shock as my body descends while my stomach is trying desperately to catch up, the squeals of the riders, the speed, the quick turns, and the surprise at the unknown in front of me all send my heart leaping inside me. This ride doesn't make me nauseous like many others do, yet I get the thrill and excitement it offers. Odd that I love the roller coaster as a ride so much and hate it in the up and downs of life's experiences just as intensely.

The difference now was that when I passed through the deep gorges of life, I moved through them quickly with hope and joy. Sure, sometimes I was gasping for air and struggling to climb to the next summit, but now I did it with an inner peace and was able to laugh, smile and feel deep joy even in the middle of the crisis. I now knew that instead of trying to move the mountains in front of me, I needed to climb them. The sudden drops into the rifts of disappointment became only tiny vacuums in my emotions, and I focused on the Spirit of God in me. I began loving this adventurous ride of life. I felt alive and vital in the hands of a mighty God.

Gib had completed his master's degree, and we had celebrated with our closest friends with an open house. We were proud of his accomplishment. Just as he finished, we took a camper trip to the southern states and the historical site of St. Augustine, Florida. We tried to envision how the oldest city in America had looked back then. We enjoyed the beautiful coastline as we drove north through Georgia and South Carolina before turning inland. We discussed the confederate states, slavery, the civil war, <u>Gone with the Wind</u> and the disagreements that split our nation. Then we hit country western music. The kids were all old enough now to really take in the history of our nation, the diversity of our people, and the fun of a well-sung ballad.

Shane's senior year began so quicky it was difficult to absorb the fact that all those years had passed since I held my first baby that crisp December morning. He had been so tiny to be the fulfillment of my life-long dream to have a baby. As he grew, I had loved every moment of being his mom. It seemed like only a moment before, but now we stood on the brink of everything changing. I was excited for him, but knew soon, too soon, he would be moving on in life and things would never be the same. When he chose a near-by Christian college I sighed quietly, thankful that he wasn't going far. Toward the end of the year, he went on choir tour and Gib went along as chaperone. They both had a great time. Friends attended his commencement, and he had his all-night party to celebrate. His open house was hugely attended as we celebrated with his friends, as well as family friends. My first-born was now a graduate, and it came too quickly.

In September he moved into the dorm and became involved in college life. He played football, joined male chorus, and his room at home became quiet. No more races to strip his bed, no more pranks he pulled on me, no more drinking directly from the milk carton. We would have to settle with seeing him on Sunday mornings at church. We all missed him, but evidently Wendy didn't let it sink in that he was gone.

One fall day Gib went to the cookie jar and found it empty. "Who ate all the chocolate chip cookies?" he demanded.

Without thinking Wendy replied. "Shane ate them." The words were barely out of her mouth when you could tell by the look on her face that couldn't be true. Shane wasn't around.

Gib stared at her, "You want to alter your story a little?"

A quick glance around the room and with a sheepish grin she admitted, "I ate them."

As happy as everything else was, church was the opposite end of the spectrum. It was in deep trouble and leading to a full church split. It felt like a divorce. I have always been a peacekeeper and felt completely helpless to stop the momentum of this rock rolling down the mountain and gathering so much junk along the way. Attempts to correct misunderstandings caused more confusion and it was becoming clear God wanted drastic change. It was a time of deep sorrow as we had experienced something so incredibly special in that church. The friends we made there would be life-long friends. We had added two families to our group of closest friends. The five families loved spending time together, and the adults became aunts and uncles to the kids. We looked forward to Sundays, special holidays, and outing together. Then, Mary Ann, Sharon and Alan all brought much love and laughter to the group. Mary and her husband, Ron, had left the church, and we learned how difficult it was going to be to sustain our time without seeing them weekly. Still, the remaining families tried to hang on, unwilling to let go of this special time.

Suddenly, in the middle of this uncertainty, my beloved Granddad died. It was March and as we drove south to Oklahoma to be with family, we watched the snow along the side of the road disappear and brown grass took its place. Finally, a few sprouts of green started appearing. Granddad Charlie was not a perfect man even in my eyes. However, he was the one person I always felt would love me no matter how naughty I was. I knew I could disappoint everyone else in my life but never him. His pride in me was not based on my performance and I was so thankful to have him. He was my fragile confidence and now he was gone.

I stood in front of the coffin and looked down at the shell of the man I loved so much. I had him for 36 years, longer than many of my friends had their grandfathers. Yet, I couldn't believe he was gone. I had always called him Charlie instead of Granddad. He would take me downtown with him and introduce me to all his friends and hold my hand as we walked the street together. We skipped, laughed, and worked in the garden together. He chased me, and we loved each other without restraint.

I noticed the hair that sprouted from his fingers, and I reached down and smoothed it as I had done so many times. They were cold. I touched his cheeks, but they didn't ripple under my fingers as before. His eyes were closed so I couldn't see them light up again as he saw me. We'd had something so very special and now it was gone. As tears slid silently down my cheeks, I felt Granny's arm around my waist.

"He's happier now," she whispered. "He's with Jesus."

"I know, but we will miss him."

She nodded her white head and I wondered how she would face each day without him. They had spent 69 years as a pair and in her sorrow, she was trying to comfort me. Looking at her strength reminded me of strength all around me; God 's strength, Gib's strength, and Granny's strength. God was talking to me, and I heard Him loud and clear.

After the service, we returned to their house, and I lingered alone outside while the rest of the family went indoors. In silence, I walked down the driveway struggling with the idea that Charlie was really gone. I noticed how many things had changed over the years. The driveway had always been gravel and now was concrete. The old tree that sheltered the drive and provided hours of climbing fun for my brother, Carl, and I was now a stump. Those things had changed but one fact had never changed. I always had Granny and Charlie.

As a kid I had spent many weeks each summer with my grandparents. I had eagerly awaited the sound of crunching gravel as his car started up the drive at noon. I would rush outside to greet him, and he would chase me into the house, and Granny would have to slow us down. He taught me to call out "doodle bugs", crack pecans between two rocks, tie up tomato plants with rags and even how to drive before I could barely see over the steering wheel. We got in trouble together for running in the house and spent hours gluing a broken vase we shattered because Granny was so angry with us. My love and admiration were genuine, and the only demand I ever made of him was his presence. Now, he couldn't fulfill that simple demand. He would never take my hand again, yodel while he worked or have me help him with his chores.

As I walked up the driveway, I remembered my first encounter with death. It had been here, on this driveway. I had a kitten named Toby. She purred and butted her head against me when I scratched her ears. I had loved the sound of a motorboat she made. She was a beautiful kitten, and her white fur was dotted with clumps of brown that looked like dust balls. That day, my brother, Carl, had tugged at her paws until she got annoyed and ran off. Carl and I had stretched out on the ground watching the clouds until Daddy came out of the house twirling his keys around his fingers. Charlie, close behind said, "Hey, you kids want to go to the ice dock? We are going to make homemade ice cream."

"Whoopee," we both yelled and raced for the car. It only took a few minutes to reach the ice dock and we waited impatiently in the backseat while Daddy went inside. He reappeared with a huge brown sack slung over his shoulder and moved awkwardly as it seemed to propel him down the steps and toward the car. Carl opened the door and Dad plopped it on the floorboard of the back seat.

"Don't eat all of it before we get home," he said with a grin.

Carl nudged me and began poking his finger through the layers of the bag until he finally had a hole big enough to pull out some ice chips.

"Do you think you could find a tiny morsel of ice for little ole me?" Charlie asked.

"Sure," Carl laughed. "Where do you want it?"

"My hand will do," Charlie responded with an open palm.

Carl took some ice, dropped it in Charlie's hand, a few more in Dad's extended hand and then some down the back of my shirt. I squealed with delight and was still struggling to get it out as we turned into the driveway. Abruptly, Daddy stopped the car.

I sat up to see over the seat. Toby was asleep in the middle of the driveway. Afraid Daddy would be angry, I jumped out of the car and ran to pick her up. There was something funny about her mouth. It was half-opened and there was blood on her nose. I bent over to touch her, but Daddy, now standing next to me, steered my hand aside and laid his on her tummy. Shaking his head, he turned to look at me "I'm sorry, Honey. She's dead. We must have run over her as we backed out."

"But she wasn't anywhere around when we left," I protested.

"Maybe she was sleeping up in the tire well," Charlie said. "It is a nice warm place for a kitty to nap."

"Probably so," continued Daddy. "She would have fallen out from the motion of the car."

"But she was alive just a few minutes ago. She can't be dead." I protested.

"I'm sorry, Honey. I really am. But just wanting her to be alive won't bring her back. It was just an accident."

I sat by my kitty and cried while my mother came out and tried to comfort me. I remember nothing of what she said. After a while, Granny came out with a shoe box. She opened it revealing a shiny blue fabric. "I thought you might like some pretty material for her to lay on."

"It's pretty," I choked.

"Put her gently in the box," she said.

I shook my head. Granny sat down on the driveway beside me. "Are you afraid to touch her?" she gently asked.

I nodded.

"Just because she is dead doesn't change the fact that she is your lovely kitten" she said as she slid her hand down Toby's back and straightened her hair. "There is nothing to be afraid of."

"But she's dead!"

"Yes, she's dead. But that is no reason to be afraid of her. Here, let me help you," She took my hand in hers and firmly guided it over Toby. Her fur was still soft, but the body underneath didn't give in to my touch. The fur rippled as it broke loose from my fingers, but she didn't purr or stretch. Finally, Granny let go and scratched Toby's head as I continued to pet her. "See, death is not something to be afraid of. Can you pick her up now and put her in the box?"

With all the love and concern I could show my kitty, I gently picked her up and sat her on the shiny, blue material. Granny arranged her so the spot of blood on her nose didn't show and then handed me the lid. I put the lid in place covering Toby. Granny stood up and I followed. She picked up the box and put it in my hands.

"Take her around back of the garage. Your Daddy's waiting there" she said gently.

I was nervous. I had never been to a funeral before, and I didn't know what to expect. Daddy was leaning on a shovel. Carl was sitting on the ground tossing dirt clots while Charlie stood nearby.

"Do you want to place her in the hole?" Daddy asked.

Before I could decide, Carl took the box from me and placed it gently on the bottom of the hole. Daddy started dropping clumps of dirt on the box and I felt Mother's hand on my shoulder. Once the dirt was all in the hole, Daddy pushed it down softly but firmly with his foot.

Then, he knelt down in front of me and said, "I really am sorry, Honey."

"I know, Daddy. It was just an accident."

They all left me alone and I sat patting the dirt. I thought about whiskers, tiny nails, pink ears, and wet noses. Finally, I went looking for Carl. He was in the garage carving on a board.

"I thought you might like a little cross for your kitty." He had tied two boards crosswise with a piece of leather cord and was carving "Toby" into the wood. He took a hammer, and I followed him to the grave where he hammered the little cross into the ground. Much later that day, we had to leave our grandparents' house to return to ours, and I had stopped by the grave to say goodbye to my kitty. I smiled at the little cross.

Now, almost thirty years later, I walked around to where the grave had been. No visible sign of Toby remained. The cross had fallen and decayed years ago and, in its place, jonquils sprouted in full yellow blooms. Toby had been a part of my life for only a few weeks but, she had been special to me, and I still remembered her after all these years. To others, she had been a lesson in the day of a child, but to me it had been the beginning of acceptance of death as a part of living. That lesson has stayed with me throughout my life, enabling me to accept death whether sudden or expected.

Now, Charlie was dead. He had been an intimate part of my entire life, and I knew I would miss him immensely. No other person in the family had the exact memories I had of him. Their memories were just as precious to them even if they weren't the same as mine. Mine belonged only to me. I wasn't afraid of death. I could touch his body like I had touched Toby 30 years before. My memories would make him always vital in my life and would remain fresh until we meet again in Heaven. Someday, we will walk the main street of Heaven, holding hands again. and he will introduce me to all his friends again. He had been constant in my life.

Standing there where Toby's grave had been, I felt a gentle drizzle fall on my shoulders. I looked up to see a bright blue sky with sunlight flooding it. Right above me was one small, leaking cloud. I smiled. God had shown His presence to me, and I was grateful. I kept my face raised so the little raindrops could wash me, and I began to sing. As the words to "How Great Thou Art" poured out of my heart, I began to sway with the rhythm. Slowly, I turned round and round, still singing and absorbing God's blessing as it rained down on me. I had a wonderful grandfather that taught me so much about love and life. I had an even greater Father, Abba, that never, never left my side. Soon, I was spinning, swaying, and dancing in the rain. God had prepared me for this loss by teaching me to keep my eyes on him and now I could dance in the rain even though

Charlie was gone. Soon, very soon, I would dance in heaven with Charlie. What joy I felt!

A few days after the funeral, we returned to Minnesota only to find the fatal crack in our church had destroyed what little hope was left. It was time for us to go. We had to leave the church and I carried a deep hurt in my heart. It took months of searching until we found a new church home. Besides our immediate family, Kathy (my little sister in Christ) joined us. Shane quickly became active in the college group and drove a bus each Sunday to pick up students from the surrounding colleges. (No surprise the bus was filled with mostly girls). Teri started in the high school group and Wendy seemed adjusted to the move but suddenly announced she didn't want to go to middle school.

As I questioned her more, tears erupted from this normally unemotional girl and I was befuddled. After a bit of coaxing, she finally said, "I don't want to be sick all the time." Reality shook me as I realized she was basing her statement on Teri's experience of middle school.

"Teri's sickness had nothing to do with being in middle school," I almost shouted.

She asked if I had been sick in middle school. I told her I wasn't, nor Dad nor Shane. Shane had even had perfect attendance. Surprisingly, she appeared relieved, nodded, smiled, and walked away. That was all the assurance she needed, and all was right in Wendy's world.

Teri's high school years began after Shane's ended. I was relieved when Teri finally found her niche. Her spot in life was music. First, she joined the choir and then a performance group called Knights Unlimited. There she formed life-long friends who helped her through rough times, and for the first time in years, she loved going to school. She was always quick and intelligent and became a straight A student. Finally, things were looking up for her.

We bought a cabin up north on a lake and began weekend trips. We brought Bill, Joan, and their kids the first weekend, and through those early trips we all began to heal from the church split and had great bonding time as we enjoyed the great outdoors. Shortly, Ron and Mary came and were quick to lend a hand as we raked, cleaned, and we all settled into this new life. All though separated into different churches now, we were careful to get together often and on all holidays. We created memories that still bring smiles and laughter.

Wendy and I were alone one fall day, and it was raining just enough that our cocker spaniel didn't want to go outside. Wendy and I tried to coax her out, but we failed. So, I grabbed her collar, drug her out the door and told Wendy to follow. "I don't have a raincoat on," she protested.

"You don't need one," I responded. "It's only water."

The three of us, Wendy, the dog and I, stood as the rain fell.

"Look, Mom! The rain looks like little frogs jumping." She pointed at a puddle where the drops were plopping into the water, resulting in an eruption of water shooting inches into the air.

I burst into giggles. "That's exactly the way it looks. Come on, let's jump too."

She looked at me with disbelief as I ran into the yard and began stomping and jumping in the water. She couldn't resist the temptation and joined me as we laughed and twisted in the rain. Even the dog caught the excitement, barking and jumping with us. Suddenly I was transported back to childhood.

Growing up in Oklahoma's "tornado alley" meant the rainstorms were often followed by something much more severe. We had to be watchful and alert for sudden changes. My favorite rains had been in late August and early September while the temperatures were still warm, but the threat of tornados lessened. Often, Carl and I felt like prisoners held captive by a mom that refused to let us go outside in the rainstorm. We wanted to run, jump, and dance in the rain. Instead, Mother cautioned us on the lightning that came with it. We were stuck inside, and rain was only a spectator sport.

One fall day Carl and I were sitting on the couch, looking longingly out at the rain when Mother surprised us saying, "There is no lightning today. Do you want to go outside and play in the rain?" We didn't even take time to put on shoes. We had to hurry before she changed her mind. We sped past her and out the back door. We ran, skipped, and giggled down the driveway. Our dog was confused by our behavior but joined in the gaiety. His tail wagged in rhythm with our whoops and squeals. A normal person would say it was a gentle rain but to us it was heaven opening up.

Puddles began to form and invited us to splash in them. We covered ourselves in water and mud. The red dirt of Oklahoma settled all over our legs and somehow spread to our faces. We tried to drink the water as it fell, and the smell of wet grass reminded us that our dream of playing in the rain was really happening. The wetter we got, the more we laughed. We had freedom and felt a little naughty. There were no rules to our new game, and we collapsed in heaps on the wet grass. Our clothes were heavy, but they couldn't stop the feeling we were flying. We looked up at the window and saw Mom laughing. "Thank you, God. Thank you, Mom," I muttered. And a priceless memory was etched on my brain and heart. Such a great memory!

Back in the present, I looked up at Wendy. She was jumping and twirling but still looking at me in disbelief. "I hope you always remember this day," I chuckled.

"Oh, I think I will always remember the day my Mom was outrageous!"

She had no idea the real significance of dancing in the rain that day. Only time would reveal it.

NEW SEASONS OF LIFE

CHAPTER 9

Change seemed to be at every turn in our lives. It started with time for another cousin, Lindy, to get married in California. Shane and Lindy were only 8 months apart and as close as cousins across the country could be. So, we all piled into the camper and headed west. Gib's parents dropped us at my sister's home, and they took off alone for a week while we stayed for the wedding. We had a marvelous time and Gib's parents returned a week later and picked up our family and we headed to the Grand Canyon. As we stood staring at the massive canyon in front of us, I was reminded of the glorious creator's hand. It was a great ending for the summer.

My friends had told me about the "revolving door syndrome" and now it was our turn to experience it first-hand. Shane decided that he didn't want a huge debt for college, so he moved home and changed schools. The University of Minnesota was not only cheaper than a private Christian school, but it also had much more to offer him in his engineering pursuits. Unlike many parents, we were thrilled to have him home. Soon, Shane and I took off to Oklahoma to celebrate my beloved Granny's 90th birthday. She was so happy as loved ones surrounded her. My Granddad had always wanted to make his 90th and she almost felt guilty for reaching it without him.

As winter settled in, my parents decided they wanted to see it first-hand all the snow and frozen lakes we talked about. They flew up and sure enough, a blizzard hit the next day. Mom pulled a chair in front of the window and sat all day watching the events. Snowplows came down the street pushing the snow into high piles along the sides. People were outside shoveling and blowing snow, and she got excited when Gib and Shane went out and used the snow blower right in front of her. Soon, the sun came out and kids came out to build snowmen. Others were cross- country skiing down the street and she was astonished that cars were out driving on the remaining snow. Later that day, the four of us drove to the grocery store and they saw the huge mountain of snow pushed to the side of the parking lot. Dad just couldn't believe it was all snow and there wasn't a mountain underneath it. However, the most excitement came the next day when we drove them north. We reached the huge Lake Mille Lacs where hundreds of ice houses were parked in organized fashion on the ice. We drove out on the lake and Daddy panicked and rolled down his window just in case we sank. We explained they plowed roads on the ice and delivered mail to the ice houses. Curious, he asked what the ice houses were like inside. We spotted smoke rising from one and stopped and knocked on the door. After explaining our father's curiosity, the two young men invited us inside. Along one wall were some bunk beds, a pot was warming stew on a little hot plate, the electricity that ran to the edge of the house kept the small heater humming and in the corner was a hole in the ice with two lines dropped in. They showed us the fish they had caught, and Daddy started laughing.

"I think this is just a way to escape your wives and drink for the weekend." The two guys burst into laughter and nodded in agreement. As we stepped back onto the ice, Daddy heard the ice shifting and thought it was cracking to the point we would sink. "Get in the car and get me off this lake!" he demanded. He said he had done that once but never again. As much fun as that adventure had been, it was entertaining to drive by the same lake the next summer and watch as their mouths dropped open. Daddy raised his voice in alarm saying, "I must have been a fool to go out there with all that water below." As the years passed, you could easily get him excited if you brought up the idea of driving on a frozen lake.

While they were visiting, Wendy had a diving meet. Mother just kept shaking her head and remembering attending Wendy's swimming lessons when she was 5. Wendy had been so afraid of the water; she wouldn't let go of the side of the pool without a life- guard to hold onto. Mother was convinced she would never swim and now she watched her in diving competition. On an early dive, Wendy hit her head on the bottom of the pool. Assured she was fine, the coach put her back into the meet and she dived better than ever before. We all joked that she needed to hit her head in order to do her best. It had been a great winter experience for my parents, and they more fully appreciated what we live with daily. They were, however, eager to return South!

A few months later, Gib's parents had their 50th anniversary and Gib and I flew to Oklahoma. His brother arrived from New Jersey, and we all went to a special restaurant only to find a room of friends waiting. They were thrilled to celebrate with their sons, special friends and greatly appreciated Jinkers for arranging it all.

Our next big change came through Shane again. He had dated different girls throughout college, but he became serious about just one, Kelly. It soon became obvious she was "the one." He was graduating with his bachelor's degree, and we had planned an open house celebration. He wanted a creative engagement, so, he decided to surprise her at **his** open house. While he opened his presents, he had arranged to have that time recorded. Kelly had just completed her associate degree, and in the stack of his presents there was one for her. When he handed her the gift to open, she laid it aside remarking this was his day. Nervous and almost shaking he demanded she open it. Although reluctant, she opened it to keep him from overreacting. When she gasped, everyone stopped talking and watched. Inside was a written proposal and a ring. She said yes and we all were thrilled that we had actually attended someone else's engagement, and it had all been recorded for posterity. Joy and fun for all. Wedding plans started in earnest.

While Shane was preparing to become a husband, the biggest change in his life so far, his job of big brother continued. Teri was completing her senior year in High School and since she didn't have a boyfriend at the time, she invited her big brother to take her to prom. He did so proudly, and they had a wonderful evening. Shane had always been the watchful and protective brother. There was a family joke about that role that referred to an incident when Teri was just a few weeks old. I needed to fetch a diaper, so I put Teri on the couch and told 5-year-old Shane to watch her. When I returned, I found Teri screaming on the floor after wiggling off the couch. Incredulously, I demanded, "I thought I told you to watch her." In the complete honesty of a child, he replied, "I did, Mom. I watched her fall off the couch." So, through the years we laughed about big brother "watching" his sisters.

Still another story of his "watching" his sisters happened when he was in high school. Gib and I attended a play across town with a huge group from Gib's work. Mid-performance they halted the show and announced there had been a tornado go through the northern suburbs. Hundreds rushed to pay phones (before cell phones) and when unable to reach our kids, we ran to our car and drove home fearing the worst. Neighborhoods all around us were hit and already police had cordoned off the areas. Our hearts were pounding as we turned into our neighborhood and saw all the homes intact. We rushed inside to find the kids sitting on the floor laughing and talking.

"We tried to call. Why didn't you answer the phone?" Gib questioned.

Teri was the first to respond, "Because we were gone. Shane took us out to see the tornado. Mom, there were houses without roofs and wires everywhere."

Multiple emotions sped through our brains. Should we get angry at their foolishness, or just rejoice they were okay? Somehow this demanded a response and I hesitated for fear I would say things I regretted. Gib, on the other hand, jumped right in. "Shane, are you nuts? Those wires were live electricity. They could have electrocuted you all. There could have been more tornadoes. There were nails all over the road and could have punctured your tires and you would have been stranded. What were you thinking?"

"I just thought it would be cool to see all the damage right away. I was watching out for the girls." Shaking his head Gib continued, "We are grateful you are all okay. However, in the future don't ever go chasing after thrills from a tornado. It isn't safe. We drove home in a total panic since you didn't answer the phone. From now on, Shane, watch your sisters with a little more wisdom." The three kids grinned at each other. They had shared a secret time they would always remember, and mom and dad would get over it. They would have the memories.

Of course, change wasn't relegated to only one person. Teri graduated from high school and was preparing to go away to college. With Shane's wedding in a few weeks, my sister, Patricia, flew in from California. We packed the trunk with all the things Teri would need at college and piled our own luggage on the top. Patricia, Teri, Wendy, and I took off for a cross-country trip to settle Teri in her dorm in Philadelphia. We laughed, watched the change in scenery as we drove East, and Patricia even learned to really read a map. What fun we had. She had come to help me drive and it was a great time together. We returned home without Teri. and as I walked down the hallway, I saw her empty bedroom and began to cry knowing things would never be the same. Her life and ours were changing. We had spent so many happy and miserable times in that bedroom and now it was empty. My little girl was no longer little. My little girl no longer lived here. It was a day we all set as a goal in life but that doesn't make it an easy moment to reach. She would fly home in a couple of weeks to attend Shane's wedding, but then she would be gone again. Doubts crept into my mind as I wondered if I had done all I was supposed to do to prepare both of them for their future. Were they both ready to "launch?" Change was definitely unsettling and a little scary.

However, there was no time for fear or to ponder questions. There were final details to attend to, arrangements to be checked, and the excitement took over any misgivings I was feeling. Shane's cousin, Lindy, surprised him and flew in from CA to make the family attendance more complete. My parents arrived, but Gib's mother had broken her hip and they hadn't been able to come. However, Aunt Jinkers had flown up alone to stand in for that side of the family. Teri returned home and we were ready to start the celebration. Patricia, her husband Newell, and some friends put on a fantastic grooms' dinner. We roasted the couple in fun and turned in early for the next day. The excitement grew and the wedding day finally arrived with a burst of glorious sunshine.

Shane looked so handsome in his white tux and never had I seen his eyes sparkle more than that day. Kelly had a custom-made dress and hat that made her appear to glow. We had fallen in love with her already, so it was even a personal pride I had when I looked at this stunning bride. Kelly and her mom had planned a superb wedding. She had chosen royal blue for her attendants and even her bouquet held some specially dyed royal blue roses. Every detail spoke to the love put into the plans. They even had an ice cream wagon at the reception and Kelly's mom had made special striped aprons for the men serving it. Friends poured in, and it was a day of pure rejoicing and commitment to God in their lives. Then, Shane and Kelly were whisked off for a short honeymoon at a bed and breakfast and then our cabin for a week alone. Once they returned from the cabin, they continued their honeymoon by driving to Oklahoma to see those who couldn't make it to the wedding. Kelly really wanted to include all the family, so she put on her wedding dress, and they spent time visiting with Gib's parents. The next day they drove down to my Granny's home and she and my Aunt Vera Mae got to see Kelly in her wedding dress. The Oklahoma family was so thrilled to have been included and get to see the bride in her dress. I was astounded at this newly married young lady who wanted to spend her honeymoon hours with those who couldn't come to her wedding. She continued that unselfishness a few months later at Christmas. Although it was her first Christmas as a married woman, she agreed to spend it with Shane's family in Oklahoma.

It was my parents' 50th wedding anniversary on Christmas day and the entire family decided to surprise them. First their kids came. Patricia and I and our spouses hid in Carl's house. They had planned to go to dinner and as Mom related that neither daughter had mentioned their coming big day, we jumped out to surprise them. Squeals of laughter rang out. Little did they know that was just the beginning. The next day the grandkids came, and the fun began. There were 18 of us gathered around the table on Christmas Day and gifts for the anniversary appeared also. After a few days the grandkids left, and the adults added another surprise - a surprise trip to Las Vegas. The surprises kept coming when we arrived at the airport to see their best friends ready to board the plane with us. It was a memorable time filled with surprises. In the midst of it all, I was so proud and thankful Kelly was so unselfish she could spend this first Christmas with in-laws. I wondered how I had been blessed with such an unselfish daughter-in-law.

Shane and Kelly's Wedding

After all the hubbub was over, back in Minnesota, it seemed odd to gather for a meal without Shane or Teri. Suddenly, we were a family of 3 instead of 5. Shane and Kelly took up residence in an apartment near the university. Shane was pursuing a graduate degree and Kelly had a job downtown. Teri flew back to Pennsylvania for college, and changes were everywhere. Even Wendy announced she wanted change. She wanted a bigger and better bedroom. We repainted Shane's bedroom and moved his stuff out. Aunt Jinkers, Wendy's soulmate, bought Wendy a full-sized bed for her new room and we decorated the walls with her gymnastic awards and ribbons. We got a new cocker spaniel, Peanut, and he moved into the new room also. Wendy and her dog became inseparable. Gymnastics filled Wendy's time and eventually filled her void of a real clique to belong to. As a freshman, she had qualified for the varsity team and the four years of competition were years of growth for her. She accepted Christ as her Savior and been baptized in a local lake by the same pastor who married Shane. She joined the church youth group, but, sadly, she never found a group of kids that she felt connected to. All these changes around her seemed not to affect her so it was a surprise when I got a phone call from her science teacher wanting to meet. She was an average to an above average student, so I went to the meeting a bit confused. He quickly announced Wendy was making a "D" in his class. Shocked, I asked why. and he showed me all the blanks where she hadn't turned in her homework.

"I don't understand," I protested. "I have seen her working on all those papers. Is there any way we can get into her locker?"

"Sure, we will get the master key in the office." We opened the door to the most organized and clean locker I had ever seen. Sure enough, stacked neatly on top of each other, were each of the pages she was missing. We pulled them out and as the teacher looked them over.

He almost gasped as he remarked, "They are all done except one problem on each page, and they all look correct. Why would she not turn in pages that are 90% done? They would all be A- or B+ work. Instead, she has zero on all of them."

Suddenly, I understood. "She is a perfectionist. In her thinking she hadn't completed the task, so she didn't want to turn them in incomplete. It doesn't make sense to you or me, but to her it was all or nothing. I don't care if she gets any credit for any of this or not. However, she WILL be turning them all in on Monday. She isn't leaving the house until they are done. "Oh, she will get partial credit for late work, but it breaks my heart because it is all worth so much and she will get so little credit," he answered.

"It will be a hard lesson for her to learn but a necessary one. She must force herself to be less than perfect. She must learn to do all she can do, and then if she gets stuck to ask for help. She has always felt asking for help shows weakness, and she is so driven to be strong. She will turn these all in. Please call me on Monday and let me know if you get them." I took all the papers and her textbook and headed home.

"Hi, Mom. How did your meeting go?" She asked without looking me in the face. "You know exactly how it went." I dropped the papers on the table and waited.

"What right do you have to get into my locker?" she shouted." The right of a mother with a daughter in trouble." I retorted. "Wendy, I want you to listen to everything I say. You may not speak, so listen without trying to figure out what you will say next. I see a pattern here. You are a perfectionist. You did nine out of ten problems on each assignment. You got to the most difficult one, number ten, and couldn't figure it out. So, instead of asking for help you quit. Then, since it was incomplete you put it in your locker and didn't turn it in. Today, your teacher looked them over and said all 9 problems on each page looked correct. If you would have turned them in, you would have had 90% on each assignment. Instead, you have a zero on them and are making a "D" and heading for an "F" in the class. Your tests have been good as you know most of the stuff, but you have a zero on all homework Your obsession to do it perfectly has screwed you up bad. Now, when you turn these in you can only get 50% instead of 90%. And my dear, you will be turning these all in on Monday. You are not leaving this house, watching TV, or using the phone until they are completed. You will sit at the dining room table every minute you aren't sleeping or eating and work until done. You may get Dad to help, or we can ask Shane to come over, but you will complete each and every assignment and turn them in on Monday. I have told your teacher to call me after school Monday to assure me he has them all. This is not up for discussion. You cannot deny or try to talk yourself out of this. You MUST and you WILL complete this work. When done, then and only then, will we talk. I know you had plans this weekend so you have 15 minutes to call friends and cancel out of everything. Then, I expect you to be at the table working. Perhaps the more you learned as the semester went on will allow you to be able to work through the early papers on your own. Good luck. You have 15 minutes."

She didn't protest. She made her calls and soon was at work at the table. When Gib came home, he checked on her and sure enough she was remembering how to do the first lessons. As the weekend progressed, Gib had to work alongside her, and we even called Shane a couple of times for clarification. By Sunday afternoon all pages were completed and stacked neatly at the end of the table.

It was time to talk so I sat down opposite her. "Now, what would you like to say?" Belligerently she said, "I have nothing to say."

"You can be angry at me, but the real anger should be directed at yourself. Wendy, you are your worst enemy. Being a perfectionist is one of the hardest things to carry around in life. It pushes people away; it prevents you from experiencing real joy. and it puts limits on what you can do. We **all** fail. The Bible teaches failure is our training ground. The only perfect one was Jesus, and since you aren't Him, you can't be perfect. You will struggle with this all your life. Teri is a perfectionist also and learned how to live with it last fall. She was a freshman in college, and suddenly, she was flunking some classes."

Curious, she asked, "What did she do about it?"

"After lots of tears and battling her own self-perception, she signed up for a study- skills class. It never entered her mind that she had no idea HOW to study. She had absorbed everything easily and school had been a snap. Then, she began to touch on ideas and subjects out of her normal realm and needed to study and learn. But she didn't know how. It was a very humbling experience for her. Wendy, you are learning that lesson now. You can let your perfectionism destroy you, or you can admit you need God's help at putting it in its right and useful place. You must make s choice. Do you want to let it control your life, or do you want to control it?"

"I don't understand all this," she admitted. "I know I screwed up, and I agree I didn't turn those papers in because they weren't finished. But where am I to go from here?"

"Honestly, from here you must decide who is going to have control of your life, goals, and emotions. You must accept yourself and realize you are human and will fail. There are positive traits to perfectionism. You are a good planner, thorough, you give attention to details. However, when you set standards for yourself that are unreachable, you hate yourself and feel guilty when you don't achieve them. This is the negative side of perfectionism. In Corinthians Paul wrote that God's grace is sufficient for us. And Matthew said whoever exalts himself will be humbled. You will struggle with this, but God wants to carry your burden and the only way to control it is to give your life, goals, and achievements to God. You must work at **wanting** to do your best but not **having** to do your best. You can control this, but it will take effort."

"All this over a few homework assignments?"

I laughed. "Oh, that life was so simple. Tomorrow, you will turn them in. From now on you can ask for help or turn papers in even if not complete. Just don't let things pile up on you again. And Wendy, remember what I have told you over and over. You are the daughter of The King. You are royalty. With that comes lots of perks but also responsibilities. Live up to being His daughter!"

"I know Mom. I guess if you make me do the work anyway I might as well do it the first time," she snickered. "Can I do something else now?"

"Sure, if all your other homework is finished in all your other classes."

She stood, laughed, and said in passing, "Never give up, Mom. Never give up!"

She was right. I never gave up. Both the girls struggled with perfectionism throughout their lives. However, they both tried to let God help change them and they succeeded in many areas. Occasionally, I would have to remind them their perfectionism was raising its ugly head. They always smiled, nodded, and said thanks for recognizing it.

One morning I woke with a heavy feeling like impending disaster. I worked through chores and the feeling didn't lift. When I finally sat down, allowing myself to think, Wendy strolled through the room. She stood facing me, all 110 pounds of muscle. Assuming my stare gave her entrance into my thoughts, she said, "I've been looking at colleges, Mom. I think I really want to compete in gymnastics at the college level, so I have been looking at ones where I have met coaches."

A blast of hot air hit me square in the face. This was the disaster I was fearing. It had reached the time for me to face that in just 1 ½ years my baby would be gone, and I would be an empty- nester. How did it happen so fast? She was still such a kid in my eyes. She had a steady boyfriend, attended prom, pushed herself in her competition, and still giggled like a small child. She did silly things like burping contests with her buddies. She had grown through a period of lying in order to look better to others, and coming home after curfew. Was she ready to begin looking for colleges? I changed the subject quickly to her dress I was making for her junior prom. I was really hoping I might distract her from talking about such a drastic change.

Before the conversation got going, the ringing phone interrupted. Daddy's voice alerted me to danger. He quickly announced that my dear, Aunt Vera Mae had unexpectedly died. What a shock. She was living with and taking care of Granny. She was never sick. He went on to explain that without warning she had a brain aneurism pop and died without regaining consciousness. This was the real disaster I had felt was coming all morning. Now, I must go to Oklahoma. I would miss Wendy's prom and I hadn't even finished her dress. Quickly. I called my dear friend, Vonnie. She was there in half an hour and started working on Wendy's dress while I packed.

Confident she would finish the design that had no pattern, I left it in her hands, and loaded up Wendy and moved her to Shane and Kelly's while we were gone. I was sad I missed her prom, but it couldn't be helped and once again, God provided others to help when we needed it. I couldn't stop thinking about how this would impact Granny, Mother, and their futures. Would Granny be able to easily enter a nursing home? Mother was still working so how would she have time to handle all Granny's needs? There were big changes on the horizon and no answers yet.

A few days later, after the funeral we had a family meeting. Finally, we all decided they should move Granny to a nursing home in the City near mom where she could drop by after work each day and visit. This would be a difficult change for Granny, but we felt she was a strong woman and could do it. My parents left to go to the city to look at nursing homes while Patricia and I stayed to care for Granny. It became a great time of bonding and lots of laughter.

One afternoon, we heard the ringing of the ice cream truck driving through the neighborhood. Patricia and I grabbed our wallets and ran to stop the small truck. The young boy was visibly shocked when he asked what we wanted to buy, and Patricia boldly answered, "Give us one each of everything you have." When I tried to protest, she stated logically that we didn't know what Granny would want today or tomorrow so we would give her choices. After loading two bags up with all the bars, we paid and took our treasure to the floor of the living room.

We spread all the bars out in front of Granny so she could see them. She squealed in laughter like a small child and pointed at one and then another. She kept giggling until she chose the largest red, white and blue one called "the Bomb." It was way too big for her to finish but she savored every suck and bite she took. She giggled about it all afternoon. The second afternoon, she asked when we were going to have our treats, so we brought them all to the floor again and let her pick. She was just as excited as the first day. Finally, she chose another large one. Each day about 2 PM she would ask for our treats and giggle in earnest at her choices. Yes, change was coming, but we were making memories to go with her through the change. Within a few days we settled her in her new abode, said our goodbyes and promised to return in a couple of months. She wasn't thrilled with her new home, but she was trying her best to be agreeable.

As summer started, we had returned for a brief visit to see Granny and upon our arrival back in Minnesota we got the call that my beloved Granny had died. Teri had gone to a summer mission trip to Wildwood, New Jersey and it was while she was there that Granny died. Therefore, Teri was unable to come for the funeral. It was no surprise Granny only lived two months after my aunt died. Vera Mae had never married, and Granny had only been "holding on" for Vera Mae to have someone to live with. Granny was more than ready to meet her Lord. A quick bladder infection and she was gone. Once again, we traveled to Oklahoma and faced another loss. She would be in Heaven with her husband and daughter now, and I would miss her so much.

As a child, I had spent so many nights at her house and would lie awake watching her when she thought I was asleep. From the screened porch where I slept, I would peek through the windows at the head of my bed and see her on the small sofa. Each night she read her Bible and devotions without fail. Then, placing her Bible on her stomach she would close her eyes and I knew she was praying. Some nights the sessions with God were short while other nights they seemed to go on for a long time. She was faithful and now God had called her home at 93. When I had grown older, she had told me she prayed for me every night and I knew that was true. As Mom and I stood beside her coffin, I mentioned to Mom that I would miss knowing she was praying for me every day. Mom had smiled when she said, "Honey, she is even closer to the throne than she was, and she is still talking directly to Him for you." That was a great comfort for me. After the funeral, we brought the flowers home and lined the back patio. A gentle, warm rain watered them, and once more God was reminding me, He was taking care of Granny, her flowers and me.

A new season of life began. I had gone so many years with the support of my Granny, Charlie, and Aunt Vera Mae. Now, they had all three had moved to Heaven and only Mom remained of that initial family group. I was deeply grateful for the lives of these three godly people. God had used them to teach me many lessons. They had encouraged and inspired me. I did not fear change and new seasons of life. God had led me through it safely and often. I knew it was inevitable. As I thought about the scripture in Ecclesiastics 3, I liked thinking about there being a time for everything. I had just passed from the season of being supported to being the one supporting others. I accepted the changes going on in my life and found I could completely relax. God's plan for me, and each of my children, was full of hope, joy, and adventure. I knew He was leading us through all the seasons of life, including this new season. Knowing that God never changes allowed me to not resist and instead to rejoice. What did He have in store for us?

COUNT HIS GOODNESS BABIES EVERYWHERE

CHAPTER 10

Adventure, I was on an adventure with God. I felt excited, apprehensive, enthusiastic, uncertain, daring and at risk. Where could God lead me? What was in store? Why couldn't He show me the next event? Would there be hazards? Would there be joy or peril? I sucked in deep and remembered how He had taught me to be content in every circumstance. Therefore, He would let it rain when I needed rain, and sunshine when the rain passed. I had nothing to fear. So, my new season in life started with peace and contentment.

In the fall of Wendy's senior year in high school it was time to be earnest in our search for the right college. We began traveling to schools that Wendy had already talked to the gymnastics coach. Meanwhile, Kelly was nearing delivery of our first grandchild, so we called often to find out how things were going. Sure enough, the baby wanted us to hurry home because it was demanding to be let out. Excusing ourselves from discussion with one of the coaches, we sped toward home. As we rushed into the hospital, we saw a tiny pink blanket wrapped around a doll-size being. Overwhelmed, I picked her up and held her close to me. To my surprise, tears of joy rolled down my cheeks and onto her face. I was holding the next generation. I had just closed out my grandparent's generation and now, here was a brand new one. I was deeply grateful to have the privilege to hold my newborn granddaughter, Elyse. Kissing her cheek, I verbally thanked God for this gift of love. I WAS A GRANDMA!

I turned to Kelly and asked, "Can she call me Granny?"

"Of course," she replied.

"I want to keep the love of my Granny alive and there is no better way than for me to love her like my Granny loved me." I really liked this new adventure!

You've heard the adage that the "other" shoe is about to drop? Well, this first shoe had been a soft, fluffy, pink slipper, and now the "other shoe" hit the ground like a heavy work boot. Bam! Gib quit his job. The company had been downsizing and he had survived multiple cuts, but the atmosphere at work had become stifling. He took an enhanced severance package and quit. Instantly we had only one income, my teaching. Now that was one BIG change. At first, he did some consulting, but that wasn't a steady income. He began searching in earnest, had interviews, we flew to a couple of interviews, but nothing fit. This part of the adventure wasn't fun. However, God kept reminding me to be happy, and I was. I had no idea how long this season of unemployment would last, but I determined to support Gib throughout.

Life didn't stop for the rest of the family. Teri moved back home. After her year in Pennsylvania, the cost of an ivy league school was prohibitive. So, she had gone two years to Oshkosh, Wisconsin, and now was switching to her third college and the fourth major. She had been indecisive about all that, but positive she had found the right boy, and she came home engaged. She would now attend the small Christian college where Shane had gone his first year, and her new major was elementary education.

Wendy chose Winona State as her school, but she was devastated when her gymnastics coach told her they intended to red shirt her for the first year. Unable to practice with the team meant she would be alone in the gym with an assistant coach. Her perfectionism raised its head, and she completely abandoned her dream to compete at the college level. Her grades plummeted along with her self-esteem. The good thing about it all came about because without daily practice she was free to socialize more and she met a great guy, Brad. He helped her through the emotional roller coaster, yet studying disappeared off her radar, and partying took its place. By the end of her freshman year, Gib and I decided she wouldn't go back in the fall. This put her relationship with Brad on hold. She returned home and enrolled in a one-year program for medical assistants for the fall. Thus, we were once again a part of the revolving door syndrome with both daughters home.

Earlier that spring Teri had thyroid problems and the doctor had removed it. Now, the heat of summer had her wiping down her neckline often when she discovered a lump under the collarbone. Sure enough, the rare event of Hodgkin's disease returning after 15 years came as a shock to all of us. She entered a full-fledged battle. Chemotherapy, massive vomiting, hair loss, and fatigue took a strain on her relationship with her fiancé. Each time I took her for treatments, she would begin barfing in the car all the way home. We carried a barf- bucket and wet wash rags with us each day. To my pleasant surprise each day after we got home, Wendy became her nurse. She carried wet rags to Teri and wiped her mouth and forehead. She tenderly emptied the bucket, rinsed everything out and returned to hold Teri's head and whisper encouragement into her ears. She was so tender and so caring I knew God had brought her home for this purpose. In the fall, Teri struggled to stay in school. The college gave her a special parking spot next to the door, but her strength continued its downward spiral. Finally, she admitted she couldn't keep up with the schoolwork and she dropped out for the rest of the semester. During this time, she and her fiancé decided they weren't destined to be together, and they ended their engagement.

Gib out of a job, Teri fighting cancer and losing her fiancé, Wendy was dropping out of college, and all could pull a person down. However, God kept reminding me through rainstorms and scripture that He was in control, and I was His daughter. Tiny Elyse reminded us that life goes on and has blessings daily.

Time began to pick up speed and I could barely keep pace with everyone. Wendy and Brad struggled to keep a long- distance relationship. Teri finished treatments, completed college and headed to Texas to teach elementary school. Gib found his niche in Real Estate, and I kept teaching. We had little time to stop and think about anything.

Then, a tiny bundle burst on the scene. Shane Vincent, our first grandson, literally burst forth all over me. I was changing his diaper in the hospital and forgetting to "cover" a boy, I was anointed with stream of urine that shot straight into the air. My shock and laughter mixed with everyone's in the room, and we all rejoiced to have this small boy, a tiny gift from God enter our lives. Now, I was Granny twice! I was able to spend the first night with them at home and took the overnight feedings so Shane and Kelly could sleep. Since I totally love babies, it was a joy for this time of bonding. I was very content that "my Shane" now had "his Shane."

The next year found Wendy and Brad engaged. Teri came home from Texas to visit, and met a fellow named Guy. Now both girls were involved in these long-distance relationships. Wendy and Brad put miles on the car between Illinois and Minnesota while Teri and Guy flew back and forth between Texas and Minnesota until I thought they should get special awards above the miles they were accumulating. Into the second year of teaching, Teri decided she really was not cut out for teaching, resigned her job as of December and was ready to return home. However, by now, we were deep into plans for a January wedding for Wendy. I told Teri she was welcome to come home, however, she would have to store her belongings somewhere as the house had to remain intact for the wedding. Guy came to the rescue. He flew to Texas, they loaded a truck and started for Minnesota. They stopped in Oklahoma City to spend the night with my parents and for Guy to meet them. Grandparents loved this one-on-one time and called afterwards to say they agreed this was a perfect match. Now, only time would tell if that was true. Finally, back in Minnesota, they unloaded all of Teri's things into an extra bedroom at Guy's house. I don't know if he realized then that Teri's things would never leave there.

As Wendy worked on last minute wedding plans, Brad worked on their future. He rented an apartment, planned a honeymoon to Door County, Wisconsin, Grandparents flew in, Patricia and Newell arrived, and along with Brad's parents, we all moved in the hotel together. We gave our house to the bridal party, and they had a slumber and make-up party and everything came together. It was a very cold day in January, but the happiness everywhere made it all seem warm. Her wedding dress originally had short sleeves, so we added long sleeves with pearls and cut-outs to match the train. Her soulmate, Aunt Jinkers, demanded her right to buy her wedding dress and she and Wendy held that secret. She chose bright red for her attendants and of course, her childhood buddy, Charie, was her maid of honor. She asked her "surrogate" uncles to serve as two of the ushers and although older than all the other attendants, Bill and Tom were so proud in their tuxedos. Joan and her daughter, Denise, were the musicians and that was so special since Denise had been Wendy's idol when she was small. I made a shiny white dress for Elyse, now five. to be her flower girl and matching white pants and a red vest for Shane Vincent. He was supposed to ride in a wagon pulled by Elyse, but at the last moment the two-year-old just wouldn't get in the wagon so Elyse walked the aisle with the Maid of Honor. Brad appeared very nervous, but all changed the moment he spotted his bride coming toward him. We had a buffet dinner and dance, and the evening was magical. My "baby" was launched. Following the honeymoon, the newlyweds settled in an apartment in the same town as Brad's parents.

Wendy and Brad's Wedding

Meanwhile, Teri and Guy were a solid couple, and I wondered if she experienced a little jealousy that her younger sister beat her to the altar. Within a few months, Shane announced grandbaby number three was on the way. Late October Destiny arrived fair headed and a cuddler. Her enormous eyes made everyone's heart melt. Before I could really get much time with her, tragedy struck again.

My Mom, my best friend for all my adult years, had undergone tests concerning blockage in her legs. She had an angiogram and that common test, successfully used many times a day, put such a strain on her heart, and she went into cardiac arrest. After paddling her three different times, she was now struggling in the ICU in Oklahoma City. I was in heavy conferences at school with parents of my 150+ students and I hesitated to leave. She appeared stable so I thought I could wait a few days. However, the second morning of conferences, I announced I couldn't wait any longer. I flew to Oklahoma and on a layover along the way, I called home to see if Gib had any news. Upon hearing his voice, I choked up and asked, "Have you heard?"

He sadly replied, "Yes, Honey. I am so sorry."

"What are you saying? Did she die?"

There was a long silence before he continued. "I'm sorry. I thought you had heard."

Stunned, I watched people going to and fro in the airport, laughing, scurrying, and smiling and I wondered how their life could be going on when mine had just crashed. I tried to climb up into God's palm, but it seemed out of my reach. I hung up from Gib and stumbled my way to my gate. A caring airline worker saw my distress and allowed me to board the plane with the crew.

As tears ran down my face I called out to God. "Please, God, send me a pastor. Not just a Christian but a pastor." I just kept repeating that over and over as I sat alone on the plane. Soon, the other passengers began boarding. I kept my face down until a gentle voice said, "Excuse me, but I have the seat next to you. I rose and let him enter and sat down again in silence. As the plane took off, I looked around to see a nearly empty plane. Why hadn't that man moved somewhere else?

"You look like this isn't a pleasant trip" he remarked.

Hoping to scare him off, I said, "It isn't. I just found out my mom died before I could get to her."

"I am a pastor and would like to help you if you will let me."

Astonished, I turned to face his soothing eyes and stared in disbelief. God had brought me a pastor. Eventually I spoke. "You are not just a pastor; you are an angel." He didn't appear shocked by my declaration. I went on to explain my desperate prayer and he only smiled and nodded.

I poured out my heart to him and he shared insights into my family as we discussed how each person would react. He was so knowledgeable like he knew each person personally. He prayed with me and by the time we landed my heart was settled. I was facing a time of mourning, but I knew I wasn't alone. Once we landed, I hurried down to get my luggage when I realized I had never thanked him. I turned, searching the area looking for him. He was not around. It seemed he had vanished. I knew God had sent him, but had he really been an angel? That thought made the hairs on my neck tingle and stand up. All I knew or sure was that he was God's messenger to me. Once again, God had provided beyond my wildest dreams.

A couple of days later the rest of my family arrived in Oklahoma. First, Wendy flew in from Chicago, and then the others came in a van from Minnesota. Guy came with Teri, and, of course, Gib. Shane. and Kelly came bringing only Destiny with them and leaving the older kids with Kelly's parents. As they entered the house, Daddy sat in his chair, and we slipped the tiny baby into his arms. He cooed and talked to her and we all sensed the realization of life unfolding before us. As we were ushering a new life in, we were ushering a precious one out.

Within a day Teri became ill and soon struggled to breath. We put her in the hospital with pneumonia and Guy stayed with her until they chased him out at night. We were able to check her out of the hospital for a few hours to attend the funeral. Because of all her problems, the Oklahoma doctors wanted to keep her in the hospital for a prolonged time. However, the doctor in Minnesota wanted her home. So, a compromise was met that allowed our family to travel with Teri in the van, stop every few hours, and give her an IV of antibiotics. Gib and Shane rigged up a hanger for the IV bag, and the morning they left I was fine until they drove away around the corner. Then, I collapsed on the ground in the front yard. I was letting my family go, I wouldn't be there to tend to Teri, and my mom was dead. I felt overwhelmed and defeated. After a while, I struggled to my feet and asked myself, "What else could go wrong?" I didn't have to wait long to see.

Early the next morning I got up to pack so I could catch a later flight home. I heard strange sounds from the basement and went downstairs to find Dad sitting on the floor in the bathroom talking to himself. He looked up at me and said simply," I don't know what to do with all this water." I suddenly realized my feet were wet and as I looked around, I saw all the discoloration of the carpet. Each bedroom was soaked, the carpets were ruined, and I discovered it was seeping in where the wall met the floor. Thus began the saga of the next couple of weeks which included changing plane reservations, dragging carpets up and outside, and moving furniture. Carl, my brother, arranged for a drainage system to be installed all around the outside of the house. Workers bustled in and out of the house repairing walls and floors. It became clear that Dad was unable to make any decisions. So, we made them for him. My sister and I sorted and hauled away mother's-soaked shoes and clothes from the closets. Phone calls to Minnesota told me Teri was recovering well, Shane's family was home and reunited, and all was well there. Even Dad's house took shape in a matter of days. The workers had hurried to paint rooms, lay new carpet, put furniture back in place and finally Dad was back in his bedroom with everything where it belonged except Mom. It was time. I had to go home. I left a defeated Daddy behind making him promise he would come to Minnesota in a month for Christmas. I needed him.

The weeks ahead brought a deeper sorrow than I had ever experienced. Without thinking, I would pick up the phone to call Mom to share something one of the kids had done and suddenly realize she wouldn't be there. I would slam it down, mad that I reopened that pain and mad she wasn't there. Since we didn't live in the same house, I didn't have her absence to remind me, and my brain would trick me into believing she was still alive across the miles. This went on for months and even years. I recreated my loss of her over and over. Daddy seemed to be in a trance. Daddy did come for Christmas, but he passed each day in a zombie state. He had always believed his entire purpose in life was to care for my mom and now she was gone. When the day came for him to leave, I went with him to the gate. I was in agony as I watched him walk away from me down the jetway to board the plane. His shoulders sagged and I was helpless to comfort him. Much of this trip through mourning he had to take alone. As the plane flew away, I noticed the rain drops on the huge windows. It should have been snow in December, yet it rained. Once again, God was talking to me.

Our trip to Oklahoma for Mom's funeral had brought about another change. Guy observed all the medical needs Teri had, how she needed a caretaker, and instead of it scaring him off, he wanted that job. We saw his patience and concern for her, and we all knew this was a match God had provided. Once back in Minnesota, he had met with Gib to ask for her hand in marriage. They discussed her needs, their love, and their future and Gib gave his blessings. Then, we waited. Weeks went by and no engagement. Later, we learned he was searching for the right ring and ordered it and waited. Finally, Teri was engaged.

Once again, we threw ourselves into planning a wedding. From the time she was a little girl, Teri loved purple. If any of us tried to wear anything purple, we were told it was HER color. Of course, the bridesmaids' dresses would be purple, and flowers would be purple. However, that wasn't enough. She decided she wanted to wear her purple shoes and wanted purple buttons down the back of her dress. After protesting, I sewed them on. Each plan we made seemed to remind me that Mom would not be there. Teri planned her wedding for April Fool's Day, and I was nervous too many jokes would be pulled. However, that wasn't the case and the day arrived with family and friends pouring in to celebrate. All was good except Mom was missing. Teri sang beautifully at her own wedding. Elyse was again the flower girl. Both Dr. Cich and Dr. Etzwiler were there to share the moment. Guy looked handsome in his tux and they made a regal couple. What a joy to see Teri looking at Guy with so much love in her eyes. A white rose sat on the organ in memory of my mom. She wasn't there physically, but she was there in Spirit. The dinner and dance were fun for all now all our children were launched. The revolving door finally stopped. We were officially empty nesters.

Teri and Guy's Wedding

Six months later, I was in Oklahoma visiting Dad when my sister called. Her first words put me on high alert. "First, let me say we are both okay. Our house burned down overnight." Unsure I had heard her right, I clarified what I had heard and asked for details. She poured out the story of careless workers that were college boys. They had wrapped oil-soaked rags up and placed them under the deck to return the next day. Instead, they ignited, and Patricia and Newell had escaped on hands and knees crawling through the smoke to escape. I was so glad I was there to soften the news for Daddy. A couple of weeks later, I flew out to California to help in any way I could and dig through the heap to find anything salvageable. The months and years to come were a terrible struggle for them emotionally. I had gathered up pictures of their early years and even had one of Newell's mother. At least they would have few tangible memories to look back on.

About the same time, Teri began having chest pains and underwent tests in the clinic and they found nothing. This continued off and on for a few months. Finally, one day she was able to get to the hospital while the pains were still raging and the tests would be more accurate. God intervened again and had the cardiologist on duty that night to be the top guy. Dr. Thatcher knew right away the problem and ordered an angiogram the next morning and for the first time in my life I lied to Teri. She was frightened and asked if that wasn't the test my Mom had that sent her into cardiac arrest. I told her no, even though I knew it was. I talked to Dr. Thatcher and gave him the family history and he had to manage our fears as well as Teri's. The angiogram would be the next morning

Gib had a terrible cold and couldn't be at the hospital during the test. A pastor friend sat with me while I waited. It wasn't long but the time drug by slowly. Teri had blockage on the back side of the heart. This area they call the "widow maker" because it is so hidden and goes undetected until there is a major and often fatal heart attack. When Dr. Thatcher came to talk, I listened intently. I kept waiting for him to say he would give her pills and send her home, but he kept talking and talking.

Finally, I interrupted him, "Are you talking about heart surgery?"

He appeared confused by my question. "Yes, what did you think I was talking about?"

"I don't know. I was going down one track and you were on another, and they weren't crossing each other. You are going to have to start all over."

"But you were engaged in the conversation and asking such good questions," he continued.

"Maybe so, but I was waiting for some 'pills and send her home answers.' Could you please begin again?" I didn't know this new doctor, and although he seemed to know what he was talking about, I was unsure. With great patience he started all over and the immensity of what he was saying finally sunk in. Teri needed by-pass surgery immediately. While he was running the angiogram, Teri kept saying to him over and over that she wanted a baby. She pleaded with him, "Please fix me so I can have a baby. He really felt the pressure of her demands. When he finally stopped talking, I went to find Teri and the two of us hugged and cried. Back in her room, a parade of doctors and techs kept us from making too many calls. Guy had used all his vacation time for the wedding and honeymoon and now we had to call him at work and tell him his bride had to have heart surgery. I reached Gib at home and began crying the moment I heard his voice. Then, I called our primary doctor (Teri's oncologist when she was an adult) to get his take on all this. He reassured me both the heart surgeon and Dr. Thatcher were the tops in their field, and if he had a loved one undergoing this, those were the doctors he would choose. Scared, unsure of this new world we entered, we continued our calls.

At last, I had to call Daddy. I slipped out to another room so Teri wouldn't have to hear the emotion. Immediately, Daddy grasped the severity of the situation and asked, "Did she have an angiogram?" I acknowledged that she had, and he became silent.

"Daddy, the angiogram went well, and she is in her room. They are preparing her for surgery tomorrow."

"How long have you known all this?"

"Less than an hour. Why?"

"I thought you were keeping this from me."

"Daddy, I love you too much to not be honest with you. I will always tell you."

Hanging up, I felt like a hypocrite. I had been honest with Daddy but not with Teri. I had told Teri a boldface lie to calm her fears and now I was telling Daddy what an honest person I was. I called Gib again and poured out my anguish. When I finally quieted Gib responded. "Tina, you are an honest person. You just tried to help Teri through a traumatic experience and calm her fears before a serious test. You can clear it up now. I am sure she will understand."

Back in her room, I approached the subject. "Teri, I lied to you." Before I could continue, she answered, "I know Mom. I knew an angiogram was what Mimi had and I knew you were not wanting me to be afraid. It's okay, Mom."

"Why didn't you call me on it?" I inquired.

"I wasn't sure if you were lying to protect me or protect yourself. I didn't know if you couldn't face the truth." Once again, I was astounded at the maturity of my daughter. Her wisdom went so far beyond her years.

Morning came after a restless night. Gib donned a mask and went to see Teri before her surgery. A pastor came and shared Psalm 91 with her and prayed and Guy hovered as closely as they allowed. She was so brave. She wasn't a little girl who could just trust what her mom and dad told her. She was an adult that had seen all the possibilities and things hidden in the shadows. She smiled and tried to encourage all of us. Again, I felt that same panic I had felt 22 years ago as they wheeled her through those forbidding doors, and she disappeared. Hours drug on as we all waited. Shane tried to distract us, and attempts were made at small talk, but the pressure seemed to suck air from the room. They gave us periodic updates throughout the surgery, but the only update I wanted was that it was over. When they finally told us the surgery was complete and she was in recovery I cried to release all the tension inside me. Once again, God had seen her through. Recovery would be weeks, but Teri was alive. The surgeon explained that the radiation she had as a child prevented her heart from growing to adult size and flexibility. The strain on her heart had caused multiple problems. The first time Dr. Thatcher came into the room Teri asked about having a baby. He deferred that conversation until he would see her in his office. Later, at the first follow-up appointment, Dr. Thatcher gave Teri a small window of time in which she could get pregnant. She must have the baby as close to the surgery as possible to be sure her heart was in good enough condition.

Teri mended slowly and soon she started trying to get pregnant. Meanwhile, Wendy was trying to get pregnant also. Although these girls were so different and not as close as many sisters, they seemed to time things in their lives to match each other.

One day a few months later Teri called me at work and asked if she could come by to see me at school as soon as the kids left. She pulled her chair up across from my desk and handed me a greeting card. "What's this?" I asked.

"Just open it and see," she replied.

To my disbelieve it was a congratulation card to the "grandmother- to-be". Breathless, I looked up at her and saw the beaming face that was so joyful she couldn't contain the happiness. We both started squealing and jumped up and ran around the desk to begin hugging, jumping, crying, and shouting. What absolute and complete joy! Teri was pregnant!!! After we calmed down and could converse, one concern Teri expressed was for her sister, Wendy. She knew Wendy was trying to get pregnant and she didn't want to discourage or hurt her. We finally decided to wait a month or two to tell her and see how things went. Teri's baby was due June 2. Of course, it would be a high-risk pregnancy, and they would plan to take it early by caesarian.

A couple of weeks later Wendy called with the joyful news she was pregnant. Her joy was curtailed a bit by her fear of having to tell Teri. She knew how desperately Teri wanted a baby and she didn't want to hurt her. Wendy's baby was due June 1. As calmly as I could, I encouraged her to go ahead and call Teri. I told Wendy that Teri would be okay and would rejoice with her so just do it and get it over with. This was their story to tell, and I held my breath waiting for one of them to call me back.

I didn't have to wait long as first Teri called laughing hysterically followed by Wendy calling with giggles and excitement. The girls were due one day apart!! How much fun the coming months were. They shared each stage of development of their babies and even one double shower. Years earlier my mom had sewn the most beautiful, lace and fluffy cover for a bassinet. She said she wanted each of her grandchildren welcomed in beauty and luxury. Kelly had used the bassinet for each of her children. My problem now was that I was going to have two grandbabies at the same time and only one bassinet. I quickly began sewing a second one using the one mother had made as a pattern. At the double shower, I presented each girl with a bassinet. We were ready to welcome our babies. Of course, we all knew Teri's baby would arrive first and that would allow for her to be home and settled before Wendy's baby came and I could make both deliveries and both home- cares. I basked in the joy and anticipation. Babies, babies everywhere. You can't get any better than that!

BOASTING, BLESSINGS, AND BURDENS

CHAPTER 11

Weeks later I was still basking in the joy of the coming births. All the pains, agony and frustration to reach this point dissolved. God had grown our faith. I thought about the meaning of faith. The dictionary defines faith as complete trust or confidence in someone or something. Through the years, there were tests of faith all along. Time after time, God honored both Teri's and my faith by showing His might and sometimes clearly saying no, but always answering. I thought I really had a lot of faith. I knew it was given to me by God. He had grown my faith in Him and in return, I could tell anyone about faith, since I knew so much about it. Right? I had silently become puffed up and self-righteous in my faith. After all, I had so much more faith than those around me (or so I thought). In small groups I silently thought I was "so much farther down the road" than the others. I (with a capital I) had done it. I had achieved great faith! Now, my faith was resulting in the birth of these two babies. What joy.

The phone rang out and shattered the silence of my day. I was frustrated it was interrupting me and answered with annoyance in my voice. Teri's voice was barely audible and had terror deep within. "What's wrong?" I pleaded.

"I haven't felt the baby move since yesterday. I called the doctor, and they want me to come in at once. Mom, what if my baby has died?" Fear gripped us. "Mom, Guy and I are already on the way, can you come to the hospital?"

Calmly I responded, "Don't jump to conclusions. We have always waited until we have all the news before, we start to worry. You must wait on God. I don't know if babies sleep for that long and not move around. So, you must wait. I will meet you at the hospital and, Teri, I am praying."

As I drove to the hospital, I began trying to imagine what could be wrong. I knew Teri had followed every detail of her care, so she had done nothing wrong. I knew she was in a close relationship with Jesus and her spiritual life was good. So, what could cause this? I appraised my own spiritual life. Lately, I had been proud that I had so much faith. I knew in my head it was a gift from God, but I had begun taking credit for it in my heart. Afterall, wasn't I a good Christian that was learning to lean on God all the time? I was proud I trusted.

It felt like a bolt of lightning struck me. Was God allowing Teri's baby to die because of my pride? Would He do such a thing? I began to sob and pulled my car off the road. I pleaded, repented, pleaded, repented, and pleaded more. "Please God, don't punish Teri for my pride. Let her baby live. She has suffered so much in her life. Give her this, please! Take what you need to from me, but not from her. Oh God, how did I ever think I had anything to do with my faith? You gave faith to me as a gift, and I have gotten puffed up about it. I have been so blind, so wrong and so far, off- base from You. Forgive me. Save Teri's baby and watch over her. I am so sorry." I stayed parked until my sobbing slowed and finally stopped. I continued to pray until peace took control again. Whatever I would find at the hospital, God was in control, not me, not the doctors, but God.

A few minutes later I was standing by the side of Teri in the ER. They had just completed tests and announced the baby was fine. The baby was turned toward her back and her movement was interior, so Teri didn't feel it. Her heartbeat was strong, and all was well. We all rejoiced and even the nurse was smiling with genuine joy to send us home with good news. I never told Teri about my session with God. However, that night Gib and I had a meeting with a small group from church. I shared with them all that had happened.

"I know that God **could** take Teri's baby because of me. What I don't know is if He **would.** I know He is just, perfectly righteous in the treatment of his creation, and He will punish when necessary. I also know He is merciful, powerful, as well as loving, and jealous of anything we put before Him. God taught me that to take pride in my spiritual standing is a sin. God owes me nothing. I owe Him everything. I don't deserve His mercy; it is His gift. His grace covers me and that is not because I did anything, but because of who He is. He humbled me and taught me to rejoice exceedingly when I am allowed to see Him working in myself and others. I had allowed Satan a stronghold in my heart concerning something I thought I had done. I must be always on my guard lest I get puffed up. God, keep me humble."

My friends rejoiced with me in the lesson I had learned as well as the health of Teri's baby. That evening as we drove home, the wind began blowing against the windows. Soon, drops of rain pinged against the windshield and sounded like a song. Again, once again, God was reminding me He was cleansing me and walking with me through the valley. I was His daughter, and He was always there and would always be there. How I loved the rain.

Following that frightful moment, I was able to rest in God. Babies were growing in tummies and excitement was mounting. Teri was truly enjoying pregnancy since she only had to take an occasional shot. The baby was producing enough insulin for both of them, and Teri was mostly shot free. Mid-April, I decided it was time to let my middle school students know of the coming excitement. The girls' due dates were before school would end and if there were any surprises, I might miss some days. So, I told them the story of two babies corning. They were delighted and often asked how things were going. A few days later a natural disaster, a flood, hit our dear friends' home in Grand Forks, North Dakota. Norm and Debi were under forced evacuation and ended up in the Cities near us with one of their sons and their dog at our home. As floodwaters, and then fire, ravaged their town, we were so grateful they were safe with us.

April came to a close as May first burst on the scene and bright sunlight flooded my empty classroom during my prep hour when Gib called.

"Wendy just called, and she thinks her water broke and is on her way to the doctor." Uncomprehending, I corrected him, "You mean Teri."

"No, I mean Wendy. She will call when she knows more."

I hung up thinking this was all wrong. It was a month too early. This was the wrong first baby, and what does she mean she **thinks** her water broke? Realizing this could be the real thing, I began laying out a weeks' worth of assignments and directions on my desk. Gib called again saying her water had broken and she was on the way to the hospital. I called the school office and sent the secretary into a panic when I announced I was leaving, and she had to find someone to cover my classes for the rest of the day. She protested but I stood firm. I called my friend who usually subbed for me, and she promised she would be there tomorrow and for as long as I needed. Within a few minutes I was in the car heading home. Gib had us packed by the time I arrived, and we took off for the 5 ½ hour drive to Illinois. We arrived at the hospital just minutes after baby boy, Casey, arrived. Kisses, pictures, hugs, baby holding, cuddling, and laughter were constant. Casey was tiny and a month early and we were so happy he was healthy. After a while, Wendy turned to Brad and asked, "Did you tell Mom about Teri?".

As Brad, Gib, and I all looked up, Brad announced, "Oh Yeah, Teri is in the hospital. She has been having contractions and they are trying to stop them."

"Good," I replied not even pausing. "She is right where she needs to be. They will get it stopped and all will be well." I honestly believed that. We went on rejoicing and looking over our tiny little guy. I had bought baby girl and baby boy clothes, so I sent Gib to the car to fetch the tiny blue outfits. What fun. We stayed until Wendy tired and then we went to their home to sleep. I sent a message to my sub, and she wrote on the board "Baby # 1 Boy, 6 pounds. Born in Illinois. Mom and baby fine."

Morning came and we decided to load our suitcases in the car "just in case" we had to take off for Minnesota. We went to see Wendy and baby Casey at the hospital. He was so tiny and so precious. She wanted me to help her shower and then we got a call. Teri would be having a Caesarean section that afternoon and we had to leave. It was a bitter-sweet time. I so wanted to stay, help Wendy, be with them the first night at home, hold my tiny grandson, but we had to head north for our 5 ½ hour drive. I called my sub and announced the pending arrival of Baby #2. She wrote the information on the board for all my classes to see and they waited in anticipation also.

We arrived in Minnesota shortly after Teri's baby girl, Ashley, was brought into this world and even before Teri had been able to hold her. Debi was there and able to be with Teri as her surrogate mom while we were driving home. Both of the "Twin Cousins" were born an exact month before their due date. Now the sub wrote on the board "Baby #2 Girl born in Minneapolis. 7+ pounds. All are well. Later she told me roars of cheers and laughter erupted each hour.

We planned to return to Illinois the next morning as Teri was expected to be in the hospital about a week, and we could be with Wendy when she brought her baby home. However, early the next morning Teri called unable to breath. I told her to alert the nurses and set out for the hospital leaving Gib at home to repack us.

As I exited the elevator and walked toward Teri's room, I noticed a bed in the hallway with an oxygen tank on it. Peeking in her room, I saw it was empty. Confused I headed to the nurse's station and announced I was Teri's mom and wanted to know where she was. A strange scene unfolded before me. Like a game, all the nurses froze in the position they were in.

Slowly, the head nurse spoke. "You don't know?" Fear gripped my stomach, and I could barely breath. "What? I don't know what?"

She came around the station and said, "Come with me, I will take you to her." At first, I followed and then I demanded, "Where are you taking me? Are you taking me to the morgue?"

"Oh, no! I'm taking you to the heart ICU."

Once I entered the Cardiac ICU the nurse explained that Teri had complications. WOW! Teri's tiny heart had not been able to pump off the extra fluid from the pregnancy and she had gone into congestive heart failure. They had called a "code Blue" on her just as Dr. Thatcher had arrived at the hospital. The team had saved her and moved her to the ICU. When I finally reached Teri's bedside, I realized I had never seen true terror in her eyes. Her voice quivered as she said, "I almost died." The nurse was pounding on her back to help loosen the mucus and she sat in bed with eyes wide filled with complete and utter fear.

I glanced into the hallway to see Dr. Thatcher approaching. I slipped from the room to question him. Yes, it had been a close call. This complication meant a variety of things. She would not be able to breast feed the baby and there would never be another baby. Their job now was to get the extra fluid from the pregnancy off her body and relieve her heart. She had been aware she was close to dying and had screamed at him to bring her the baby. He had quietly told her he would save her, but she must listen to him and do what he said. He calmed her and her hysteria slowed and her heart and breathing became normal. She was moved to the ICU, and they had finally brought Ashley to her, but now the baby was back in the nursery.

I spent most of the next hours in the nursery holding and rocking Ashley, as her mother fought once again to win the battle of ridding her body of all the excess fluid. As the baby of a diabetic, Ashley had been producing enough insulin for mother and baby while in the womb. Now, they had to slowly bring her down from an insulin high. She had a tiny board taped to her arm with an IV inserted and she would fling it around waving her arm above her head. I would sing to her and try to hold her arm in place. She quieted with the sound of music and both Teri and Ashley made great strides in recovery. Joan and Bill came and sat with me in a room off the nursery as they loved and supported us all and prayed before leaving.

After a couple of days, Teri was out of danger but would remain in a regular hospital room for a few days. We quickly made the drive back to Wendy. How gracious God was to allow us "speedy" trips back and forth between Minnesota and Illinois without speeding tickets. We made so many trips those first few days our car could have run on automatic pilot. It was exciting, fun, nerve racking, and many more emotions. However, the most pronounced emotion was thankfulness.

In spite of early births, Teri's congestive heart failure, Teri's baby having adjustments as extra insulin left her body, and Wendy's baby developing jaundice, God had granted both babies and mothers a joyful delivery. What a beautiful fulfillment of dreams to become mothers. And to think they did it all within 21 hours of each other. Outrageous Sisters!

Casey was small and seemed miniature after holding Ashley. Wendy took to motherhood instantly and she and baby thrived. Once Teri was ready to come home from the hospital we returned to Minnesota. Guy and I were working but Gib was more flexible since he was in real estate. Therefore, he took the overnight feedings so Teri could sleep. He would sit in front of the TV to feed her and watch Hercules. He said he was teaching Ashley to be mighty. When I returned to work, my classes cheered and wanted all the fun details. Later, I heard from parents the excitement was carried to most dinner tables for discussion each night.

School let out for the summer, and I was free to enjoy those babies. The first few months were delightful, stressful, and exciting. We went to Illinois every two to three weeks to watch our boy change and grow. Teri needed lots of help as she was very weak, and Ashley was with us many hours a day. Toward the end of the summer Gib and I went on a trip that would change our direction in life. We went on a short term mission trip to Hungary to teach conversational English and it proved to be the beginning of a metamorphosis in our lives. God was transforming us in ways we didn't see or understand yet.

They say time speeds by when you are having fun, and we were having fun. Our babies grew. Gib was traveling some to Atlanta and while he was gone, Teri began to have terrible chest pains. Suddenly, we were back in emergency surgery for a second by-pass. It was agony for Gib as the surgery took place on a Sunday and communication with the hospital was impossible, so he went without contact for hours until I finally reached him when it was all over. Teri was fine but it had been rugged.

Life became a strange normal. Teri slowly recovered and the twin cousins grew into toddlers. As the little ones grew, we got together as much as possible. Gib soon started a new job in Atlanta. John had his own computer programming company and it had long been a dream of his and Gib's to work together. We had met John and Jan at our earlier church. They had been in the college class we taught. We had become close friends and kept that friendship alive for years. Now, Gib would become a long-distance worker. With the internet, all was possible. It worked out that we were able to spend more time with Jan and John and that was a bonus. We were determined to keep life-long friends across the miles and the guys working together cemented that even more. It was great having two steady incomes again.

Wendy and Brad were healthy and ready for another baby. This time I was privileged to get to be in the delivery room when Quinn joined the family. Brad and Wendy had their completed family. Casey was dark headed like Wendy, but Quinn was lightheaded with curly hair, and we all thought he was a miniature Brad. I loved bathing, cuddling, and feeding him and when Wendy went back to work, I looked forward to the moments Casey took a nap and I could grab a quick nap if Quinn slept too. It was a fun exhaustion.

The next summer we returned for our third trip to teach young people English in Hungary. Many of the same students returned to camp and it was a joy to see them. The English camp provided the missionaries with a basis for follow-up and although we came to help them, they brought such joy and blessings to us. The blessings felt like raindrops that fell first on our heads and then would trickle down into every part of our being. Short-term mission trips would allow us to take care of our families at home, keep our jobs, and still be able to share the gospel and support missionaries internationally. We were being transformed into new creatures with new purposes. Our summers would never be the same.

Gib and I were approaching our 40th wedding anniversary. We feared that if we waited to celebrate until our 50th all our parents would have died, and we wanted to celebrate with them. We had already lost Mom and in May Aunt Jinkers had passed on too. (Although she was 97, her life seemed too short.) Missing both of them, we decided on a big celebration for our 40th and not wait. Gib's parents drove up from Oklahoma, and my brother, Carl with Cheryl brought Daddy. Gib's East Coast family flew in, and my sister, Patricia and Newell flew in from California. There were other guests that came from long distances, and we had a dinner and dance and rekindling of relationships. Dr. Thatcher and Dr. Cich made it and we all rejoiced. The little kids loved dancing, and everyone had a special time to celebrate. We were so happy we hadn't waited.

For a while now, Teri had been voicing her desire to have another baby, but she knew she couldn't survive another pregnancy and delivery. So, she and Guy began searching out the possibility of adoption. They wanted an infant and the country that opened for them was Viet Nam. One fall day, an email came with the picture of a tiny, black-headed Vietnamese girl a few weeks old. It was love at first sight for all of us. Ashley could barely contain her excitement. From the time she was small, Ashley had played with dolls. She didn't pretend she was the mommy of the doll, but the big sister, and now this would make her dream come true.

Guy would have to travel alone to Viet Nam, submit all the paperwork, meet Karissa, and return home without her as the paperwork was completed. A few weeks later, Teri, Guy, Ashley and Gib mounted the plane for a trip half-way around the world to fetch the baby God had created for them. We were all so happy. As they were doing all the legal paperwork needed to bring her home, I was waiting with great excitement and going to work each day.

While they were in Viet Nam, unexpected tragedy hit a family dear to us. A baby died suddenly and then the mother committed suicide. I went to the funeral alone. Satan got hold of my heart and brain and began whispering that I would be in their place soon. At night, I dreamed the plane would crash on the return flight killing all of them. I woke up shaking and covered in sweat. I buried my fears and went to work pretending all was fine. I assumed God would take care of it and didn't spend time lifting my problem to the throne. Then the nightmares began happening in the daytime. It seemed so undeniable that I couldn't discern what was my imagination and what was reality. Still, I told no one.

Teri called from Viet Nam. She was crying and said the American Embassy was holding up the paperwork and my family was prevented from leaving Viet Nam. I cried with her a little on the phone but still told them nothing about what was happening to me. I felt like an oyster. I kept trying to add layers of protection around me, building my safe "pearl" and surely nothing would happen. After the phone call, I broke down and called Shane and Kelly. I was so lost, so low, so afraid, so confused. Kelly stayed on the phone talking and praying with me and she sent Shane to spend the night with me. By the time he arrived I was much better, but I so needed human contact and Shane's presence was a great comfort.

Days passed before they were able to board the plane to fly to Los Angeles. There, they would spend the night. I stayed busy while they flew, and I rejoiced they were on American soil. The next morning, they started the final leg home and I paced for hours with the fear of the plane going down between California and Minnesota.

Finally, they arrived, and I went to meet them at the airport. Once I saw on the console that the plane had landed and at the gate, I became giddy with excitement. First down the escalator were Gib and Ashley. I rushed to them and hugged and kissed them. Next was Guy and after a quick hug I turned to see Teri carrying a little bundle that was watching everything and everyone around her. What an alert almost 4-month-old! Karissa had no fear and came to me at once. I barely fought back tears of joy and relief as I didn't want to frighten her, and the rest of the family had no idea what had been happening to me.

During the next few hours, we shared their experiences, and I told them of our family friends' tragedy and what had happened to me. They chastised me for keeping it all to myself, and, although I had kept it to myself to protect them from worrying, I understood now that silence had given Satan a stronghold. I hadn't asked for help. I had thought I should be able to do it all myself. I was so wrong.

Nestled in the heart of my loved ones, I relaxed and began to bond with my new granddaughter. Everyone else was suffering from jet lag, but not that baby. She was wide awake. After they all went to bed, I spread a blanket on the floor in the living room and laid down with Karissa. She cooed and talked, and I watched and fell in love. Most of the night we stayed up until she finally dosed off about 3 AM. Content that my family was safe, I drifted into deep sleep with no nightmares.

The next morning Teri related an incredible story of God's love. She had silently worried she might not love her adopted daughter the same way she did her biological one. She had kept this fear in her heart and told no one. The day they arrived at the hospital in Viet Nam, a nurse had unceremoniously, and unexpectedly, dropped Karissa into Teri's arms. Mom and baby looked at each other.

Teri described it saying. "Our eyes locked on to each other. Instantly, I knew Karissa was completely mine. Miraculously, Karissa seemed to know I was her mom. From that moment on, Karissa didn't want me out of her sight. Mom, I've heard of love at first sight, and now I have experienced it."

It was true. Karissa only wanted to take a bottle from Teri. If Teri wasn't holding her, she would anxiously search the room and only relax when she saw Teri. Like glue, they were bonded. Karissa would laugh at everything Ashley did to entertain her. Ashley wanted Karissa to hurry and be able to crawl or walk so she could get around.

Too curious to stay still, Karissa quickly became a roller. She would roll and roll to get across the room in a hurry. This became a problem when they put up the Christmas tree. She would roll under the tree and play with the dangling ornaments. The tree had to be redecorated with unbreakable ornaments down low and they tied the tree to the celling to be sure she didn't pull it over. The days, weeks, and months passed with pure joy as the entire family bonded.

When Karissa was about 10 months old, Teri became ill and had to be hospitalized with pneumonia. Karissa had no idea what happened to her mom. She had just disappeared. Teri was in the ICU for days with tubes running in and out of her and not wanting to scare Karissa, we didn't take her to see Teri. Teri's infection had gone septic on her and as the infection flowed through her bloodstream, her entire body was fighting a rampaging inflammation We were forced to put Teri into a coma to allow her body to heal. It was a fearful time. When awake, fearing she was dying, Teri would whisper to me a simple question. "Why would God give me a baby after so long and then take me away?" I tried to encourage her and tell her she wasn't dying, and she would recover, and all would be good again. She showed no reaction, just stared at me when I said that.

While Teri was in the hospital, Ashley was to have a birthday party. The hospital called that morning to say Teri was in trouble and I rushed to the hospital while Guy attempted to put on a party. Once Teri was out of danger, I went to help Guy only to realize I had no energy for a bunch of energetic little girls. I grabbed Karissa's car seat, abandoned Guy, and went home. Shane's family was at my house, so I sent Shane Vincent and Elyse back to help Guy. The little girls loved having Shane Vincent to chase all over the house and the party was a huge success. Best of all, Guy survived.

At last, Teri was transferred to a regular hospital room, and she anxiously awaited her baby's arrival. Guy carried the little one in and tried to set her on Teri's bed. Karissa sent up an alarm and grabbed her Daddy around the neck and turned her face away from Teri. If Karissa could have verbalized what she was thinking, she would have accused Teri of deserting her and she made it clear she was now a Daddy's girl. That never changed. No matter what we tried in the future, Karissa wanted Daddy. Teri was devastated. Her health had stolen from her once again, and now it took her baby. She tried to hide her broken heart, but her eyes said it all.

Through all of Teri's problems, I hadn't really asked God why. I was willing to accept whatever was in store for her and try to learn whatever lesson God was teaching us. Yet now I wanted to question Him. He had formed and forged that faith through the fires of suffering. She had been able to fight her way back up out of each valley and her trust in Him had only wavered for a quick moment. Now, I saw a gradual withdrawal in her. God had fulfilled her greatest dreams, but now she was on shaky ground. I began praying for her spirit and emotions. I knew her pain and it crippled me. Karissa was still affectionate and fun, but the depth of the connection was gone. Teri did all the "right" things, nurturing her daughters, while her deep, deep joy was threatened.

I beseeched God to teach her to abide in Him. I knew I could share her burden but never take it away from her. I reminded Teri that Karissa's earlier and complete dependency on her had really been unhealthy. She really did need both parents and God was teaching her that. I encouraged Teri to climb up into the palm of God and she only nodded.

One day I asked, "Teri, how are you really doing?"

She opened her heart and said, "I am dismayed. Always, God has prepared me for what was coming. This time I was completely unprepared. I have been to the mountain top with Him. I have been to the valley and walked in the shadow of death, and I have trusted Him through it all. Don't get me wrong here. Just because I don't feel like dancing in the rain with you, doesn't mean I am losing it. I am unshaken in my trust in God. I am just wounded. This goes way beyond my selfish desire to be Karissa's favored one. It goes to my desire for her to be happy no matter what. Because of my health I will not always be there for her. It is important she know Guy will be. I know God has a reason for everything. I am still abiding in Him. I just need to rest and heal a little. Don't worry about me, Mom. I still keep my eyes on the hills where my strength comes from."

Relieved, I said, "That's so right! Climb up into His palm and rest. We may not know what the future holds, but we know Who holds it. I am praying for you."

"I have no doubt about that, Mom, and it helps a lot."

Teri was going through a fiery ordeal, and I was helpless to make it easier for her. I kept reminding her she was the daughter of the King. He had left her a part of Himself in her heart and the Holy Spirit was there to comfort her. Angels were nearby and would also comfort her. We spoke daily and over the phone we began praising God and thanking Him even when we didn't feel like celebrating. I could only help her keep her eyes upward and slowly she began to heal.

One day she commented, "Too bad it isn't raining." "Why?" I asked.

Because I am ready to dance in the rain," she giggled. Teri was strong again!

AWAKENING

CHAPTER 12

Blessings are mysterious. God allows us to be a blessing to others and then covers us with so many blessings when we aren't looking for them. I guess that is why they call them "showers of blessings." We had three children and their spouses that loved Jesus, seven grandchildren that were loved and coming into personal relationships with Jesus, and relationships so deep with friends and family that we had a tiny glimpse of what heaven would be like. Gib and I had been active and ministered in church all our lives. We had served in almost every capacity there was. We had been able to travel the United States, and much of the world. God had sustained us through so many trials and now He began to stretch us in ways we didn't expect.

With our love of travel, people and adventure, God sparked a tiny flame of curiosity as to what He was doing around the world. It started simply with an invitation to join a team going to Hungary to teach English for a week. It would be a natural fit for me as a teacher and a stretch for Gib, but we would team teach. That started our first three short term mission trips. We were unaware of the door God was opening would lead to twenty more trips and six major lessons He had in store for us.

The first lessons He taught us was true humility. It was easier to pay our own way for a trip, but God would not have that. The church required we raise money and prayer support, and we quickly learned why. These trips involved teams. Not just of a team of "goers," but a team of supporters.

We had prayer teams supporting us. What fascinated me though were the financial supporters. What an awakening I had when I stood in a country where my friends were unable to go and experienced an event they would love. I would lock that experience in my heart with their name on it and share it with them when I returned. Suddenly, the trips became theirs and not just mine. What a joy to take them with me. We always took a list of our supporters with us and prayed for them while we were gone as they were praying for us. The most beautiful support we ever received was two dollars. A single woman on a very tight budget gave what she could. I folded those two dollars and put them in my pocket each morning of that trip and often slipped my fingers around them to remind me of those that sent me.

The church had a commissioning of the team before we left on a trip. This was deeply moving for us. First, it reminded the congregation that their people would be out on the field and would need their prayers. Then, it reminded us we were representatives of God and this fellowship of believers. That carried responsibility. Finally, and most importantly, it reminded us that this was God's trip, not ours.

Our second lesson was to see God's protection over us, the team, and even our possessions. When we had failed plane connections or long layovers, He used those times to bond our team into a family. If suitcases missed a flight, He provided alternate things until all arrived. Most evident was His constant protection of the team itself. Over and over, He cared for each team member's needs. Every trip had at least one story of how God provided for physical needs. On one trip a member fell down some cement steps and it looked quite serious. The missionary rushed her back to our dorms in his car while the rest of the team took public transportation and prayed all the way back that she wasn't too badly injured. Shortly, I stood by her bed, and she looked fantastic. Her comment was so simple, "No need to worry. The first pains and problems went away. Oh, I have some scratches and bruises, but God took care of me, and I will be 100% by morning." And she was!

Another show of God's hand on us was on the plane trip home from that same trip. As we checked in for the overseas flight home, all but one team member was upgraded to first class. Attempts to get her moved forward failed and we all settled into our seats. One team member was seated by a young woman searching for a place to donate money to help others. As she heard about the orphanage we worked in, her heart was moved, and she soon became a large donor and supporter of that orphanage. Meanwhile, the member in the back of the plane was ministering to a woman in a desperate crisis in her life. Coincidence? I think not.

God showed up for us even when we checked in for our flights. Expecting to pay extra for oversized keyboards or heavy computers, He whisked us through check-in with no extra costs. In other countries He passed our extra materials through customs without penalties. It became a game to watch what He would do next or who He would use to expedite our belongings.

Our third lesson was so basic we almost missed its importance. We discovered early that the road to success in helping the missionaries with boots on the ground was simple. First, we needed to really listen to their needs. This included financial, emotional, relational, and spiritual needs. Sometimes, all they needed was the assurance that they were not alone, and our church was praying for them and wanting to help any way we could. We were their partners. These were ordinary people who chose to listen to the call of God and leave their homeland to share the greatest story ever told. They gave up many family events, but the joy they had sharing the love of Jesus was reward for them. We saw their day-to-day struggles and we came along- side them to encourage and help as we could. Sure, they had education in the Bible and even in survival techniques and areas we weren't qualified in. Yet, as we walked with them in their daily work, we saw that they all had one similar trait. From Eastern Europe, to Latin America, to Asia we discovered they all loved people. They were willing to care, love, invest time and patiently wait for the Holy Spirit to bring understanding in the hearts and minds of those they worked with. They were a diverse group of people. Some were speakers, teachers, mentors, Bible scholars, computer experts, audio producers, writers, organizers, and guidance counselors. Some were single, some married and some with families.

One example of the how the missionaries touched our lives and humbled us was an experience in India. I was traveling in a small car with women to a meeting. As the driver wove between hundreds of people in the streets of this city in India I was overwhelmed at the throngs of people.

Never had I seen so many people. It reminded me of a wheat field in Kansas and they flowed like wind blowing them back and forth in front, behind and beside us. I turned to see the wife of the native missionary sitting in the back with tears flowing down her face. She spoke barely above a whisper, "Thousands and thousands of people are lost, and they don't even know it." Her heart was breaking for her people. We listened, absorbed all we saw, and we praised God for allowing us to walk alongside these missionaries and their people. We prayed for them fervently and developed a deep love and concern for God's workers everywhere.

The fourth lesson in making mission trips successful was simply being willing to return over and over to the same place and build relationships. Eastern Europe was hungry for the outside world and the Good News was new to most of them. Having lived in a Godless society for so long, they were hungry to hear what we had to say. Whether there or Asia, we found the people needed to be loved. Everyone wanted us to come again and again, and each trip got harder and harder to leave and return home. One leader in a village in India expressed it so beautifully when he said, "Somewhere back in history we must be related. Only family would care enough to keep returning and loving us."

Our fifth lesson taught us the ways the Holy Spirit worked in different cultures. In India we saw miracles of healing God used to awaken the hearts of people. Many were saved when they saw the power of God. In Ukraine we saw the students from countries controlled by fear, come to learn English and find safety in Jesus. We saw joy beyond circumstances in all areas of deep poverty. We learned to live, love, and earn respect before we had a right to share our hope in Christ. We worshiped in so many languages and sang "How Great Thou Art" in English alongside someone singing it in their language and our tears of joy flowed together. We watched translators, some Christians, and some non-Christians, explode with enthusiasm along with the English speakers. They would translate and repeat so rapidly, and if our pastor would raise his arm, they raised theirs. As he whispered, they whispered. As he shouted, they shouted. One time as he was speaking rapidly, Pastor Bob said "Gracias," and the translator said, "thank you." They continued without a pause never realizing they had changed languages for a moment.

Whether we did medical camps, construction, repair work, teaching

English, teacher training, family camps or sports days each was important. If we held babies, taught Bible lessons, ran children's programs, visited in homes, or passed out materials, the one thing all had in common was people in need of love. The world over, people needed people. We made life-long friends with those we served with as well as those we served. We have stayed in contact with missionaries and students all over the world. and a few are our closest friends even today. No matter what method or approach the Spirit used to touch the lives in each culture, He needs real hands and feet to touch the people and what a privilege to be used.

On one trip to Ukraine, I sat listening to a dynamic Russian woman tell her story. I was struck with the irony of the situation. I remembered the "duck and cover" drills I had done as a child. We were taught that the Russians wanted to bury us and hated us and now, I was listening to a Russian telling of her exact drills she did as a child and the fears she had of our country. Olga quieted and inquired, "Why are you looking at me like that?"

"I am fascinated that I was always taught to fear you, a Russian, and now I am rapidly becoming your friend. It is such a wonder I have this chance to really get to know you."

She was silent for a moment and then said, "When 'the wall' fell and Americans were allowed to enter Russia. A short-term mission team came to Russia and needed a translator. I got the job and traveled with them translating all they shared about Jesus. I remembered that early Russian authors had written about God, and I was curious. All my life I had been told He didn't exist, and now these people were saying He did. When they left, they gave me a Bible. I began reading and discovered a living God between those pages. I saw His covenants with Israel and the fulfilment of His promise in sending a Messiah. I trusted that Jesus was who He said He was, and I became a believer. Now, I want to share His truth with everyone. That is why I am here at this university in Ukraine. That is why our paths have crossed. God orchestrated our lives and brought us together." A I thought about her words, I could see how God had orchestrated it all. Those first contacts to her had been willing to go. She had been touched by their sincerity and the Bible they left behind. Now, we had responded and been willing to go and was allowed to see God working in this fantastic woman. There were no miracles of healing here, only willingness of others and the power of the Word. From that moment on, Olga became a part of my life and my family.

Macedonia held another jewel awaiting our discovery. Brian and Elizabeth were putting on a family camp and needed help. We took a team to supply crafts, games, support in any way they needed. Here, we saw the investments in lives and everyday living examples change the people's hearts and enable them to hear the Spirit speaking. The language barrier prevented us from having deep conversations with the families, but it allowed us to get to know the Richards family in depth. The kids wormed their way into our laps and hearts. and once again we had friends that would last a lifetime. Many of the rough times ahead for either family were shared through the years. Again, God orchestrated our paths, and our lives became one.

We saw results of miracles performed, beatings for sharing the gospel, fear tactics that ended up strengthening faith, gentle love and acceptance, and many other techniques used to touch the people God sought. As varied and unique as the people, the manner of reaching them was just as unique. What a creative and wondrous God we saw in action.

Yet, our deepest lesson was still to come. At home, everything was changing rapidly. We had sold our cabin as we never had time to get up there anymore. We sold our home and bought on a lake in town. This would allow us to have the lake fun and never leave town. Then, God opened a door that changed everything. Africa – we were going to Kenya on a mission trip. Our mission pastor, Bob, had lived there for years and now we were putting together a team to go. Teri called and asked, "Mom, do you think I could go to Africa?"

The thought almost made me hysterical with fear. "I really doubt it, Teri. I guess you would have to clear it with your doctor and with Pastor Bob." I was sure they would both refuse. I put it out of my mind and didn't even bother to pray about it. When she called back a few days later announcing they had both said okay. I wanted to protest and scream. Teri was going to Africa!? Instead, I called Bob. "What were you thinking?" I demanded.

"Tina, it will be fine. Remember, I lived there for so many years. There is good medical care, and we can watch her closely. God will protect her." He seemed so confident.

So, now I did start seriously praying. Soon, our son, Shane, called and declared he and his oldest daughter, Elyse, had signed up to go also. We would be teaching in a school in the slums of Nairobi and visiting many ministries in the area. All our other trips had taken weeks of preparation. This one was no exception. We each took one suitcase of personal things and one suitcase of materials to use and leave behind. As the time neared, anticipation was high. What would Africa be like? What was poverty there like compared to the rest of the places we had seen?

Lesson six began quietly and transformed me slowly. In the midst of all the planning, God began teaching me the most profound of all lessons, deep, deep gratitude. God shook my soul to the core, and I was overwhelmed with a depth of thankfulness and awe. God had given us a new home, our kids had caught the desire to go on a mission trip, we were going to Africa, and we were going with Pastor Bob. I felt my heart was going to explode with gratitude. Little did I know this was just the beginning. Wrapped up in my own experience I failed to see the quandary Wendy was experiencing. Before we left, she told me how frightened she was we were going. When I asked if she was afraid of Africa her answer was so basic. "No, Mom. I'm afraid because my entire family is going on the same plane. My mom, dad, brother, sister, and a niece. What if it crashes?" I flashed back to the panic I had when Teri's family and Gib went to Viet Nam. My heart went out to her. I had been so wrapped up in joy at going with my kids on a mission trip, I had never realized her dilemma. All I could do was hug her and remind her that God had led each of us to go, and He was in control. I promised to pray for peace for her.

Pastor Bob had shared an old African saying with us. "Once you taste the waters of Africa you will never be content until you return again." That nailed it! Each of us fell in love with Africa. When I think back on all we experienced, warmth floods into every cell of my being. We really had a great awakening.

First, we were to teach lessons in the grade school set on the edge of a slum, Kinyago-Dandora. The primary school offered education, healthcare, clean water, food, and nutrition. Started in 1987, it was already one of the top schools in the area. This slum, located next to the city dump, offered no hope to the inhabitants. Our first glimpse came as we turned in by the dump. We saw children dangerously riding atop the garbage trucks and as the huge vehicles dumped their loads in huge piles, the kids rode the trash to the ground. Often, they were temporarily buried and had to burrow their way to the top of the pile. They wanted to be first to uncover any hidden treasure within the trash that they could sell. Overhead vultures circled, waiting, just waiting. As the trash hit the ground people rose like ants out of nearby piles and scoured the newly arrived trash. Picking, clawing, and fighting to find something they could use, trade, or sell, they dug in the leftovers of others. Their desperation broke our hearts. Then, we turned a little downhill toward the school.

As the vans turned into the schoolyard we were surrounded with bodies. Students yelling greetings, reaching out hands, yanking doors open and pulling us out. We felt like rock stars that were being mobbed by fans. They were so excited to see us. Never had we been welcomed with so much enthusiasm. That enthusiasm lasted the entire week. These children and teachers were so grateful for any and everything we did, and we fell in love with each child and couldn't hug enough. We laughed, taught, prayed, shared stories, listened and listened, and our hearts grew until we thought they would burst. When we brought out the balloons complete havoc erupted. Gib was mobbed as they pushed and shoved to grab a balloon. Joy was everywhere. It penetrated your soul. This school sat on the side of a hill and the slum stretched out below us. We didn't enter that slum because it was too dangerous. Little children who were unable to attend school would gather on the ground outside the fence next to each classroom and listen to our lessons. Everyone was so eager to learn and desperate to gain an education to escape the poverty they lived in. The lessons we brought, and the visual aids were received with such zeal that we wished we had brought more. The teachers had grown up in the slums themselves, got an education, and returned to work in the slums and help others get an education. When money was short, they often continued teaching without pay. They were committed to the community.

Each evening Bob had arranged for other ministries to have dinner with us and share their stories. We took a few days to visit self-help ministries where they taught skills to help people with finding work. We bought handmade products that would remind us daily of them once we returned home. We met young people and heard their stories of overcoming things so few of us had ever experienced. Most had been students at Day Star University and like the teachers, they had returned to their own communities after getting an education. They were helping build infrastructure and community planning as well as finding aid for those in need. The commitment to their own people was a beacon of hope for the younger kids.

Since Kenya had been under British control for so long, English was one of the official languages and made communication easy. We were able to get involved in the lives of the teachers and the kids. It was so rewarding. We. like other team members, decided to sponsor a child through Kenya Children's Fund. We prayed, hoped, and invested our lives in the success of the young boy we supported.

One day we made a walking trip down into another slum in the Mathare Valley. This was our first trip into the gates of bowels of the inferno. We were surrounded by leaders of the church as we made our way over packed down trash and filth. We crossed a bridge over the river that ran through the valley. We saw people washing clothes in water containing sewage. We saw men making alcoholic drinks from the same water. The banks of the water were covered with filth. The stench reached our nostrils and burned. Then, we were in the heart of huts, lean-to shanties built from old tin and mud. Less than 6' x 8' inside, they had no beds, no running water, and no electricity. A family of four or more lived here. They hung hammocks to sleep at night or lay on pieces of cardboard. Although they had cut windows in the tin to allow light inside, they had to close them at night to protect themselves from the high crime. Fear was high because of rapes, beatings, theft, and even murder all around them. The average income was less than $1.00 per day if they could find work. HIV was rampant with one out of three adults having it. Many households were run by juveniles since parents had died from AIDS. Over 600,000 people lived here in 3 square miles area. This is as great a number of people living crammed together as many of our cities that are 80-100 square miles, and they were doing it in only 3. Public toilets were few and shared by 100 people per toilet. Some used plastic garbage bags and tossed them into the river at night. I saw a man selling the skeleton of a fish he had coated and fried. What a delicacy for some family. Fish bones would be a great celebration. Health problems like malaria, cholera, tetanus, and polio were everywhere.

Contrast this with women standing their toddlers in the street and pouring a bucket of water over them to wash them. Instead of sadness, they were smiling and nodding to us. The tiny children said, "How r u?" It was the only greeting they knew, and they repeated it over and over. To our astonishment, we saw joy everywhere. Smiles, nods, greetings, laughter were all around us in this hopeless place. Finally, in the heart of this filth and poverty we reached the school. It was an oasis in the center of valley of hopelessness. If this slum was safer than Kinyago, what must that one be like?

Again, teachers and students met us with great enthusiasm. Here, in the middle of this poverty that was worse than any we had seen, even in India, there was joy. The local pastor had started it all by simply feeding a few kids, and then trying to teach a few to read. It grew and grew until there was a school. Now, there are only 3-4 schools in the area to educate over 70,000 kids. They put on a performance for us with native dancing and song. The rhythms seeped into our lifeblood, and we were soon swaying and feeling exhilaration. Students slipped their hands into ours and walked with us. The classrooms were the same lean-to shanties with long wooden boards to sit on and a long thin board to write on. The children sat shoulder to shoulder in a dark room. Unlike American school, there were no discipline problems, and everyone was eager to learn. Any student unwilling to adapt was removed. There was always another ready to take their place. The main technique for learning was rote and not student involvement. With hopelessness all around us, there were shoots of tiny plants of hope rearing up in this school. Education would give these kids a chance. There was no escape from their surroundings, so they were making the best of where they were. Still, in this pit, we saw deep gratitude for learning, teachers, opportunity, and even for our presence.

As we climbed back out of the valley that day, tears flowed from all of us. Pastor Bob led us in prayer acknowledging to God that He had broken our hearts in the things that broke His. We all knew we would never be the same. As I opened my eyes realization flooded over me. God had taught me humility, shown His protection, taught me to listen and build relations. Now, to the inner core of my being He was creating in me a new heart. One so filled with gratitude that I couldn't contain it. He was awakening my soul to how His heart was broken as He viewed what His creations were doing to each other. I was awakening to the desperation of humans not reconciled with God. I was broken, challenged, and filled with gratitude that He had allowed me to see His heart and how He loved me and every person he created. Africa was becoming my great awakening. Yes, we had taken a drink of the waters of Africa, and we would return.

Armed with this heart filled with thankfulness, our mission work was ended. Each member had the opportunity to pay for themselves for an extra side trip for a safari. No one refused. It was a beautiful way to end the trip. We were able to meet, debrief, and share all that we had experienced. We had morning and evening game- drives to see the animals in their habitat. We could experience the uniqueness of Africa without the pain of poverty. Elyse, our granddaughter, turned 16 while on Safari. As the Maasai waiters sang their unique birthday greeting, I closed my eyes and listened to the distinctive music of Africa. "Oh God, you are so wondrous. You love these people, and you have taught me to love them too. Thank you for allowing me this privilege. Help me to adequately share what you are doing when I return home."

Africa has so many problems and so many wonders wrapped in the same package. Beautiful, frightening, exciting, dangerous, glorious, and perplexing are all part of the landscape of the Serengeti as well as the cities. Someone once said that when you leave Africa, as the plane lifts, you feel that more than leaving a continent you are leaving state of mind. Africa had our minds. We knew we had to return.

A year later, in preparation for our second trip to Kenya, Teri and I put together a teacher training program. We had learned that the teachers didn't have training just willingness, so we wanted to help. We spent hours making a workbook to hand out with lesson ideas on how to use natural materials surrounding them. We put in games, ways to involve students in the learning process, puzzles, songs, and actual lesson plans. We held the program in the hotel where we stayed, and the night before the training I entered the conference room to check it out. The tables were set in a rectangle and glasses for water, pens and workbooks were already in place on the tables. It looked so professional and I felt so inadequate. What could I really offer these teachers? Who was I to think I knew what they needed? Bob entered behind me and commented that it all looked ready. I stared up at him, "Everything is ready but me."

"Why?" he asked.

"I feel so inadequate. I have trained and mentored many teachers in my career. However, they were Americans and in a culture I knew. I am in uncharted territory now. What if all I prepared is useless for them?"

"Tina, anything, and I mean anything you have to offer them is a prize. These people are so grateful they will love you for just being here. Anything else is just icing on the cake."

He was so right. The next day they received everything we brought and presented with such grace and thankfulness. Teri and I were humbled. Never had I seen this level of acceptance and appreciation in any workshops I had done in America. They gave us yet another reason to fall more deeply in love. Africa was in our blood.

Gib and I returned again and then missed a couple of years going to Africa. One year we kept Teri and Guy's daughters so Guy could go with her. We continued returning to other countries on mission trips, ministering wherever we could, but Africa was never far from our hearts. A few years later, summer came, and we returned to Kenya for our third time. Things appeared normal at first until we learned there had been unrest and riots because of crooked elections. The slums had erupted in violence and some of our students had been raped and others had seen people murdered in front of them. While at school, the students were able to escape the chaos and subtract their minds from the horror they had lived through. However, each night they were forced to return to uncertainty and fear. I had learned years earlier that for many students, school hours were the best hours of their day. Home and neighborhood brought no joy or comfort. Here, they returned to no dinner, violence, and disease that surrounded them, with no hope of basic needs being met. There were no playgrounds, no basketball courts, no open fields to gather for a football game. Only darkness, hunger and fear awaited them. An artificial calm had crept in and although still nervous, the students continued as if nothing was bothering them.

Suddenly, one morning we were in the classrooms when I heard the sound of shots suddenly ringing out. As the children ran from the classroom and I feared for their safety. Once I ran outside, I saw all of them dancing in the rain and I realized the sounds were not shots but rain on the tin roofs. That's when I saw the joy they had in this God- given gift. Their land desperately needed water. They sat out every utensil they had to catch the precious drops as they fell. Realizing their complete reliance on God, I thought back over the journey that brought me here not only to Africa, but to the face of faith. That was the day I looked across the compound and watched Teri dance with joy.

I recognized God's hand in each step along my journey. He had prepared me before each new adventure. I had learned to be happy in all circumstances. I had learned to see Him in action in even the smallest of events. I had learned to trust Him to take care of me and others. I so had walked through the valleys and reached the mountaintops with Him. I had learned not to fear tomorrow and know He was in control. I had learned there is a season for everything, and He had led me through so many of those seasons. Now, using a little girl, He had taken my hand and was teaching me to always dance.

So, that day as I twirled and danced with fervor and eagerness, I rejoiced at all I had learned and looked forward to all He still had in store for me. He had awakened my soul and I was so grateful I didn't know if I knew how to worship Him as completely as my heart yearned to do. I whispered to Him, "Let the rain fall, and let me catch the blessings. Let me praise you and declare you throughout every moment of my life. Help me to remain grateful every moment of everyday. Keep awakening my spirit to yours. As I praise your name, remind me not to wait for a storm to pass but even if it is pouring to dance in the rain."

UNEXPECTED GAINS AND LOSSES

CHAPTER 13

We don't keep score in life often. However, over a five-year period it would be easy to think of life in pro and con events. We passed through a period of loss. It started with my dad's memory loss getting serious enough we needed to put him in a care facility. He was over 90 and we feared for his safety. One morning, his caretaker arrived to find him and his car missing and his glasses still on the shelf. Since he was legally blind without them, my brother called the police immediately. It wasn't till late in the day before we heard from a nursing home in Texas that they had Dad. Evidently, he had taken off driving from Oklahoma City and ran out of gas in Texas. Carl and Cheryl drove down to bring him back to Oklahoma City and he claimed he was just going to my grandparents' home. Now, he had to go to a facility that was locked so he couldn't escape. With a heavy heart, Carl found a suitable home and he moved Dad.

Next, came the unexpected death of Gib's mom. Of course, I knew that with all three parents over 90, they wouldn't last long. However, none were "ill", so each death came unexpectedly. The following year Dad died in February and Gib's dad died in December. Only nine months later, Gib's only brother, Len, died suddenly in September. Not only was it unexpected, it also wasn't even in our list of possibilities. He had a flareup of blood pressure and then, in a few hours, he was gone from a burst aneurysm. Emotions ran the gambit for his immediate family as well as us. This loss wasn't old age. This loss should never have happened. This not only stunned but stabbed us. It seemed the losses were coming one after another.

Nestled between the losses, we began to experience some gains. Teri was approaching her 40th birthday. She never thought she would live long enough to reach that milestone. She began planning a huge celebration. She wanted to be surrounded by those that she loved and had supported her through so much. She planned a dinner- dance, and all were invited. Knowing some loved ones had already passed on, Teri was thrilled when others rearranged schedules and flew in, drove in, or arrived any way they could to celebrate. Gib's brother's death brought great sadness for Teri as he had been so looking forward to celebrating with her. However, Jeff came to represent Uncle Len and family and Teri was thrilled to have him there. Then, Patricia, my sister, broke her toe and she and Newell were unable to come. However, family and friends (even those confined to wheelchairs because of major back surgery) came, and rejoiced, celebrating the miraculous 40 years of Teri's life. She shared her gratefulness with everyone, recognized a number of special people and then we all danced and celebrated her life together. Teri had experienced so many loses in her life, it was a beautiful blessing to watch her celebrate the years God had given her.

A new season of life was on the horizon as it was time for me to retire from teaching. At the same time, Gib's parents' estate was closed, and we pondered the proper way to recognize their impact on our lives. It seemed only proper to use the money we inherited to take the entire family on a trip. Grandpa and Grandma's love for travel would continue through the next generations. We didn't have a huge camper to take everyone, so we called a full family conference. We discussed a cruise, Hawaii, and Europe until we settled on a trip to Italy. All 15 of us set out for 10 days on a once-in-a-lifetime adventure. From Venice to Rome, we traveled together. I spent many hours planning a trip of joy for everyone from six-years-old Karissa to 65-year-old Gib.

Gondolas, masks, dungeons, water taxis and pigeons filled our days in Venice. Then, on to Florence in the huge bus we had rented. Quick naps along the way and we were ready for the art, cathedrals, and Gates of Paradise. Leaving the beautiful art, and on to our Tuscany villa and paradise. We had rented a family villa that sat atop a hill with a 360-degree view of the surrounding area. We had rented the entire villa and adjoining buildings and delighted in the two swimming pools, an authentic Italian meal prepared by the host's mother, and a view straight from a picture book. We wished we could stay there forever, and we fell in love with Tuscany.

Although most of our evening meals were preplanned, we came to a night without any ideas and our host sent us down the side of the hill to a magnificent restaurant. There, we were seated outside divided between two tables. Gib gave us all guidelines for ordering, and we all sipped wine and awaited our meal. The waiters came out of the kitchen on their way to the other table carrying steaks the size of large roasts. First one, then another, then another. Gib was on his feet and over to the other table. "What have you ordered?" he demanded. Shane and Teri were speechless. Finally, one said, "There was a misunderstanding. It was in kilos, and we thought we ordered right."

"Evidently not," Gib responded. Two steaks were over three pounds each. A third one was over two pounds. This meant almost eight pounds of meat for five people. Gib stumbled back to our table and sat down in shock. I leaned over to him and said, "Relax, they are just spending their inheritance." Wendy almost yelled, "Well, it's my inheritance too." I burst into laughter and said, "So, go get some of your inheritance."

Quickly, everyone at our table grabbed our plates and went to the other table and got our part of the steaks. We all ate an absolutely fantastic meal and once done, the kids started trickling back up the hill to the villa while Gib and I waited for the bill. As they traveled through the darkness, they heard a scream. Shane Vincent said, "Well I guess Granddad just got the bill." (In reality, the scream came from a small girl who had fallen into cacti.) That meal was over $1,000 and became the family joke for years to come. At Christmas, we hung a bag of coal for Shane and Teri in place of their stocking as a joke and more laughter.

The trip continued through Cortona, Pisa, Sienna, and on to Rome. In Rome, the boutique hotel staff bought watermelon to celebrate the 4th of July with them and they took excellent care of us. Daily we thought of Aunt Jinkers and her love for ice cream. Each day, in the heat of afternoon, we sought out a gelato shop and licked our cones in her honor. We thanked Gib's parents nightly for this wonderful trip. The churches, statues, fountains, Circus Maximus, Colosseum, Forum, Pantheon and Vatican City were visited even in the extreme heat. We banked memories that would last a lifetime and Kelly made each family a photo book of the trip so each of us could look back on it and smile.

Family in Italy in 2008

Still basking in the memories of the trip, Fall came with an unexpected, fantastic gain. A new family burst into our lives and became a part of us. Will Lopes became the music pastor at our church and our family adopted him and his wife with open arms. Nelly gave birth and brought a week-old little gal, Camila, into our lives. Nelly and I shared the baby's first bath and many other firsts together. Will was from Brazil and Nelly was from Dominican Republic and their Hispanic background opened us up to many new adventures and times of laughter. Of course, I was able to get my "baby fix" by helping with the little one and Teri saw Will as the little brother she never had. Shane had to teach Will the art of car ownership, I taught Nelly to paint, and she soon changed room colors on a whim, and we all helped them learn the ways of surviving suburbia in America. What great fun we all had! They were now a new branch of our family tree.

My brother, Carl and Cheryl came to Minnesota, and we traveled to Canada and a quick trip to northern Minnesota. It was the last trip we took before Gib announced he was joining me in retirement. I loved to tease him that he just couldn't handle me having freedom without him. With all of us retired, Patricia and I decided the two couples should go on a trip together. After much discussion we chose a four-week trip to Australia and New Zealand. What fun we had. The four of us saw all the tourist sites with our favorite being the tiny penguins in southern Australia. They were so cute and so fun to watch. We celebrated Gib's retirement and his 66th birthday together. It was a special time together and great celebration of life.

Also in the gains category, we continued mission trips and even made a trip to Israel and Jordan. Soon, Gib was ready to return to Africa, but I was having second thoughts. Afterall, we had already been to Kenya three times, and I was feeling guilty about going on a trip with the wrong motives. The blessings God poured out on us were so immense that it was easy to forget we were supposed to be a blessing to others. Instead, I had come to yearn for the blessings I experienced myself. I was selfish and wanted to experience the joy and contentment that Africa and its people gave me. Therefore, my reasons for going were wrong. My motives weren't pure, so I felt I shouldn't go. However, Gib felt as strongly the other way. He felt God was calling us to return. After praying and not receiving a clear answer I decided to yield to my husband's direction and go. Once again, Teri, along with her best friend, Shannon, and I prepared a teacher training seminar as well as the regular lessons for the week in the classrooms. Teri's oldest daughter, Ashley, was going too. Little did I know this trip will be filled with so many gains within a huge loss.

Gib and I left a few days earlier than the team and traveled to Spain to investigate the possibility of a STMT (short term mission trip) in the future. We met the African team in the Netherlands before traveling on to Kenya together. As they arrived, Teri was exhausted. She had overworked and under slept in preparation those last few days and arrived completely exhausted. We spent the first day in light tourist experience allowing the team to recover from jet lag. The next morning as we prepared to go to the school, Teri's roommate, Shannon, came to tell us Teri was ill. I went to her room to find her crying, weak and sick. Too weak to go with us, the team left her behind in the hotel to rest for the day and went on to minister at the school. That evening when we returned to the hotel, Teri had grown weaker and quite pale. Concerned, but not afraid, we all went to bed early to be ready for the next day. Before dawn Shannon knocked on our door once again and said Teri was having trouble breathing. We carried her to our room that was closer to the hotel desk. After discussion and prayer, it was decided I would remain behind with her and try to nurse her to health. However, as the day progressed, Teri's health deteriorated.

By mid-afternoon she called out to me. "Mom hurry, it is going septic on me." Having had sepsis three times before, she knew the way her body felt when it took over. Once again, infection was racing through her blood stream throughout her body. Our time was limited. Teri was in a life-death crisis. We had to go the hospital at once. The hotel called a taxi and then Pastor Bob. We couldn't wait for Bob, so the staff loaded Teri into the waiting taxi and just as we started to leave, Bob arrived and climbed into our taxi. At the ER they had trouble registering any blood pressure for Teri, and the staff went into full crisis mode. Teri was in danger, and they reacted swiftly. Doctors, nurses, and techs surrounded her and worked over her. They were superb and refused to give up on her. Then, Dr. Silverstein entered. He was an American from Chicago, and head honcho of the hospital, he stepped in and started giving orders. Pastor Bob remembered him from years earlier. As we stood against the window and watched, I was amazed at the knowledge, care, accuracy, and reactions of everyone on the team. They were fighting for Teri's life and they did everything as well or better than the hospital in the states. Eventually, she was transferred to the ICU with fluid in the top two lobes of her lungs.

As I followed her bed into the ICU, I felt like I had entered the show M.A.S. H. Beds lined each side of the room with no walls or dividers between patients. The doctors were at an open station at the end of the room and never were out of sight of their patients. Teri's voice was so weak they couldn't hear her call, so they gave her a bell to ring. Most of the time she was the only patient awake. I was able to be with her for 15 minutes and then spent 45 minutes waiting on a chair outside. She was terrified. She knew how extremely sick she was. Pneumonia, infection rushing through her blood stream, her heart barely able to keep up and her gasping for air and all agitated in body and mind. She would look around the room seeing strangers all around, a foreign country, nothing looking familiar, and she was often near panic. I would pray with her, sing to her quietly and read scripture. Between my visits she would try to sleep. I observed the staff washing down every inch of the ICU three times per day. That included even washing the tops of the rails holding the curtains. Once per day an inspector came with white gloves and ran his hands across all surfaces to be sure they were clean. If he discovered any problem, the cleaning team came back and did it all over again. Everyone was so caring, took their jobs so seriously, and were so very gentle with both of us that we felt pampered and protected.

During waiting time between seeing her, I passed my time reading through the Bible, and emailing a plea to all our prayer warriors to get on their knees and pray. In a matter of hours there were prayer groups all over the world holding Teri up before the Throne. I find it difficult to explain how a person can actually feel they are being prayed for, but it is a real phenomenon. I was scooped up out of these strange surroundings and nestled in the palm of God's hand. Teri told me. "Mom, something special is happening. I can feel people praying for me. I feel the presence of God and it's like an angel is sitting on my pillow." Perhaps one was.

Meanwhile, it was necessary for me to contact our travel insurance in the U.S. I was unable to reach the international connection and I met one brick wall after another. Eventually, I contacted Kelly, my daughter-in-law, with the information, and she called the insurance for me. Within an hour they called me. They questioned me and announced we had Teri in the correct hospital, and they knew Dr. Silverstein and he was great. From that moment on they took over all needs we had. Kelly continued to run interference in every way we needed.

Time crept by slowly as I waited to see Teri. I was torn between my desire to be serving at the school with the team and my need to be with her. The team was able to do all the lessons and ministry they had planned despite two missing members. Teri's daughter, Ashley, showed her maturity and functioned well as she focused on the tasks before her, leaving the care of her mom to me. I admired the way she related to the adults on the team, trusted God, while trusting the doctors and me to care for her mom.

Three very long days passed, and Teri slowly gained strength and her body started responding to the antibiotics. Still frightened she told me of dreaming she would die on the trip home. I quickly squashed that idea. "Teri, I don't care if it takes us a month to get you home, we will get you there safely. We can wait till you are ready to travel and then go a little way. We can stay there for days until you are ready for the next leg and so on. We will skip from city to city as needed. You will make it, Dear." She smiled, relieved, and never brought that fear up again.

I had lots of time to ponder everything going on around me. My loss was small compared to Teri's. In the eye of the storm, I rested in God's hand, and I focused on Teri's greater loss. She was unable to be with the people she had grown to love so much. All the hours of preparation were lost to her. She had lost her health. Yet, even in the middle of loss, Teri had experienced gain. She had the privilege of being the focus of an international prayer marathon that lifted her directly to God. She had felt the support and she had come to completely trust Dr. Silverstein. We had seen the wonder of God's hand in the first emergency team that fought so valiantly to save her. I had told her of the efficiency of Kelly and how Ashley's faith was growing daily. She had simply smiled, nodded, and slipped into peaceful sleep.

Day four Teri finally graduated to a regular private room. Dr. Silverstein told the nurses to ignore all rules of visitation as I was welcome to be with Teri 24/7 if I wanted. There was a huge, padded window seat where I stretched out and rested whenever Teri slept. She felt secure and often opened her eyes, spotted me, smiled, and went back to sleep. Slowly she got better. She began asking Dr. Silverstein when she was going to get out of the hospital. He shook his head and looked her straight in the eye. "Missy, when they brought you in here, I didn't know if you would leave here in a body bag. I'm not letting you go until I am ready so just relax."

Each morning it became harder for me to see the team off. Finally, I began crying and voiced how much I missed going to serve. Gib and Bob volunteered to stay and let me go instead. However, that wasn't practical for multiple reasons and with their encouragement, I knuckled down and returned to the hospital. As I entered the hospital that day, I took notice of the signs. Each pointed a different direction with a title of the department. That is, all except for one. That sign had no department listed, only one doctor's name - Dr. Silverstein. It was clear the impact this man had on the hospital and on our lives. No other name appeared on any sign. He certainly stood alone. Later, as I walked down the hallway of the hospital with him, I saw all the staff step to the side and bow their head toward him. These people saw this doctor as their hero. Their respect for him was clear and overwhelming to behold. Once again, I saw the hand of God on each aspect of this entire experience.

The most shocking thing in all this was the finances. Before Teri could be admitted to the hospital, I had to pay a down payment of $7.000 since she was entering the ICU. I went to the business office and gave them my credit card. Gib wasn't with me, and since we paid it off every month, I had no idea what the upper limit of our card was. To my surprise, it cleared quickly. Evidently, Bob related the story to our driver, Elias, and the transportation group asked Bob to tell me they would take up a collection to cover Teri's cost. I was completely humbled.

These fellow believers barely made enough money to feed their families, yet they were willing to sacrificially give us money. They saw us as part of the family of God in need, and they wanted to help. I was amazed at how quickly they had responded. Even though we didn't need their help, their willingness to help was deeply appreciated.

Even more astonishing, when Gib set down to settle final bills, they actually gave him money back Teri had had multiple tests including EKG's, CAT Scans, X-rays, three days in the ICU, and a week in a private room, and the total bill was less than $7,000. This proved hard for an American to comprehend. Of course, Dr. Silverstein's bill wasn't included, and it was much more in line with American expectations. Still, in the end, all expenses were covered by the travel insurance.

The next experience that was so precious came on the weekend. Teri had different visitors come to see her. They had ridden on the bus for one hour one way, stayed only 15 minutes so not to tire her, and then rode back home another hour. While there, they gathered round her bed and beseeched the Lord on her behalf. Never have I heard such heartfelt petitions and boldness before God. They were passionate, believing in the Great Physician, and asking for Him to intervene in Teri's life. I couldn't stop the grateful tears that snuck out of my eyes. What a privilege to witness such love and trust in Jesus. Later, Teri remarked, "Mom, I can't believe those people. They took all that time, spent their money for transportation, and came many miles to see me. I have had more visitors in the hospital in Kenya than I do in the hospital in Minneapolis. Wow! It is such a sacrifice for them." That's exactly what I saw - sacrifice.

The final day of the mission trip culminated in a time for the teacher training seminar and, of course, Teri couldn't go. Gib and Ashley spent the day with her at the hospital in order to free me up for the seminar. Once we were ready to begin, Bob got everyone singing. I closed my eyes and listened to the most beautiful sound I had ever heard. They began chanting and responding, and I thought I was being lifted to heaven. Their voices resounded off the walls and landed in my heart. How these people loved the Lord!

I stood to face them. They all knew Teri and loved her, and I shared her progress, and they began to clap. Overcome with their love, I opened our seminar with words from my heart.

"In America we have made a huge mistake. Our heroes are our movie stars and professional athletes. We don't choose them because of their positive lifestyle. We choose them because they entertain us. Now, I find myself standing in the presence of true heroes. I am speaking about you. You escaped the slums, got an education, and could have a totally different life free of the desperation of the slums. Instead, you have chosen to come back to help others. Your love for your people is the true meaning of love and sacrifice. You have continued to teach even when you don't get paid. You travel long distances each day by bus and on foot just to be there for each other and your students. Your presence is the only stabilizing factor in the lives of many of these children and you rise to the occasion. I don't know if what Teri, Shannon, and I prepared for you today will be of much help to you. However, I do know that your presence here has been a great help for me. I stand in the presence of giants, and you are my heroes."

Unable to go on, I looked to Bob in desperation. He rose and started singing and they all rose and sang with him. Our hearts united in praise and after a while we were ready for a day of work. We dug in, shared ideas, techniques, and materials and when we broke for lunch, I think every person in the room hugged me. The afternoon sped by, and Shannon and I felt we had given them materials, ideas, encouragement, and hope. It closed with hugs and tears wrapped in one. The week of stress was over, the mission trip was done, and I only wished Teri could have experienced this heavenly high with me.

The next day Ashley and I left Gib in Nairobi with Teri and went on safari with the team. Pastor Bob had been under so much strain. He felt responsible for the team and for Teri. He was her pastor and friend and wanted to minister to her, but the demands of making the team function well rested on his shoulders. As the week progressed, so did his kidney stones. By the time we went on safari he was in full blown distress and torment. Unwilling to separate from the team and go to the hospital himself, he traveled with us trying to encourage others. The team began to pray for relief for him knowing the long plane rides home would be excruciating. God touched his body and Bob endured. Once we landed in Minnesota, he drove himself directly to the hospital.

The travel insurance was fantastic. They sent a paramedic over. He would be responsible for Teri. Once she was released from the hospital, he would make all decisions about her care. He would decide when to travel, when to interrupt the trip if needed, and once back in the U.S. he would decide if she was to go home or the hospital. Gib would stay in Africa and travel home with Teri and the paramedic. I would go with Ashley and the team ahead. Weary, the team left without Teri and Gib.

Fortunately, they were able to come the very next day. Gib related how they were treated like celebrities on the plane and flew first class. They were able to rest not only on the plane, but in the first-class lounges and that allowed Teri to endure the trip well. When they arrived in Minnesota Shane, Wendy, and I rushed to the airport to meet them only to find them sitting outside the international wing. They had been excused from customs and ushered out quickly. Teri was tired but looked better than when she had first arrived in Kenya twelve days earlier. She was able to go home without a hospital stay.

Each time Teri had gone to Africa she had gotten ill afterwards. She had suffered from pneumonia each time and now the doctor finally told her she couldn't go again. She had already reached her own conclusion that that had been her final trip. Africa changed all of us forever. It was like nowhere else on earth. It will always be in our hearts. God showed us real heroes. We will see them again in Heaven.

As the days and weeks passed, Teri and I analyzed our trip separately. When we finally talked, we discussed all the blessings that had been poured out on us in our time of need. From the moment she became sick God extended His hand and used His people all over the world to touch our lives. From doctors, to drivers, to prayer warriors, insurance providers, and people, people, people. God had used Kelly, heroes, Pastor Bob, the team, and unselfish Kenyans to humble us before God. The trip was not a failure. Sure, it was different than we expected, it wouldn't have been of our choosing, but it had been the most powerful use of God's people we had ever seen. We were so grateful for each experience. Once again, He had proven the trips were His trips not ours.

Loss cannot really be compared to gain. We can never replace the lost lives of our parents and brother. They left a hole in our hearts. We can never regain the loss of Teri's health, her lack of being able to serve in Kenya, and her sorrow at not getting to say goodbye to all the teachers and staff she loved so much. However, even through those losses, God sustained us. He had led us through new seasons of life, and He had always been there.

Looking back on the unexpected gains and blessings we could see how He had not only sustained us, but heaped joy, love and insights on us. We had celebrated her 40 + years of life, added a new branch to our family tree, had multiple trips, and been allowed to meet real heroes, and passionate believers. We'd had time to stop and ponder, and we found God waiting for us.

The losses had been immense. Oddly, they didn't feel overwhelming. In the center of the storm God had showered us with confidence, insights, and peace. Teri and I discussed the depth of the verse, Philippians 3:8 "I count everything as loss because of the surpassing worth of knowing Christ Jesus my Lord." We had been allowed to have first-hand experiences capturing the depth of God's love for us. We learned to rejoice in all we had experienced and now we anxiously awaited the next adventure He had in store for us. Whether we face gains or loses we could say, "Lead on God, and we will follow!

CAN I JUST ESCAPE?

CHAPTER 14

Excitement was in the air. We had added a new baby with the birth of Natalia for Will and Nelly. We had kept little Camila overnight while her parents went to the hospital, and she was sound asleep by the time Will called with the news. First thing the next morning we took Camila to the hospital. Without hesitation, she climbed into the bed with Mommy and baby sister, and we captured a precious family picture. What joy to have this tiny ball of love and Teri could hardly wait to get to the hospital to see her. How we loved that family that had become such a part of us.

Spring was upon us, and in a few months our first grandchild was to marry. We were giving a shower for Elyse in just two days, and Wendy was flying in from Illinois for it. Once again, Teri needed me to take her to the ER. She couldn't breathe. Guy would oversee the girls, so, off Teri and I went for another sleepless night in the ER. By morning she was admitted to the hospital, and they determined the valves into the chambers of her heart were leaking from too much pressure. Therefore, they needed to slow down her heart and that meant adjusting her medication. Leaving her in their competent hands, I headed to the airport to pick up Wendy.

Once she was updated on Teri, we began planning, checking over our lists, and preparing for the shower the following day. Since friends were coming from out of town for the shower, the men decided to have a "Man Cave Party" for themselves. We cleared out the garage, brought in the grill and turned them loose with the guide to show them his wares and how to cook them. Saturday was nippy and all the men were bundled up and we were happy the "girl" party was inside the house. Mid -morning Teri was released from the hospital in time for the shower, and joy, laughter, and fun were had by all. That night after all was cleaned up, Wendy called me to her bedroom.

"Mom, you have had lumps in your breasts before. Were they solid or soft?"

"Mostly soft, sometimes tender, sometimes moveable. Why?"

"I have a solid lump." She lowered her head as she spoke. She showed me and it was as solid as a rock and not just tiny.

"It is probably nothing but get in to see a doctor as soon as you get home." I advised.

She saw a doctor the next week and that's when all things spun out of control. Quickly she was sent to a surgeon as he was the one to order ultrasounds and after appointments were made, we waited without worry because it was really nothing! Right?

A few days later Gib turned the car into the underground parking lot of a huge convention center. Along with our friends, Tom and Leann, we were to help usher people in the right direction through the maze of hallways. Leann shared a funny joke and the four of us continued laughing. Gib's cell phone rang, interrupting our laughter, and he clicked the button to answer. Suddenly, through the car speakers, the car was filled with the serious voice of Brad. As he began to speak, I suddenly remembered today was the day Wendy was to have an ultrasound on the lump in her breast. She had told me about it earlier, but I had already shifted into positive. It would be nothing. This is my healthy girl and I had had lumps that were nothing. So, I hadn't really given it a second thought. Yet, Brad's voice sounded ominous.

"Hello, this is Brad. I am here with your daughter, and we just left the doctor. The ultrasound was unable to pass through the mass."

"I don't know what that means," I said. Already, my stomach was tightening.

"It's not good. It shows the mass is solid and we must go on to have a biopsy." Silence surrounded all of us.

"Brad, can Wendy hear me?"

"Yes, I have you on speaker phone."

I started to give her a pep talk but all that came out of my mouth was a pleading sound. "I love you, Wendy." Then, the tears began to flow. I couldn't say more. I couldn't shift into a positive place. Why had I gone about my normal day without thinking about her having this test? How could I have acted like everything was fine when nothing was? I couldn't speak and I heard Wendy crying in the background. Finally, pulling myself together, I tried to cover the tremble in my voice by speaking louder. "Wendy, I will call you in a couple of hours. We are getting ready to go inside a convention and direct people where to go for the meeting. I will call you once I am home. Wendy, I love you!"

Brad reassured me that she heard me and said they were on their way home and would await our return call. I needed time to process this. What does it mean? Can it still be nothing? As tears flowed, Leann, who was sitting behind me, put her hands on my shoulders and gave me a virtual hug.

"I can't believe I got so busy today I forgot she had this test. I can't believe . . ." my voice trailed off. Gib reached across the seat and took my hand and squeezed it. After a few deep breaths, I sucked in a full lung of air, opened the door. and stood up. Leann quickly stood beside me, and unsure of what to do, she placed her hand on my shoulder again. I wiped the tears away, shifted into the positive and then said, "We must go inside. We are a little late. I will deal with this after the convention starts." Gib was by my side and wordlessly we began to walk toward the elevators hand in hand. I drew all the strength I could from him through his hand.

It was seemingly easy to shift into a mode of directing and helping others. A smile, a nod, pointing directions, greeting, and an occasional laugh passed the hour without the heaviness on my shoulders being unbearable. I understood how performers can "let the show go on." The trick was simple. Focus only on the task in front of you. Allow the other world to sit quietly and wait. Finally, the crowd dwindled, Gib could handle the rest, so I slipped off to a corner and pulled out my cell phone. What would I be able to say to her that would encourage her?

"Hello," Wendy's voice sounded small and vulnerable.

"Hi, sweetheart," I said. "I am still at the convention but was able to slip away so I could call you. How are you doing?"

I heard her clear her throat and when she spoke her voice was strong and unwavering. "I am fine. We have an appointment to see the surgeon on Wednesday so there will be no more news until then."

I closed my eyes and pictured her sitting herself up straight, putting on armor. and toughening to talk to her Mommy. How I wished I could reach across those miles and wrap her in my arms as I had done so many times when she was hurt. Instead, a phone was the best I could do.

"Did they give you any more information?" I asked.

"They only said they couldn't make any predictions and only a biopsy would tell us what we need to know. They wouldn't say it was cancer and they wouldn't say it's not."

Again, that heavy silence surrounded us. I didn't want to give her false hope, but I couldn't think of anything logical to say. Finally, a few words tumbled out, "I am so sorry I am not there. I still hope this will be nothing. However, I am glad you will get a biopsy so we know for sure and can put this behind us." Silence. She didn't believe this was nothing.

Gib motioned for me to return to my post. "I have to go, honey. I will call again when I get home."

"Don't do that, Mom. Brad is here and I am okay, and I need to process this. I really am okay. And Mom, I love you too." Her voice broke and I heard her disconnect. How can this be happening?

The days that followed were a blur. In the middle of these unsure days, Gib and I found our new church pulsating with love and support. They were beginning to be a strength to sustain us. Wendy decided she didn't need me to come for the biopsy as we wouldn't get results for a few days after that anyway. So, we waited for results. And then, once again, I heard Brad's serious voice.

"The biopsy shows cancer."

The only words I could speak were swear words. Aware I was swearing I seemed unable to stop myself. It was the only word that fit. I couldn't ask anything, I couldn't add anything, I could only think that swear word over and over. Later, Wendy told me Brad kept saying, "All she did was swear. I've never heard your mom swear and that is all she said over and over." As I hung up the phone, the tears flowed, and Gib knew by my actions even though my words wouldn't come out. We held each other, trying to get the world to stop spinning and the chaos to stop. It didn't.

The next afternoon, I went outside along the lake and lay down on the bank. I allowed the beauty of creation to pan out before me. I was awed by the many hues of green and blue. "Wow, God, you are such an artist, and you must really like blue and green." Suddenly, an enormous shadow fell over me. I looked up to see what was blocking the sun and watched a magnificent eagle swoop down toward the water. He was playing, and he tilted himself, so his wing almost touched the water and then turned straight and ascended up, up, up. Caught in an airstream, he soared and let his massive wings rest. Smiling, I sat up and watched. First, he turned this way and then that way. He put on a show of splendor for me. Finally, he again swooped down to the water and grasped a fish in his talons. Again, he flew just barely above me as he mounted up on the skies and flew away with his dinner. How wondrous!

Could it only have been one day since my world had crashed and Brad had said that awful word, cancer? My healthy baby had breast cancer. My world had begun to shake and shake till I felt it was an earthquake. This couldn't be true. No way would God let this happen to a second daughter. No way would He demand this of me. Usually the encourager, I became the one destroyed. I couldn't talk to Wendy again. I couldn't let her hear my agony. I couldn't hear her agony. I was defeated.

Yesterday hours had passed before I had escaped to this same place on the lake, waiting for God to intervene. The battle lay ahead along with the pain, the treatments, the surgeries, and the fear, such heavy fear. Would I be strong enough to fight for or with her? Could I withstand her agony and her pain? Each thought had burned itself into my brain. I had prayed so much the last few days as Wendy had appointment after appointment. Now, God's answer wasn't what I wanted, and He seemed so very far away. I had taken my Bible with me to the lake and now I pulled it into my lap unsure if I could focus on it. It fell open to Isaiah 40 and I began to read verse 31. "But they who wait for the LORD shall renew their strength; they shall mount up with wings like eagles; they shall run and not be weary; they shall walk and not faint."

I had begun to pray. "God, I am too weak for this. I need you to send me an eagle. I can't walk this path. I need to soar." Slowly, I had felt a strange sensation. I felt I was being lifted up onto the back of an eagle. Keeping my eyes closed for fear the feeling would disappear, I felt the eagle begin to climb. Soon I saw in my mind the clouds around me. Tentatively,

I opened my eyes and looked down to see my home below me. That was where all the misery was. Yet, I was above it. I was soaring, I was free of pain and agony that the word "Cancer" brings. Again, I had closed my eyes and soared and soared. The wind was beneath us, and my eagle and I just floated. Strength began to replace fear while contentment replaced insecurity. My God was bigger than all those problems below me. As my confidence grew, my eagle began to descend. I wanted to stay up there, but I knew I had to come back to reality. I also knew that God had sent my eagle, and I could call my eagle back anytime I needed him. God had given me an escape plan. The problems were still there, but so was God. I smiled when I opened my eyes and saw my home surrounding me. I was not safe in my home; I was safe in God. What a joy. He would be there for the battle ahead. He would lead me, Gib, Wendy, and Brad through each step. And I could soar whenever I needed to. What a relief.

Now today, as I stretched out in the sun, I closed my eyes remembering yesterday's soaring. Today, God had sent a real live eagle to remind me He not only had the situation in hand, but He had plans to help me each step of the way. Today as I opened my eyes to soak in the greens and blues, I could smile that God loved me, my family, and the world He created. Wendy was His. He would give her strength. I could teach her about my eagle and give her an escape plan too. It really would be okay. The colors were so vibrant, just like my Lord. They were just another touch of the master artist. He loved color and He had placed that same love of color in each of my daughters.

Both girls had their favorite colors since they were small. Teri loved purple and Wendy loved red. Shane kept bouncing between blue and green and was never obsessed like his sisters.

Wendy was known for her red shoes. We would go to Shane's little league games, and she would go to the adjoining playground. She was easy to spot with her red shoes and even one of the other mothers called her "Red Shoes" instead of her name. When shopping for new shoes she only wanted to try on red ones. Whenever I bought black or white ones, they sat in the closet unused most of the time and were donated later in perfect condition. One day when she was only about 4 or 5, we were going to church and Wendy had a peach-colored dress on. She looked so cute until I saw the red patent leather shoes.

"Nope," I said firmly. "You have to put on your black shoes. That dress looks terrible with red shoes. You can change shoes when we get home from church. Go change now into the black ones and hurry."

She returned quickly and asked if she looked okay. "Yes, the black looks great. Get your little Bible and meet us in the garage."

Shortly she ran into the garage, climbed into her seat with Bible in hand, and we started off to church. As we turned into the parking lot, I turned to give last minute instructions and noticed for the first time, red shoes in all their glory. Swallowing hard I tried to control my anger, "What are you doing in red shoes?" I demanded.

With a gentle smile and ducking her head, she responded barely above a whisper,

"I just thought red shoes are happier." With that, she hopped out of the car and skipped down the sidewalk into the church.

Teri was just as obsessed with purple. As far as she was concerned it was "her" color and no one else in the family should ever wear it. Whenever she found a shirt, dress or pants that were purple, she wanted them no matter if they looked good on her or not.

These colors remained with the girls forever. Wendy wedding done in red and Teri's in purple. Their homes reflected their colors. Teri's adult bedroom was purple and Wendy's accent color was red. There was no question in anyone's mind as to their favorites.

Now, I wondered if God's favorites were peaceful colors of blues and greens. I sensed He was reminding me that I could trust Him to be there throughout the battle ahead. I would have my eagle. I would have my God. I would have strength well beyond my personal faculties as I would have His strength. Today, I was finally ready to get up off the bank of the lake and head back inside to face the chores that lay ahead. I thanked Him once again.

We had made phone calls and spread requests for prayer. As of yet, we didn't know the next step, but it was obvious we would clear our calendars and head to Illinois. The next few weeks would be filled with tests, putting in a port for delivery of the chemo, and other preparations.

Earlier, my sister and her husband had planned to come to Minnesota to see Teri and me dance in a recital together. We had taken tap dancing lessons as a way for Teri to get physical activity and now were to be in a recital. Patricia just couldn't miss it! They came to the recital, and then the four of us took off on a week trip through Wisconsin, into Illinois, and ending in Wendy's town. We were there for her birthday and cooked steaks to celebrate. It was a delightful time. It was a pause as battle plans were being readied.

Two weeks after they left, we returned to Illinois for "chemo training." Explanations, plans, and meds were introduced to us in detail. The cancer was invasive ductal carcinoma, and it was the aggressive triple negative. That meant the 3 hormone receptors were negative. At one time the medical field had thought that would be a good thing. However, they soon discovered that triple negative was not good. It was highly probable her cancer would return.

Once home from the doctor's Wendy cleaned carpets and we scrubbed the house to be ready for the siege. She announced she would cut her lovely, long, black hair so it wouldn't be so traumatic when it begins to fall out. She was readying herself for battle. Brad was trying to deal with it in his own way. He was constantly talking, fretting, worrying, and asking "what if" questions. Wendy would often walk away from him and shake her head saying he just kept repeating the same things over and over, and he had to let it go and stop worrying. It seemed they were on different tracks heading for the same station. I could see her stiffen her back and sit up straighter. This was not going to beat her. Chemo would start two days after Elyse's wedding. Teri made it down to see her, and the sisters encouraged each other, and both took on the appearances of warriors. Our Coleman women were ready.

The sun shone bright on the day of Elyse's wedding. It was to be outdoors, and the weather was gorgeous. They had chosen a "garden" venue that was perfect and filled with family and friends. The bride was the most beautiful and radiant I had ever seen her, and Shane was bursting with pride and holding back tears to see his daughter so grown up and lovely. Wendy's family had come from Illinois, and we gathered to rejoice with Elyse. Wendy's hair was short and bouncy, and she and Teri looked more like sisters than ever before. Teri sat down behind Wendy, and we took a close-up picture of their faces which would become our favorite for years to come. The problems were laid aside for a few hours and we all reveled in our joy. The next morning Wendy's family as well as Gib and I set out for Illinois. Her first treatment would be the next day.

Wendy and Teri at Elyse's Wedding

The day after her first chemo I was devastated when I woke to pain and itching. I had shingles. I was going to have to leave Wendy so as not to give them to her. I wanted to scream, cry, yell, or whatever it took to make them go away. I wasn't sure if Wendy needed me to be there, but I knew I needed to be with her. I had had the single shot five years before, so perhaps it would be a light case. I had never read that it was only 50-80% effective. Since Wendy was just starting treatments, her immune system wasn't compromised, and she was in no danger. Wendy's doctor arranged for me to get an antiviral shot before leaving Illinois. Still, I felt like a naughty child being sent home by the principal. There just wasn't time for me to be sick. Teri was continuing to have problems and needed more testing; Wendy was having chemo and now I had shingles. What was happening to the "Coleman women?" As it turned out, I had an extremely light case, and they were gone within a week. Somehow, Teri, Wendy and I must figure out how to support each other across the miles when one was having a problem and needed the others.

I bought a pink ribbon charm, the symbol for breast cancer awareness, and put it on a chain around my neck. Often, I found myself stroking my necklace and thinking of Wendy. Yet, something was missing. Gib removed a tiny silver heart from my high school charm bracelet and put it on the chain alongside the ribbon. Now, Teri was there too. It was a tangible way to have my girls by me. Teri noticed there was nothing on the chain to represent Shane. So, I shopped until I found an "S" and put it beside the girls. My three were always "touching" distance from me. As we sang choruses in church, I would stroke my kids. With Gib on one side and Leann sitting on the other side holding my hand, I felt my girls were with me. I couldn't protect them from pain, I couldn't take their place, but I could pray for the empty spots in their souls to be filled with the Holy Spirit. I would be their cheerleader, encourager, and constant companion even if not physically there. Countless others here and around the world were standing in the gap and praying for both of them. Shane was suffering deeply as he prayed for his sisters.

I wanted my girls to have complete eternal joy. I would teach them to have their own eagle to soar on above the pain. I would have them memorize Isaiah 40:31. I would always remind them they were daughters of THE KING and they always had angels with them and, the Holy Spirit never left them. The King had them in His arms every moment. Needless to say, we couldn't run from what lay ahead. So, we would stand and fight. Our fight song would be Joshua 1:9 " Have I not commanded you? Be strong and courageous. Do not be frightened, and do not be dismayed, for the LORD your God is with you wherever you go."

We would run the race, He would keep us from becoming weary, and we WOULD SOAR. Afterall, my daughters were warriors.

FEAR, HOPE, AND WAIT

CHAPTER 15

Wendy's battle had begun. Between treatments, Wendy had shots to bring up her counts following the treatments. This plan would last four sessions and then she would begin another group of 12 sessions of different drugs. Once done with chemo, she would have radiation. With this timeline and no setbacks, we should be done by Christmas. She would lose her hair, but they predicted she probably wouldn't be too sick.

Those predictions proved correct. It was often hard to realize she was undergoing chemo. During the next three weeks Wendy never missed a day of work. She was only a little nauseated. She had almost normal energy and it was so unlike Teri's last bout with chemo that I wondered if what they were giving her was doing its job. However, as the days passed, we met with the doctor often and he always announced things were going great. The first rounds appeared to be flying by with very little side effects.

When we first discovered Wendy had breast cancer, I had warned Wendy that I had something I couldn't remove from my calendar. Gib and I had planned a European 50th wedding anniversary trip. Our reservations had been made, and money paid down. She was doing so well; it wasn't going to be a problem. She only had one treatment left in this first round as we made final preparations for our trip.

Two days before leaving I went shopping for a new purse. I have no idea what happened, but suddenly I was aware I didn't have my phone. Panic set in. This was to be my connection to Wendy while I was in Europe. Close to hysteria, I began retracing my steps and finding nothing. A woman and her daughter saw my distress and asked to help. I had her to call Gib on her phone, and he came to the mall. She stayed with me until he arrived. I will admit it was the closest to a complete meltdown I have ever experienced. Reality and fear tightened their hold on me, and I was in a panic mode. We searched, and all the while, Gib kept reassuring me we would be able to reach Wendy on his phone, and my breathing slowed a little. We were standing near a checkout site when Gib tried calling my phone. We heard it ringing. It was inside a drawer at the checkout station. The worker pulled it from the drawer and said it was found in the men's dressing room a few minutes earlier. Evidently, whoever had taken it discovered it was locked and they didn't know how to open it so they just left it in the dressing room. Even now I have no idea how and when it disappeared from me. Had I tried it out in a purse and left it there? Had I laid it down while inspecting purses? Had I left my backpack open, and they removed it? I had no idea. I only knew that God returned it. I realized the deep fear I had in leaving the country with my daughters ill. I realized I had closed myself in a protective shield not even admitting to myself my fears. This trip was going to be so good for Gib and me, and yet the girls would never leave my thoughts.

Thankfully, we already felt surrounded by God' s family in our new church. So, it wasn't a surprise that the day before we left for Europe, our new Pastor preached a sermon that was meant for us. It was God's timing and so affirming that I just had to share it with the girls. I quickly sent this email to the girls.

God took me to church this morning. First, we sang familiar choruses so I could close my eyes and sing to Him. The words were all about how great, loving, and strong He is.

I stroked my necklace with your two charms on it and felt you there with me. Then, Pastor Todd preached on John 16: 16 - 24. It was written for the three of us in this battle together. I will list a few things that made the biggest impact on me below.

Many of the trials in this world are "fall out" consequences of this fallen world we live in. The question is not if you have trial; but do these challenges keep you from accepting Jesus as your Lord. It's NOT just in asking Him to forgive and save us but knowing deep in our soul the truth of the resurrection is the only real joy we can live by. Read on and hopefully you will understand "real joy" more. Here is what I gleaned from his sermon.

1. <u>Life can be confusing and difficult</u> (John 16 vs. 16-18) Circumstances put us into questioning states. We ask Why? Where are you God? I thought you loved me, and on and on. No matter the problems we have cancer, heart, parenting, chronic illness, financial, jobs etc. they all remind us that life is not neat.

*2. <u>Resurrection truth produces lasting joy</u>. (Vs. 19-22) Vs. 20 is the key and should be a verse you claim over and over. "Truly, truly, I say to you, you will weep and lament, but the world will rejoice. You will be sorrowful, but your sorrow will turn into joy." Weeping will continue for the night, but the real joy comes in the morning. Unlike the world, we have joy so deep it will not be taken away from us This is a promise in the Bible, but we must trust. But Satan tries to fill us with a lie and he tells us we won't suffer if we just have more faith. This is a lie straight from Satan. Nowhere does the Bible even hint at this. **Our deep joy must be founded only in the cross.** II Cor. 4:16-18 Here is vs. 16 – 17. "Though our outer self is wasting away, our inner self is being renewed day by day. For this light momentary affliction is preparing for us an eternal weight of glory beyond all comparison". (Wow! We are really getting prepared!)*

Here is a question without an answer: Could we experience pure joy <u>without</u> experiencing sorrow? (Just think about that for a minute)

Back to end the section in John 16 vs. 23. " . . . Whatever you ask of the Father in my name, he will give it to you."

This doesn't mean He will give me a new car if I ask in the name of Jesus. Instead, it means, with deep penetrating prayer, He will take away our temporary sorrow and trade it for eternal joy.

I stop relating the sermon here to tell you this is what I want for both of you as you wage your battle. COMPLETE ETERNAL JOY. I rest in Him so often I can truly say I have it. I have shared with you how I crawl up in His hands when I am too weary for battle, but I still have eternal joy. I mount up on the wings of eagles when I need to "fly" above the trials, and I have complete joy. There are no easy ways out of the battles before each of you. As a mom, you know how you wish you could protect your children from painful things. It can't always be done. If I hurt deeply because I can't take your place, think how much more deeply it grieves the Holy Spirit when we don't let Him do his job and bring us eternal peace and joy.

*So, I challenge both of you to take every fear, frustration, questions, anger, etc. and give them to the Holy Spirit, and then ask Him in the name of Jesus to replace the empty spots in your soul with joy: deep, full, wonderful joy that **you are the daughters of the King.** Don't let Satan have control of your spirit. Instead, ask in the name of Jesus to be given eternal joy. You are both fighters. You are united in love for each other and love for your families. You both are waging enormous battles I cannot take away. But I have learned I can be your cheerleader, constant companion (in spirit when I can't be there in person), your encourager, and your reminder of Who has the control of your life. It is scary to give control of your life up. But, once you do, nothing anyone can do to you will stop the joy. The physical pain and discomfort, the fears of the unknown, the frustration as to why you have to do this, will all become not only bearable, but steppingstones to a 'bigger and better life.*

I will be out of the country for twenty days, but not out of your hearts; there are no miles in eternity and Heaven. I will be raising you up to the Lord many times during the day while I touch my necklace. Granny, Mimi, Grandma and Jinkers are already in Heaven, and they are in this fight with you. They are standing by the throne lifting you up. Many here on earth are praying and having their friends praying for you. **You are the daughter of the King!** *You are already His and you will continue to be victorious. WOW! What a great God we have. God is good. God is good all the time! Love and more love, Mom*

Now it was time for Gib and me to leave. Both girls were in an okay place. Teri had learned she would not be having heart valve replacement at this time, and Wendy was in a set routine with little to no side effects. God had set us a time to escape, and we were ready. Armed with my necklace to stroke, and IPads and phones set on an international plan, we set off. It had been 40 years since we had lived there, and we were anxious to see the changes and reminisce the years spent there.

Our first stop landed us in Geneva. As the plane descended, we felt like pilgrims coming home after a long absence. We rented a car and drove across the border into France and the tiny town, Ferney Voltaire, France, we had called home for three years. We found our quaint village was no longer so quaint. It had become a bustling small town. We still strolled down main street, bought lunch, ate in the park, and stopped at the fountain where Shane had ridden his bike with Teri perched on the handlebars. This was where he caught the bus into Switzerland each morning to attend an international school. We drove by our apartment building where we had lived and then by the house where we had spent the last year. As we passed Teri's French school, little children played, and we expected her to pop out with her tiny pack on her back. Driving up the valley we realized the only thing missing was the backseat full of kids.

We stayed in the Auberge des Chasseurs, the same place where we had stayed 40 years before when we first moved there. Nestled on the side of the Jura mountains our view of the valley stretched out in front of us and was crowned by Mt. Blanc strutting her stuff above the low hanging clouds of white cotton candy. The Alps across the way seemed so close. The same open beams on the ceiling of the restaurant were there, still painted with flowers and vines. Ignoring the jet lag, we basked in the sun beside the pool and relaxed. We were home!

The next few mornings, we drove into Geneva and walked by the hospital where Wendy had been born. We attended the Fete de Geneve and the fireworks on the lake. We strolled through old town and found our church where we had spent many hours with friends. As we stood by the lake and watched the jet of water shooting into the sky, we were suddenly transported back to days that had been quieter and less chaotic. It was nostalgic and refreshing. We strolled into the shop where we bought cuckoo clocks for $50 only to find smaller ones starting at $300. Prices of everything had risen so much even though the city still held its charm. Walking hand -in-hand it was almost as if none of the pain at home existed.

After spending time with friends of long ago, we left Geneva and drove through the stunning landscape of Switzerland. Each Alpine village had flower boxes lining the windows just like a painted postcard. The drive through the mountains and leaving the area filled us with emotions of thankfulness, nostalgia, and regret that we were having to leave our paradise.

On to Paris only to discover it wasn't as much fun as 40 years ago. Now, it was too full of people. We rediscovered the beauty of Notre Dame, the Champs Elysees, and did a few touristy things. However, we most enjoyed the ride on the river Seine. We saw the changes the years had made on the city and were glad we had seen it when it wasn't so crowded. As the official celebration of our anniversary, we again attended a show at the Moulin Rouge. The only negatives were mostly frustrations. Gib lost, or had pickpocketed, his phone. Then, I got stung by a wasp and being allergic, it caused days of swelling, pain, and itching. We spoke to the girls every other night, and both were doing well so we found we could completely relax. It was time to leave France and Gib could hardly wait to get on the Autobahn. His lead foot stomped on the pedal, and we flew through Germany. I couldn't get him to slow down so I took out my book and read so I didn't have to watch my impending death.

Soon, we reached the town of Rothenberg and loved being within the walled city. The cobblestoned streets, huge central square, and friendliest people gave a gaiety to the town that transcended the ages. In the evening everyone gathered in a huge square filled with long picnic tables. The local restaurants sat up grills and we ate brats along with the local shop keepers as a fiddler and accordion player strolled through the crowd. It was delightful. We walked, ate, strolled, sang, and relished the joy the people had. It was absolutely a step back into a time when time was set at a different and refreshing pace. It was difficult to leave knowing our next stop would be a much busier city.

To our surprise, Prague, Czech Republic, was our favorite city, and we enjoyed it on a Segway. What fun we had as we rolled around town to discover new sites. This city often called the Venice of the North was filled with old structures. We climbed the hill to the castle and viewed the bridges that had not been bombed during WWII. Through the centuries, the country had been conquered often. Most recently by the Germans and the Russians. The people had no love for either. We took a dinner cruise, attended a folk tour that included dancing and singing, and enjoyed the food and people.

One day our joy of the city sobered when we entered the Jewish sector. At one time there were 120,000 Jews in this city, and now there were only 5,000. Most were sent to Auschwitz and died there. Inside a synagogue we saw a room where pictures Jewish children had drawn were preserved. They depicted the deportations, ghetto, and fences of the death camps. Then, the names! Oh, the names! On the walls of the synagogue were written each name of over 80,000 that had died in this area. Our hearts were so heavy. This scene would stay in our minds and hearts forever.

Leaving this behind we continued to the rebuilt city of Dresden, Germany. It stands as a tribute to the people who were determined to restore it to its pre-war glory. They had done just that. It was stunning.

Our final stop was Berlin and the history of the cold war we had lived through. We visited Checkpoint Charlie, the outline of the wall, and walking through history we had only watched in newscasts. There is now a museum on the rise of Hitler that actually frightened us as we recognized similarities of things happening in America and we could see how government control could destroy a society. Of course, we don't have a dictator like Hitler, but we do have so many people filled with hatred.

It was there, in Berlin, one night when we called home that we were faced with a surprise. Wendy's face popped into view with a totally bald head. Shocked, I said, "Oh, your hair must have fallen out."

"It was starting to, and I hated that, so I shaved it off. What do you think?"

"Wow, it is different, but you really look cute," I lied.

Gib chimed in that he and Wendy now looked like twins with two bald heads. We joked, laughed caught up on events and then hung up. I fell back in my chair and fought tears. Seeing her bald broke my heart. I was actually glad I was in Europe and not face- to- face with her as she would see the pain in my eyes. After sitting there a while, I looked up to see water running down the huge windows of the hotel lobby. Once again, it was raining. Once again God was reminding me, He was there with me. In the weeks to come, I got used to seeing her bald but never got used to the necessity of it. It was a constant reminder of the battle we were fighting.

When we boarded the plane to return to the states, I hesitated. Gib said, "What's wrong?"

My response was from the depths of my heart. "If we had ended our trip in Geneva instead of starting it there, I might not have been able to get on the plane home. I so long to be there again, to live in the quiet, the peace and beauty of the area. It was definitely ideal."

Gib had no response, only nodded. Now, we winged our way back to the reality awaiting us. Our trip had given us an escape for a few days, but now our trip to "Dreamland" was over.

Gib and Tina on a boat on the Vltava River in Prague

Once we returned from Europe, we learned Kelly had fallen and injured her ankle while on a trip to the Boundary Waters in Northern Minnesota. Nothing was broken but it was quite painful. Shane and Kelly had bought a new home and were in the process of packing things for moving. It was going to be a painful experience with her injuries, and quite inconvenient especially since we wouldn't be around to help her much. However, one Saturday I went out to help Shane clean out his barn that had been his junk area. He had a large dumpster, and we began pulling junk from piles in the barn and throwing it in the dumpster. Following the third color of carpet I drug out and tossed, I just had to ask, "Where did all this come from?" Sheepishly he answered, "It is from multiple remodeling's we have done. Some of that is from 3 times ago."

I started laughing and laughing. I reminded him how he never wanted to throw his "precious" things away when he was growing up. He saved every shoe box, filled them, labeled them, and stacked them sky- high in his closet. He was a pack rat turned human. This was a great excuse to get him to clean and throw things out and we laughed at each old thing we drug out. Some objects had memories and others didn't or were even difficult to recognize. It felt good to throw, throw, throw. We worked, laughed, and carried out the job while having a great time.

Wendy was starting her next round of 12 sessions of chemo so Gib and I started leaving on Fridays at noon so we could drive there in time for our grandson Casey's football games. We had the weekend together, treatment on Monday, I did whatever was needed on Tuesday and as she was usually fine, we left on Wednesday. We repeated it two weeks later.

At the beginning Wendy had Brad help her clean the house before we arrived. I objected saying I could do the cleaning. Too proud to let that go, she kept trying to keep it up. Bored and frustrated, I found hidden spots to clean that no working woman had time to address. One afternoon she called and asked what I was doing. I described the spot I was cleaning and said, "If you won't give me assignments, I will find my own spots. I can't just sit here." That was when she gave in and let me take over the cleaning. Sometimes I made dinners and froze them. The Moms of the football and baseball teams the boys were on, volunteered to bring in meals, so we set them up for Wednesday nights. That would help her survive till the weekend when Brad was home.

Everything seemed to be going as planned until Brad called one night to explain he had a "stalker". As the details emerged, we learned that he had a disgruntled female employee who felt he had betrayed her. She was fired for multiple problems, and she began to harass Brad claiming it was his fault. She left her messages and threats in their yard written on tennis balls, and even followed his car. Brad's company installed an alarm system in their home and the police were canvassing the area. Gib put dead bolt locks on all the doors. This continued to develop over weeks until the restraining order sent her over the edge, and she even attacked a policeman while inside the police station. They sent her to a hospital for a few days of observation, and we all relaxed a bit. We prayed for her mental health while each of us had to learn to trust God not only in the battle but also for the safety of the entire family. Once she was free again, the fear of what she might do was always there, just under the surface keeping us alert. A little later Brad faced her in court, and it was obvious how disturbed she was. Threatened with long jail time, she backed off and the threats stopped. Still, we wondered if she would suddenly reappear. We constantly prayed hedges of thorns around the family.

One thing that was a huge hurtle for Wendy was asking for help. I remembered how I had struggled with that lesson so many years before. When Teri was seven, I had determined she would see only strength in me, so I had battled her cancer with an unwavering attitude. I had allowed others to help only if they did it without asking or had a specific thing they asked to do. One day, Pastor sat me down and said, "Tina, you are cheating others"

"What are you talking about?" I asked totally confused.

"You are a helper and giver. You get great joy from helping others." he continued.

"So?"

"So, then why do you cheat others out of their blessing? They want to help you. They want real joy from doing something for you. But you are so determined to be strong, to be independent, to do it yourself, that you are cheating them out of their blessing. You need to let go and let others benefit from being helpers and givers. You don't appear just to be strong but to be "standoffish". He smiled as he placed his huge hand on my shoulder.

A thunderbolt struck me. "I never thought of it like that," I replied.

"I know," he said. "But each of us have to learn to receive as well as to give. Jesus came to serve, but he allowed others to help Him serve and to serve Him. He set the example. You are strong and in many ways that is good. However, He wants you to be weak enough to rely on Him but also to rely on His people. He has put them into your life for your blessings and for their blessings. Allow them to be blessed."

I never forgot those words. As I pondered what he had said, I realized I had always prided myself in my strength through Him, but I never saw that that strength could be a stumbling block to others. I began to see the lack of asking for help was a thing of pride in my own abilities. I had always thought asking for help was a sign of weakness. I certainly didn't want to humble myself and confess I couldn't do it all. I had no problem asking God for help. But asking His people to carry some of my burden had been out of the question. How self-righteous was that? I had no idea that asking for help was actually brave and showed wisdom. After all, God gave Adam a helpmate. Sure, sometimes I was so deep in survival mode I wasn't aware I even needed help. Usually, I was just too stubborn. How arrogant of me to think others should innately know I needed help. Realizing I was cheating others out of a blessing changed everything. It wasn't easy to change, let go and ask. When I tried to do it, I found both me and the other person received so many blessings for it. It took years to learn and a lesson I still fight, even today.

Now, Wendy needed to learn that same lesson. Quickly, she learned not to refuse most offers of help. However, she seemed completely unable to initiate a call for help. She had seen me toughen myself for battle, and now I saw the same attributes in her. She needed strength for the battle, but like me, she needed to learn to rely not just on God but on God's people. Letting go the control of anything in her life went totally against her private, perfectionist being. I shared with her what I had learned and that being too self-sufficient was a type of pride. God had never meant for us to do things alone. Leaving the ideas with her, I could only pray for her. She would struggle with it forever.

As the year ended, I sat down to analyze what I had experienced. None of us had been able to control what happened to us. Cancer, shingles, chemo, injuries, and frustration had all crashed into our daily lives. Then, in the midst of those events, God touched us through providing helpmates, and always showing up for us. Sometimes He put us in the eye of a hurricane, where we rested in peace. We had lost phones, lost heart, and even lost our way some days. Yet, we discovered joys in our church, friends, celebrations, and even trips. Sure, there had been tears, but there had been laughter too.

I pulled out my Bible, as I had done so often, and let it fall open to see where He took me. To my surprise, it opened to my life-verse in Isaiah. I reread the words so deeply ingrained in me. What a surprise when I suddenly was aware of a tiny word I had always rushed by every time I read or recited the verse. *It was such a tiny word* - WAIT. Isaiah 40:31 "But they who WAIT for the Lord shall renew their strength . . ."

How many times had a I rushed through this part and on to mounting up on my eagle? It was so hard to daily give up all control, all fears, all concerns, all desires and just wait. Yet He was telling me to not rush ahead of Him. I had been forced to wait many times. Yet, the waiting came because it was demanded of me not because I chose. I saw He wanted me to choose to wait and then, and only then, could my strength be renewed. This was not a one-time lesson. It was a daily and even hourly necessity. It needed to become a deeply ingrained habit of surrender and waiting. Wow! I had a new lesson I needed Him to teach me as well as show me how to teach Wendy. Once again, I found myself returning to my life verse of Isaiah 40: 31 and seeing that tiny four-letter word. It stood out to me now like it was written in a bold font that demanded a huge challenge. I needed to wait, wait, wait. I still had so much to learn.

ADVENTURES AWAIT

CHAPTER 16

Adventure. That's a big word. The dictionary defines it as an unusual and exciting experience that could be hazardous, bold, or risky. Sound exciting? It often is a pursuit and creates a psychological arousal to achieve it. Sounds like a Bilbo (the Hobbit) idea of adventure. Yet aren't we all on an adventure all the time? Sometimes life is unusual and exciting. Sometimes it is risky and hazardous. Sometimes we must be bold, and sometimes we just float along and let the adventure happen. It would be easier to float. I'd love not taking responsibility for anything and just let life happen. I guess I would love to remain a child and let others do the hard work. I want my great adventure to be simple. I want to lie on the ground and watch the clouds. I want to climb a tree and look down on unsuspecting passersby. I want to spend hours doing absolutely nothing and smiling all that time. I want to race my brother, ride a bike for hours, play catch with my dog, pretend I'm a princess, fall asleep in the sun, and eat meals prepared by someone else. I want my boldness to allow me to carefully walk across a tree that has fallen across a creek or shoot a BB gun at a target.

What kind of adventure can I have now? Sure, I can jump on a plane and wing to exotic places. Perhaps I could try parasailing or deep-sea scuba diving. I'm not daring enough to try mountain climbing or bungy cord jumping. I certainly won't sing solos or learn to pilot a plane.

What adventure awaits me?

I have decided to be daring and undaunted, audacious, and unflinching.

Calling on my inner strength I decide to do it! What an accomplishment. I get out of bed to face the day and whatever it holds. I am a swashbuckling daredevil!

It wasn't long before I wished I could climb back into that bed. Darn it all, Daddy, why did you teach me to be so responsible? I had awakened that morning in my room at Wendy's house. I made no attempt at ignoring reality. Wendy was undergoing radiation therapy and her skin was holding up well with use of lotions. She had completed seven of the proposed 36 treatments. Her hair was regrowing and was about one inch long. Overall, she was doing well. Brad's stalker was quiet. Sure, she had a restraining order, but we all knew that was just a piece of paper if she chose to act on her frustrations. All appeared quiet here. So, why was I battling life? I made up my empty bed. Since I was missing Gib who was in Minnesota helping Teri's family, I just patted his pillow.

Watching over Wendy's family wasn't the only concern. Teri had called last night declaring I had sold her my car with a target on its back. Three months earlier a deer had run right into the side of her and yesterday she had been rear ended. Now, with whiplash, she was wearing a neck brace, and would be starting treatments to restore her neck and shoulders. Any injury to her was a major one since her bones and muscles were so weak. Thank heavens Gib was there to drive the girls to school, dance lessons, and other activities.

On our nightly phone call, Gib had told me that Shane and Kelly were still paying two house payments as their house hadn't sold although they had moved to a new home three months earlier, and yet another prayer request.to add to my list. I was coming to Wendy's every couple of weeks now, and often Gib remained at home. It was odd being separated from Gib after 50 years of being side-by-side every day. Sure, we talked daily at least once, but it was odd not to have his hand to hold, his blue eyes to stare at. and his surprised look at things I said. Perhaps all that had made my rising more difficult this morning. No time now to dwell on those things. I needed to turn my thoughts to Wendy's family.

As the boys continued their busy schedules with sports, school, and workouts, their different personalities surfaced even more. Casey, now a sophomore in high school, was all smiles. He laughed a lot, always had friends over, hated to read or do homework, and was highly protective of his personal space. He had no desire to talk about God, cancer, or anything deep. However, he could make everyone relax and laugh at his antics. He had many friends and they all seemed to adore him. Quinn, an 8th grader, was the quiet guy that took school and learning seriously and read voraciously. However, when he opened his mouth no matter what came out astounded you. Either he shared insights and knowledge from all his reading about any topic, or he tried to aggravate the conversation by throwing in outlandish thoughts just to rile things up.

Neither boy asked questions about Wendy and her cancer, so I made it a top priority to inform them about any developments, new treatments, tests etc. They always listened, soaked it up, but never asked any questions. All the chaos going on around them had become the "new normal," and they adapted to each change. Things seemed to be running smoothly so it was time I ventured my way back to Minnesota and Gib.

Stress was a constant companion and reared its head in odd ways. Once home, I woke one morning with a "crick" in my neck. Thinking it would go away quickly, I went about my chores with a slight downward turn of my head. By evening, I couldn't lift my head up straight. It quickly became a matter for intense treatment. The ultrasounds, chiropractic adjustments, ice packs and muscle relaxers had their jobs cut out for them. Nothing was breaking the hold on my neck. I couldn't drive or do many of my chores. Still, life went on and I was needed. So, I painfully drug myself back to Illinois. Since I couldn't do all the housework, I engaged the boys and Brad to help, and the silly muscle spasms took weeks to completely disappear. Underneath everything was a rolling current of stress. I even began gaining weight as I found myself relying on comfort foods. Was the rest of the family doing better without their bodies betraying them?

Spring was forcing its way into the frigid north. As tiny flowers began to poke through the soil, trees began to bud, and Easter was on its way. I decided to write letters to the boys explaining the events of Palm Sunday, the last week of Christ's life, and Easter. Wendy set the letters aside and gave them to the boys on the appropriate days. Meanwhile, Wendy completed radiation, had a body PET scan and no cancer was found. We were thrilled.

Wendy and Brad suggested a big adventure. They invited us to go with them on a trip to celebrate the treatments completion and the disappearance of cancer. They wanted to go to Dominican Republic over New Year's Eve. We would have eight months to plan and anticipate. What fun!

Thrilled at Wendy's news and Teri doing fine, Gib and I sprung an escape for a ten day adventure to visit my sister in California and the Napa Valley Vineyards. We felt someone from this cold country should check out palm trees, sunshine and strolling without a coat. We would sacrifice and do it for everyone. After returning to the cold north, we got friends Leon and Pauline to travel with us to Illinois for five days. Leon suggested we take the train, so we set out on an adventure. The four of us had a delightful time, stayed in the hotel near Wendy's, grilled steaks, and dreamed with Brad about how he could finish his basement. How much fun we had, and I could get use to this calm and relaxing life.

One evening in May, when I was back in Minnesota, the phone rang, and I heard a sobbing Wendy on the other end. Crying too hard for me to understand her words I only got four words - Brad, work, ambulance, and hospital. I sucked in deeply. Had the stalker gotten to him? Gunshots? Knives? I started praying even as I continued talking. Calmly, I told her I could not understand anything except those four words. Slowly, she explained that she was in the car on the way to the hospital and Brad had been taken by ambulance to the hospital with chest pains.

"Mom, he could be having a heart attack," she cried. It seems insane that a heart attack would be a relief, but I was so happy it wasn't the stalker that I am sure she thought I sounded heartless when I responded calmly, "I want you to pull the car over and stop."

She protested wildly, "I need to get to the hospital."

"I realize that. He will be fine. They will be able to take care of him. But you are crying too hard to safely drive. You won't be fine if you have a wreck." I raised my voice and demanded, "Pull over NOW!"

I waited till she found a parking lot before I continued. "Wendy, he is young and strong. Don't be afraid." I began praying over the phone for peace, confidence, and trust in the Great Physician. As I heard her crying lessen and then stop, I added, "Okay, now you are ready to continue to the hospital. Have faith, my dear. Dad and I, and your siblings will be praying. Call again when you know something. Remember, he will be fine."

And he was. It wasn't a heart attack, but stress- related tension. His blood pressure had skyrocketed, and they brought him under control, and he was home in a day and fully recovered and was back to work in a couple of days. Stress had reared its head again, this time in Brad. This was one adventure we were glad was over. It was for a week or two before I told Wendy that I had feared it was the stalker. She laughed and said she hadn't thought about that at all. I realized then, they had put the stalker on the back burner and didn't worry about her. After all, they had bigger problems to face.

Summer arrived and Gib and I had the opportunity to take a second trip to Israel. Pastor Todd led us on this new adventure. It quickly freed our imagination. As we sat on the hill where the Sermon on the Mount took place, we imagined Jesus standing there. A stark change came over us as we looked down into the massive calm valley below and imaged the violence that will erupt in the final days at the war of Armageddon. From the Dead Sea to the Sea of Galilee we soaked in being in the land of our Savior.

For the second time we stood atop the Masada and were inspired by Israeli love and devotion for their country. Then, we took the deeply emotional walk along the path Jesus took dragging the cross to Golgotha. Later, we were overcome with joy at the top of the hill where Christ ascended. Emotions were spinning and twirling in our brains as we walked where Jesus, Peter, John, and the disciples gathered. The Bible came alive, and our minds soaked up everything we could. It and much more was deeply moving, and the images would be with us forever. What a beautiful adventure tucked between onerous ones.

While we were in Israel, Wendy had her 42nd birthday. We delayed celebrating until we returned all gathered for the fourth of July. Wendy's crew came to Minnesota, and we all played on the lake with jet skis and boats. Friends we'd met in Macedonia now lived in Arkansas and drove up for the holiday. Olga, from Russia, also arrived to complete the gathering. Fireworks, barbecues, laughter, and people sleeping in every room of the house made for a joyful time together. It was a wonderful adventure in love and joy.

A week after everyone left, Gib began to complain of a back pain like he had never had before. It wasn't overly severe, but it was constant. Next, he began to vomit. I don't think he had done that since we were in college. Hours passed as he didn't get better and the pain in his back increased. He lay in the bathroom by the toilet and kept vomiting. We finally loaded him into the car for a trip to the ER and a diagnosis of kidney stones. We had no family history of stones, so this was all foreign to us. He needed to have a stent put in but had to wait a week for the baby aspirin he was on to leave his system. They hoped to blast those stones at that time. However, the stones had wedged themselves outside the kidney but right next to it, so the blasting was difficult.

With the stent in place and more scans, they were able to line things up and blast away. Five days later the stent was pulled, and his saga was over, and recovery began. This was time for the girls to feel sorry for their dad instead of the other way around. The constant stress of Teri's heart, Wendy's cancer, the driving back and forth, the chaotic lifestyle was taking its toll on family member number three. Another painful adventure to add to the list.

Teri sensed her chances to travel were dwindling, so she decided a trip was in order to California Disneyland, and Universal City. We had a huge garage sale, and the proceeds would pay for the entrance fees into the parks. Luckily, I had a collector's bicycle to sell. It was a black and white Hop-a-long Cassidy bike and the money we got for it paid for two or three of the tickets. It was especially an adventure for Ashley and Karissa as they loved the rides, the beauty of California and the escape from the chaos of their daily lives. Teri soaked in the sun and the laughter, and we all had a great adventure.

Like a carrot dangling in front of us, we kept planning and thinking about our big adventure to Dominican Republic to celebrate with Wendy's family. We would close out the year there and have New Year's Eve in style. It sounded like the perfect ending of a tense filled year. We planned, dreamed, paid deposits, and waited for the day we would all go. The boys would be out of school for the holidays, and we would leave right after Christmas. What fun awaited us!

Once again, the unexpected, grabbed hold of us like a vise. Early December, Wendy had a swelling under her arm. A new mass appeared under her arm on a mammogram. The doctor decided to do a biopsy and announced the results wouldn't be known until after we returned from Dominican Republic. He said we were to go, have a wonderful time and leave all this behind. Stunned, we were determined to try to put away the fears in an unopened container that would be retrieved later.

Finally, the time came, and Gib and I drove to Wendy's. I had an intense cold, Brad had an ear infection, and Gib wrenched his back. Wendy, still terribly afraid of flying, held her breath and we all boarded the plane determined this trip would be wonderful. We taxied out for takeoff, stopped, waited, turned around, and went back to the terminal. The main generator was working fine but the back-up one was dead. After a while, they said we were ready to go and Wendy put her head down and said, "Why? Why does this happen to me every time I fly? I'm the nervous flier in the family and it always happens to me!" Of course, once in the air we had to hit turbulence a few times, so that she was especially relieved when we finally landed in our island paradise.

Restaurants, pools, swim up bars, sunshine, whirlpools, massages, sand, sweat, water sports, buffets, and on and on would describe our stay. Then, Wendy announced, "Absolutely not! No one will go on a helicopter ride or para- sailing. I want my family safe!" So, we settled for watching scuba diving and kayaking. For our own adventure, we decided to go zip lining. Because of his back, Gib decided to stay at the hotel while the rest of us set out to experience the jungle from above. As they got us fitted and tied into the equipment, they began to describe our trips and I knew I was in trouble. The first clue was when he said, "Use your stomach muscles and pull up your legs."

I responded, "Where are those muscles? I lost mine about 15 years ago." Everyone laughed but I was serious.

Next, he said, "Lean back and relax." I thought I could do that.

Finally, he said, "Look at the beautiful view below." Okay, that part I could manage.

So, we climbed the first "fire tower" to a platform and the "take-off" area. The others went first. Determined to enjoy it, I stepped up, hooked up and took off. I pulled my legs up and leaned back. I even looked below me. This was easy and fun. I had just completed the first of 12 runs. This meant I had to climb another forest ranger's tower 11 more times, pull up my legs 11 more times and lean back. The first six were fun. Sometimes when I leaned back, I would spin. This didn't seem right. Sometimes, I fought the spinning and tried to keep myself facing forward. I soon became more interested in looking for the young man "receiving" me at the other end than looking at the view below. Then, it became work. When I reached run #8, I was already tired. The kids took off in front of me and when it was my turn I hooked up and took off. About three- fourths of the way down I stopped. I didn't just slow down, I came to a complete stop. Below me, the valley stretched out with the nearest ground 12 feet below. No help there. I tried to nudge myself on, but nothing happened.

Finally, the "receiving" boy yelled, "turn around backwards. Put your hands on the wire above and walk yourself in." Following his instructions, I tried to move. Slowly, I budged a little. Then the spasms started. My back had a mind of its own and the spasms began to cripple me. The boy kept yelling, I kept trying, and tears kept rolling down my face. The pain was terrible, I was stranded, I no longer found this fun and I wanted this over. Crying, determined not to rot on a cable, I drug my body toward the platform. I moved so slowly. Finally, as I neared the platform, the ground got nearer, and a boy yelled from below for me to extend my leg. He grabbed my foot and pulled me to the platform. With tears flowing from the pain, the boy released me. Standing on the platform I informed him I was done and wanted to return to the center. Looking confused he said, "Sorry lady, you are passed the area of no return. You have to go all the way to the end. If you wanted to quit, you had to do it at run #six. Now, you have to finish the last four."

I was done mentally but not physically. I had to go on to the next tower and continue. Frustrated, I stomped down the path and up the ladder to see a worried Wendy waiting. "Where have you been, Mom? Are you okay?"

"I got stuck on the last run. Apparently, I must finish the course to return to the center. I'll tell you all about it at the end. Let's just get this over with."

Run #9 was more of an endurance test for the "receiver" than for me. Determined, I wouldn't get stuck again, I refused to slow down as I approached. He was waving his arms and yelling "slow down", but I just kept going full speed. He wrapped his arms around me and rode me to a stop. "Lady, why wouldn't you slow down?"

I told him about being stuck and he informed me that run #8 was the only one that goes up at the end. I wouldn't have any more problems. So, I could slow down.

"Lady, how old are you?"

"I am 69", I replied.

"Wow! He shouted. You should get some special Grandma award. Wow." I guess in Dominican 69-year-old people don't do things like that.

Once back at the center, I told the family my experience and we all laughed till our sides hurt. I was so happy Gib hadn't tried it. The ride in the open-air bus to the site was rough and bumpy enough and he certainly couldn't have held himself upright with his back in the shape it was in. He would have had back spasms on the first run! While we were out zip lining Gib was having whirlpools, massages, and walking the beaches. I was happy to have tried it once, but I was more thankful it was over, and I knew I would never need to go Zip- lining again. It was just too many trips and a painful journey for me.

New Year's Eve brought a party that covered the entire complex. Latino music, acrobats, noise, drinks, fun and more fun. We had hilarious hats, sang, yelled, danced, laughed, and forgot for a moment all the problems that awaited us back in the States. There was no snow here like at home. There were no below zero temps, no cancer, no heart problems, just paradise. For a week we had kept busy having fun and pushed all the other thoughts far away. Then, "Auld Lange Syne" played, and the thoughts and fears returned. Will the coming year bring an end to this battle? Will there be more chemo? Is the thing under her arm cancer? Uncertainty once again reigns.

The one certainty that existed throughout the year had been adventures. Most were exciting, and unusual. A few were bold and risky. Some demanded an emotional readjustment. Some were hard work while others were only floating on clouds. But all were adventures. They were not as dramatic as Abraham's or Moses' adventures. They were not as demanding and risky as Paul's. We hadn't walked on water with Jesus or didn't even have dreams where we fought with His angels. I did, however, discover that God was with me on each adventure.

As the year closed, I sat down with my Bible and thought back over all the good and bad adventures I had experienced. I searched the Bible to see what I could find about adventure. I quickly discovered the adventure itself wasn't the most important part of the story. Instead, I found how I allowed God to walk me through the experience was paramount. I had my heart set on Him, and He had blessed me. I began praising God for each adventure, both good and bad that He had led me through. I had lacked nothing. He had showered me with sunshine all around. Gib had not always been there to hold my hand, but I had walked many paths with His hand holding mine. I knew He would not stop so long as I allowed Him to lead. Whatever adventure awaited me, I knew I could claim Psalm 91:11-12 for myself. "For He will command His angels concerning you to guard you in all your ways. On their hands they will bear you up, lest you strike your foot against a stone."

Between God and His angels, I was armed for battle. Nothing could or would beat me or my family. Death and fear had lost their grip on me. My family had an army of angels to protect us and as long as we stayed united with God, we would be ready for the next adventure!

DÉJÀ VU

CHAPTER 17

With our dream adventure ending, we winged our way back to the States. It had been all we had hoped for, and we were refreshed. Still, there was a nagging doubt beneath the surface. What did the biopsy show? Gib and I continued to Minnesota, leaving Wendy and Brad to settle in and await Wendy's appointment.

We didn't wait long. Once again, I picked up the phone to hear Brad's voice. As much as I loved that boy, I was hating hearing his voice on the other end. He only said three words and I mentally left the conversation. "It is cancer."

Although I wasn't swearing this time, I felt the exact frustration and anger I had felt two years ago. This couldn't be happening again. We were right back where we started, and all the same questions were there. What lies ahead? Why? Will everyone be strong enough to do this? Brad rambled on with information about genetic testing, being sure this was the same cancer, pre-op stuff and things my brain would not process. WENDY HAS CANCER AGAIN! That's all I heard.

I wanted to yell at God that this wasn't the kind of adventure I wanted to go on. I had been on this train to the abyss once, and I didn't want to go again. Hadn't we cleared our calendars and gone for surgery before? Was there a lesson we hadn't learned the first time around? I knew Wendy was trying to absorb this news just like I was. Neither of us trusted ourselves to talk to each other yet. So, I promised Brad we would be there for the surgery, and we hung up.

The only bright spot in all of this was the surgeon. Wendy loved that doctor. He was a Christian, listened well, was down to earth, always concerned about her needs and fears, and gave an aura of confidence. She was very loyal to all her doctors but this one was a notch above the others.

The day before the surgery, Gib, Teri, and I traveled to Illinois. While Wendy was in surgery, I noticed Teri had a perplexed look on her face. When I questioned her, she said, "I had no idea what torture the waiting period was like. I only knew the patient's side. This is horrible and I am so sorry to have sent you through this so many times."

"Teri, you never chose this path for yourself just like Wendy had no choice. Those of us that love you do have a choice. We choose to be by your side. Waiting is hard but a part of the path we are on together. You are not responsible for any difficulty it has been for Dad and me. We are all in this boat together and will be forever."

We hugged and continued waiting while Brad paced and moved around. Finally, the surgeon came and shared that once again he thought he had it all. He placed a drain tube under Wendy's arm and removed a five cm mass that had three small tumors connected to it. The original mass in the breast had been four- and- a- half cm so this was even larger. He related that she would have considerable pain, and the drain would stay in place for a while. She would be wearing a sling to hold her arm still. We took our wounded girl home a few days later. With every movement or slight twinge, pain shot through her instantly. Wendy held herself rigid and always had a pillow to cradle her arm. Friends dropped by with flowers and meals. She was grateful but tried not to move.

Since Gib was still undergoing physical therapy for his back and Teri had only a week of pills she took, it was time for them to return to Minnesota. I remained to "mommy" Wendy. Brad was back at work and the boys returned to school.

Wendy needed another PET scan to figure out if cancer was anywhere else in her body. But for now, she needed to regain strength. Gib returned the next weekend, and it was time for me to go home. We left with Wendy's arm still held tightly to her body. As we went out the door, she tried to lighten the atmosphere when she yelled, "I'm sure going to miss my slave." We left laughing.

Since Teri had been sick for so long, she had missed many days and even weeks of homeschooling. Karissa had fallen behind and needed help and scheduled teaching times to catch up and move forward. So, whenever I was in Minnesota, Karissa and I spent every morning together studying. I looked forward to spending time with an energetic, healthy gal. Since I had taught for 30 years, it was second nature to me, and I enjoyed watching her grow and learn. We laughed together through lessons, and I even made her cry in frustration. However, we stuck it out and she quickly moved forward. To this day she loves to tell others I was the only teacher that made her cry.

Teri was too fragile herself to homeschool Karissa. With brittle bones, she could no longer sit for extended time, and she wore braces on her neck, knee, and back. Her stamina was decreasing and there wasn't a clear answer as to why. Her leaking heart valve was draining her strength while her diabetes and overall health were contributing to a downward spiral. Walking was becoming a chore. She bought a cane to help and attempted to stand straight. She complained very little. Although she was in constant pain, she was determined to show her little sister her support. She set out to crochet a prayer shawl for Wendy to keep her warm while she had chemo. Teri solicited favorite Bible verses and colors from each family member. She would create a family prayer shawl with everyone represented to surround her. It was a beautiful idea but a devastatingly painful undertaking. Still, she worked on it daily. Watching her determination was inspiring. Teri knew the shawl was symbolic of belonging to God and normally worn by the male. However, she wanted to surround Wendy with love and reminders of prayers and people of God who were holding her up.

Finally, ten days after surgery, Wendy had the drain pulled and began exercising her arm. She would walk her fingers up the wall and her goal was to reach above her head. She tirelessly worked toward her goal and was soon victorious. She returned to work and her friends there celebrated her return. Now it was time to start over again. Like before, she cut her beautiful black hair very short in preparation for losing it. As I sat through the "chemo training" on the new drugs I felt an unpleasant familiar sensation. I had been here before. All this had done no good. Was there anything different this time? The new PET Scan showed no cancer anywhere else, so she started the chemo with hope.

We were warned the new chemo would be rougher than the first. Each treatment would take two to three hours. There would be 8 cycles. It would affect her bones so they would be watching that as well as blood counts. If they drop, her immune systems will decrease, and the possibility of infection would rise. The treatments would take 6 months to complete. She would have 2 weeks on, one week off and repeat. It sounded ominous and overwhelming, even more so than the first time around. This didn't seem like a fleeting Deja Vu but a nightmare that kept replaying over and over.

I rarely had time to stop and think. Gib and I still tried to help both families and keep the husbands working. Guy was a steady rock, honed, and shaped after living with Teri's illness for so long. He was a born caregiver. Brad, on the other hand, was openly suffering. Brad would leave work and show up at Wendy's chemo even though I was already there. He so wanted to relieve Wendy of it all and he felt so helpless. Again, I declared Tuesdays as "Wendy days". I asked the family to pray for her off and on during the day. It united us all with one goal for one day a week. Despite everything, Wendy went about her daily life with spunk and determination to keep life as normal as possible. Other than allowing me to keep her house clean and leave a few cooked meals behind, she gave up as little control of her life as possible. Any tears of self-pity were spent when she was alone.

There seemed to be so little time between crises and needs were all around us. Shane and Kelly were doing all they could to lend a hand especially in driving Teri's girls thus relieving Gib of the constant job. Spring was trying to fight against the retreating winter and one day I looked at Teri and realized how very tiny and fragile she was. She had lost so much weight and was down to 110 pounds. I had been concentrating on Wendy so much, Teri's gradual shrinking had slipped by me. She was struggling with eye problems, muscle weakness, and stress on her bones. Now, her body was betraying her and not processing food correctly. She appeared brittle and so very delicate. Still, she continued working on the prayer shawl. Teri's muscles, eyes, and fingers all suffered greatly, but she was determined to complete it. Finally, it was done.

Teri traveled to Illinois with us to present her precious gift to her sister. Wendy's response was typical "Wendy." Fighting not to show any emotion and certainly not to cry, Wendy fought to keep control. She ducked her head and read each scripture Teri had written out from each family member without looking up. Teri pointed out each panel and the color each person chose. Quietly, barely above a whisper, Wendy only said, "Thank you," while she stroked each panel. It was so obvious she couldn't say more without "losing it". Teri, on the other hand, so wanted her sister to let down that protective shield and show her deep feelings. Teri was so open with her feelings and could not understand why Wendy was so protective of hers. It hurt to see Wendy fighting for control and Teri disappointed in her response.

Later, when Teri was out of earshot, I told Wendy how much pain it was for Teri to make it. Wendy barely spoke above a whisper when she said, "I know Mom, I really know." Yet, Wendy never expressed the depth of her feelings to Teri. Multiple times Wendy told me that Teri was her hero, the strongest person she knew. I repeated that to Teri, but it wasn't the same as it would have been had Wendy been able to say it to her directly.

Wendy and Teri with the Prayer Shawl

It had been a very long time since I had danced in the rain. Also, I rarely climbed up into God's palm or soared on the back of my eagle. I seemed to just live one day at a time without trying to recapture the nearness of God. I was slowly being drained of my reserve strength and as it ebbed from me, I seemed unaware. I had undergone cataract surgeries, kept teaching Karissa, helped Casey prepare for his ACT's, tended to my daughters, and I was barely holding on. I had done nothing new to deepen my relationship with God. After all He had taught me, I still floated on past experiences. Instead of facing my neglect of God, I thought a trip would make it better. We needed a break, so Gib and I took off to Oklahoma City. It was my brother Carl's birthday and we celebrated with him. Gib and Carl zip-lined across the Oklahoma river. Sure, it wasn't as dramatic as the ones in Dominicans, but Gib finally got to do it. We left there and headed to Arkansas to visit our life-long friends Ron and Mary. I soaked up the sunshine, love, and support from these who had been with us since the beginning. Finally, we returned to Minnesota. On the way home a large swelling on my face began to itch. Without warning, once again I developed shingles a second time. **NO, NO, NO!** I've already been here and done this. Enough of this Déjà Vu stuff. I want off this merry-go-round.

I didn't have time for this. My daughters needed me! It felt like a punishment. I struggled with anger that my body was losing the battle of holding it all together through each crisis. I cried out to God to take away the shingles. This time they were on my face, but my eyes weren't involved. It wasn't until much later that I realized that God used the shingles to slow me down, force me to withdraw a few days and rest. It was a reenergizing time for me. Between the original shingles shot and the shot they gave me to speed the recovery it was only a matter of a couple of weeks until the spots on my face dried up and the pain subsided. I didn't avoid God, but I didn't really seek Him out either. I wasn't angry at Him for allowing this, but I was completely frustrated.

During that time Wendy was developing lots of scar tissue from her surgery in her armpit. She needed a scan to see what was going on. She started radiation treatments, and meanwhile, Teri had been taken to the hospital with vomiting. and they grasped more understanding of the lack of processing her body was doing.

I turned to my prayer warriors. There are so many that sink to their knees when I called. They are the strength I need when the battle is so widespread. From Spain, Macedonia, Turkey, Russia, Kenya, and Ukraine prayers rose along with all our stateside friends and family. Finally, feeling defeated, I did what I should have done all along. I climbed into the palm of the huge, outstretched hand of my Father and let my warriors hold me up in prayer. Escape was all I could do. I felt so helpless. I couldn't stop this crushing tide.

Then, one evening I heard the birds outside my window. They weren't calling to each other. They were singing. They sounded like a recital, and their performance was magnificent. The unique thing was that I could hear different types of birds participating. I had never heard this combination before and never heard it since. I stopped what I was doing and went out on the screened porch and sat down. I closed my eyes and allowed my hearing to sharpen as I felt transported to a cloud. I began praising God and thanking Him for this beauty He was allowing me to experience. I slowly began singing with the birds. "How great is our God, sing with me how great is our God." As I sang, my spirits lifted, and I felt energized and filled with contentment. I opened my eyes to see the sun slipping down behind the trees on the west side of the lake. The orange and pink in the sky was reflected on the still lake and once again I thanked God. He had provided for me, and if I stopped to absorb it, to feel it, to experience His magnificence, He would restore my soul. Praising Him always brought me back to Him. He would be my strength. Once again, I had no doubt He had provided it for me. This kind of Déjà vu I liked!

Back to daily life and Teri had a colonoscopy and they found five polyps. They told her she had a genetic leaning toward problems and to warn her siblings to get their own colonoscopy and believe me, she took delight in the panicked expression Shane had when she announced he had to have one. She loved teasing him, asking each time she saw him if he had scheduled it, and demanding to know when he finally was brave enough to do it. Once again, she was hospitalized for severe vomiting and once again, they were unsure what was causing it all. They seemed unable to grasp more understanding of the problems of what her body was doing.

Wendy had yet another surgery, number three, to remove scar tissue under her arm. Once inside her wound, they found more cancer. It had metastasized locally, and the doctor, once again, thought he removed all of it.

Quickly the crispness of fall surrounded us. Our trips to Illinois again took us in time for football games on Friday nights. One night as we prepared to enter the stadium a light drizzle fell on us. There was no place here to dance in the rain, so I closed my eyes, turned my face upward and let the warm water dance on my cheeks. Wendy touched my arm and said, "Wake up, Mom. You must keep walking. No dancing in the rain here." We laughed and smiled at our inside joke.

Later, it began to rain harder. As the game continued, it began to pour, and as we rose to cheer, I began to dance around to stay warm. Wendy tugged on my sleeve and shouted above the crowd, "You can't count this as dancing in the rain, Mom." I replied, "I can if I can smile while I am doing it. Although it is a lot harder when it is pouring this hard."

No matter the weather or how she really felt, Wendy made every game. She would be there to cheer and support her boys. Sometimes we sat in bright sunshine and other times we huddled under umbrellas. As the season progressed, the cold touched deep into our bones, but there we sat cheering or defeated. She had started radiation treatments again, but she tried to act like nothing affected her. My two daughters were fighting different battles, but both were enduring much and suffering in silence. What brave girls they were!

Fall was a perfect time to travel to South America, so Gib and I took a quick tour to Peru. Machu Pichu had always been on our bucket lists, and we wanted to go while we were still strong enough to make the climb to the top. It didn't disappoint us. Hidden back in the mountains invading groups didn't discover it, and it remained untouched for decades. Another hidden jewel was found on Lake Titicaca. Indigenous people had built their homes on reeds cut from the lake and floated so far out into this gigantic lake that, once again, invaders didn't discover them. Today, most young people attend school on the mainland, and I fear this unique type of life will disappear with coming generations. The tour was refreshing, educational, and extremely enjoyable.

Thanksgiving brought Wendy's family to Minnesota and the entire family was in one place again. I looked around the room at my children and their spouses. Each child had the perfect match for their personalities. Kelly kept Shane organized and from running just on emotions. She kept him grounded and gave him the mental stimulations he needed. Demonstrations of their love and attraction was never far away. Guy was the steady rudder Teri needed in her daily up and downs and his sense of humor kept her laughing. She always said he might not talk all the time like others, but when he did, you needed to listen as he had wisdom. Throughout this ordeal I missed spending time with Guy as he was so busy trying to work, do all the jobs Teri was supposed to handle, as well as being the most involved Dad through it all. Their mutual respect was evident.

Brad was the uninhibited extrovert to counter Wendy's closed personality. He was a worrier to her unflappable personality and the energy she needed to keep going. He was growing in his abilities to care for Wendy, and he often made her laugh when all seemed dark.

Each of the seven grandkids had a unique personality. Each home they had been reared in reflected in their thinking. They were all intelligent and had interesting interests and sense of humors. Each one could hold their own in a conversation so there was never a dull moment when they were together. When all our kids and grandkids were there, the sound level rose and kept rising throughout the day. I watched the interaction of the personalities. There was competition to tell the best story or make the group laugh. The younger ones hung around to hear the stories of their parents' childhood played out in front of them. It was rare to get us all together and I absorbed and took part in every moment I could. Those treasured moments would replay in my heart for years to come

Finally, December arrived, and another PET scan showed what we feared. Wendy was NOT cancer free. She had a tumor behind the scar tissue in her arm pit. Her primary oncologist announced she was maxed out on the radiation she could have and sadly, the last chemo had been the best one when there had been a recurrence. The surgeon, however, was not ready to give up. He wanted to try another surgery. We closed out another year with uncertainty.

A year had passed, and it all seemed like a Déjà Vu dream. Once again, we were leaving the year behind with uncertainty ahead. Once again, Wendy had recurring cancer. Once again there was a tumor under her arm hiding behind scar tissue. Once again, I had that odd sensation I was in the same place, same conversation, same bubble I had been in before. Once again Teri was suffering and in danger. I hated this Déjà Vu feeling. I seemed helpless to fight it. Even in the cold, I stepped out on the back porch and looked at the naked trees and frozen lake before me. I knew that the Bible taught that no matter how we suffered, the glory that awaits us in Heaven would be far greater. I was having trouble looking that far into the future. This demanded a triumphant outlook from me, and I wasn't sure I had that right now.

Was I losing heart? These past two years seemed forever. They didn't seem temporary or momentary. I had been concentrating on the seen things, the temporal and fleeting things. I knew God wanted me to concentrate on the unseen or eternal things. How weak I felt. I kept climbing mountains with God only to fall with a crash to the valley of discontent. Would I ever learn? Could I keep my eyes on the eternal, dance in the rain, and have a positive outlook on life?

I looked up into the sky and saw a burst of rare color for December. A ray of sunshine fought through the clouds and spilled bright pinks and orange toward the earth. My Almighty, all-powerful God, took time to touch this downtrodden, defeated woman. Then, the colors seemed to be sucked back up into the heavens and the clouds closed in around the space where they had been. Still, I knew they weren't gone, just hidden from view. Thank you, Abba, for being there even when hidden from view. Thank you for reminding me you were, are, and always will be there with me forever.

REALITY

CHAPTER 18

I have often wondered if my perspective of life was different than most other people. Afterall, I have met so many miserable, angry, and unhappy people, and I can't understand where they are coming from. We all look at life from earlier experiences, existing events, and our own attitudes. Yet, I do believe there are certain realities that exist. For example, God is real. God had walked beside me, held me up, and been my friend. That is reality to me. Of that, I am absolutely sure. Yet, even with all the experiences I have had with Him, I don't see Him clearly. I can't grasp His glory. That too is a reality. I know the Bible describes that we see in a mirror dimly. I want to see God face-to-face. I want to understand the same way He fully understands me. So, as I walk through uncertainty I yearn for His guiding hand. I have known Him since childhood and still I learn more about Him daily. Now, as the new year burst into being, I needed His perspective instead of mine. Reality was painful. Both my girls had major problems.

Wendy had her fourth surgery. A new tumor was just below the skin under the arm. Because of where it sat, it didn't get blood flow. Therefore, it got no chemo. It had been free to grow. During surgery, fluid flowed from the area and after they removed the tumor the hole seeped constantly. The margins around the tumor were clear and we were grateful. This time the surgeon left the incision open. He wanted it to heal from the inside out, so the cancer had no chance to regrow in the closed skin. This meant she had a hole under her arm that needed tending multiple times a day. Even this didn't stop her from working. She took her gauze pads etc. with her to work and rebandaged the wound herself in the restroom. We waited to see if it would heal.

In Minnesota, Teri needed cataract surgery. But the morning before the planned surgery, the doctor called to say he was unwilling to do it. She was disheartened. Without the surgery she would be unable to drive and be independent. It wasn't long until a second doctor called with a tiny thread of hope. He thought he might have a lens that works with astigmatism (an identified problem for her) and he made an appointment to see her in a week giving him time to research it more. The alternative would be a regular cataract surgery with a cornea specialist and then very thick lens (like coke bottle thickness) he said. Again, we prayed and waited. Everyone was searching for answers. Teri's eye problems continued unsolved for week after week as she rode a roller coaster of hope, disappointment, hope, disappointment, hope, and disappointment. Finally, she was able to have surgery, and new "normal" glasses to help her.

Gib was averaging 5-10 trips a week to either her doctors or rides the girls needed. We began calling him "hockey mom" as that endearing term for the mom on the road all the time, except it now was Granddad on the road. I was still homeschooling Karissa three days per week. Ashley was a junior at an Arts Academy in St Paul and in dance lessons most days of the week. Guy kept working and holding on as we all tried to juggle our schedules.

Not only did Wendy's incision not heal, but it also seemed to grow. Now it was about four" long, two" high and 1 ½" deep. It wasn't bloody, but it oozed a smelly pus-like liquid. She wound it tight during the day while at work, using tape and layers of gauze. At night we would wrap an Ace bandage all around her body without any tape to give her skin relief. Our "Wendy Day" remained on Tuesdays since that was treatment day. Everyone continued to pray every Tuesday for her. It was encouraging and fun to hear on emails and Facebook how people were remembering times they shared with Wendy. Casey was now a senior and discussing where he would go to college. Wendy took out a map and drew a circle. He could choose any college within 200 miles of home. So, the search began. Quinn was a sophomore in high school and carefully watched the process knowing in two years he would be doing the same thing.

Meanwhile, back in Minnesota, Gib joined the staff at church as volunteer Director of Missions. That would add more responsibility to him and perhaps a bit of distraction from the mess around us. God had placed missions in the forefront of our lives and minds and, this was a natural progression for him. He hoped to encourage missionaries, increase the number of short-term mission trips and encourage the congregation in their quest to touch the lives of the missionaries.

Shane and Kelly flew to Florida to spend a few days with our "extended family" of Will and Nelly. Will had taken a job on staff at a church there, and we all missed them constantly. A big year loomed ahead for Shane and Kelly. They had two kids graduating from college in the spring and his youngest daughter, Destiny, would be getting married. They had busy days ahead.

It was time for some light- hearted fun, so we planned a wedding shower for Destiny and prayed both our Teri and Wendy would make it. At the last-minute Teri had been hospitalized, so her attendance looked questionable. Wendy braved her fear of flying and flew in from Chicago the day before. The morning of the shower, Teri was released and arrived home looking good. Both girls wanted to be included in their niece's coming wedding. We had lots of games, laughter, food, and gifts. and it was a time of celebration.

The next weeks were filled with graduations and open houses. Wendy's oldest, Casey, graduated from high school. Shane's youngest two graduated from college at the same time. Details of plans for Destiny's wedding kept everyone busy until the big day came. Wendy's family arrived, and we were all gathered to launch another couple. God supplied health for both girls so they could be a part of it.

Fall brought big changes. Casey had settled on the University of Iowa, and Wendy had to leave her first- born miles from home. I remember that uncertainty a mom feels. Will they make the right friends? Will they lean on God? Will they remember all the lessons I taught them? Who will take care of them when they get sick? The questions go on and on. I reminded her this was a time of trust. God had loaned her this precious boy, and now she had to trust God to watch over him. I advised her to cry her heart out once she left him, as a good cry is needed to flow all the junk from her body. I even suggested perhaps a good cry would drain her underarm. No one could make it easier on a mom except God. So, they launched him, and she returned home to start yet another chemo. After only one treatment Wendy's tumor began to shrink. She finally admitted the discomfort under her arm was immense. As the tumor reduced, her pain levels went down. How she yearned for the tumor to go away and the hole to heal up so she could sleep again on the left side, her favorite. She quickly shifted from frustration mode to battle mode, and she was off and running again. She was determined to beat this monster that invaded her body.

I wrote her an email telling her how much I admired her. It said:

I have thought of you so much the last few days. The battle you have fought has made you a stronger person. You have always been a fighter and you are an inspiration to so many people. I can only attribute your strength to God. You have fought with tenacity, and we joke about you and Teri being the little pink bunnies on the TV commercial. It is so true.

Your family wants to fight alongside you. We want to share your tough days as well as the encouraging ones. I hope you feel the love from all of us. We want to hold your arms up like Aaron and Hur did for Moses as Joshua led the Israelites into battle. You can gain so much strength from all of us. With our united front, your impact on others can be limitless. Unexpectantly, we have heard from others how your determination, perseverance, and reliance on God has inspired them to re-evaluate their own walk with the Lord.

You always said Teri is your hero. Well, my dear, you too, are a hero. Never underestimate your influence on others. It is great. Just give God the credit for your strength, and perhaps those around you that don't have a personal relationship with Christ will better understand the source of your strength.

Thank you for allowing me to come alongside you in your fight and giving me the chance to receive blessings because of it. How had I been so fortunate to have two pink bunnies that

just keep going and going? How proud Granny and Mimi are
as they look down from heaven and see the mighty woman
you have become. Keep fighting and keep your contagious
smile. March into battle, my pink bunny, march! Love, Mom

Gib and I went on a trip to visit our missionaries in Mexico. After time with them we returned to Mexico City with intentions of being tourists. The first day I missed the bottom step in the Cathedral and fell twisting and turning my ankle. It swelled rapidly, and we hobbled across the square to our hotel. It was scary looking. After a call home to a doctor friend, I tried to stand on my ankle and discovered I could although very painful. It wasn't broken, just badly bruised. Swollen, turning purple, and throbbing, the skin grew taut as it stretched. I tried ice, elevating it, resting, and wrapping it firmly so we could just get by. Gib went shopping and found me a three-legged cane. Fearing we might never get to return to Mexico City, I wanted to see as much of it as I could. In the square below our hotel, I spotted double-decker buses. So, with the cane on one side and Gib on the other I hobbled, mounted the steps to the top level, and sat myself down ready to take in the sights. We took all the tours they offered and saw Mexico City from on high. I hobbled, when necessary, rested when I could, and we even saw the pyramids outside the city with a personal guide. Finally, we flew home and went directly to the orthopedic urgent care from the airport. It wasn't broken but an extreme sprain. It would take two weeks to even start improving, and then four to six weeks before I could start exercising. The recovery took months and included everything from wearing a boot, doing PT, and getting shots in the ankle. I understate when I say, "what a pain." It slowed me down, but there was no time for stopping.

With boot on my ankle, we travelled back to Wendy's. She had another CT scan showing tumors under the arm growing, one in the bicep and one under the clavicle. The cancer was no longer maintained. They would try a new chemo. For the first time the doctor said that the chemo promised to "prolong life" not cure. Like Wendy, I buried that thought deep within me. Sure, I would think about it later. I would bring it out of my depth to examine it. But, for now, it was buried. A simpler way to explain it is to simply say I was in denial. Treatment began and after just three treatments the main tumor was shrinking, the other two were nowhere to be found. Hope surfaced again. Could we, just could we, WIPE THIS MONSTER OUT?

One trip down to Illinois, we left the Twin Cities late, and Wendy was frustrated we would be arriving late. What she didn't know was that we were bringing Shane with us and therefore, waited until he was off work on Friday to leave. She spotted him as he climbed out of the car and was already crying when he entered the house. She fell into her big brother's arms, and he held her in a tight bear hug. It was one wonderful surprise.

The holidays were quickly approaching. Wendy's family would not come to Minnesota for Thanksgiving but would be here for Christmas. She continued to tolerate the chemo well with side effects she could handle. She felt good enough to travel to Iowa to the parents' weekend and spend some time with Casey.

Teri's 48th birthday came and was a day of remembrance. We had walked through so many valleys and climbed so many mountains that I sent her a long email. Here is what I said.

I can't believe time has marched on so far since the first time that tiny baby was placed in my arms, and I thought someone had accidentally given me the Gerber baby. You were so beautiful even back then. The joy of that day has been compounded day, after day, after day.

We could measure your life by illness after illness, but I'd rather measure it by joy after joy. Much of your early years had to do with my mom, Mimi. She came when you were born, and she loved talking and cooing to you. Later, she loved combing your curly hair, and the way you smiled when you said her name. Once, when you were four, we were in Oklahoma for Christmas, and as you walked in the front door Mimi gasped. You were dressed in a long black coat with a hood trimmed in white fur. You looked straight off the set of "Dr. Zhivago" movie, and it took Mimi's breath away.

You were a joy to have around except when you got into Shane's room and took his things. So, we put a special "child proof" knob on the door only to have you figure it out in one day. Then, we chose a lock mounted high, out of your reach to keep you out.

When cancer hit, you taught me so much about faith and joy that year as we went back and forth to the University for radiation treatments. The lives you touched have never been the same and your undying spirit touched many in the medical field.

You struggled with diabetes, middle school, and finding your way, but the music program at high school was a great anchor for you. I loved your high school years, your friends, your abilities.! You kept going even through depression and discouragement.

You always had ups and downs, but you always endured. Your faith has helped you through so much and it has been an example and challenge to me and others. You recently said I never said I was proud of you. I have no excuse for not saying that, as I have been so proud of you all my life. Perhaps I thought you could just see it in me. It is even difficult to voice my pride as it is so deep. There have been times when I thought you were so far ahead of me in faith that I would never catch up. We are joined through love and pain in the heart. As a parent I have said and done hurtful things. Please forgive me. I didn't have all the knowledge I needed to be the best mom. If I could start over today, how wise a parent I would be!

The woman you have become is a wondrous person. You chose the right man for you, and the two of you have endured many difficult days yet both of you still smile. The evidence of your mother- influence on your daughters is clear and vast. You are a GREAT mom, and I am so proud of the job you have done with them. They are stamped with your influence and what a great stamp!

You are often hard on yourself. You have always set a very high bar for yourself, and one backward step made you stress out. Your perfectionism helped sometimes and devastated you at other times. However, your final product is always above everyone else's expectations. You are respected by so many. Others have told me they are in awe of you. They are from all areas of your life.

Do you remember watching TV with Mimi? When that little pink bunny came on and marched around beating its drum, Mimi would giggle and clap. Everyone would laugh. That bunny never ran out of energy. It never quit. He just kept going and going. He certainly reminds me of your spirit.

I don't know what the future holds. I pray the coming year will bring you the chance to conquer pain. Dad and I have prayed for you so often that if I knelt each time my knees would be destroyed. Why God has allowed so many things to happen to you will be a question that will be answered when we stand at His Thone. In the meantime, my little pink bunny, may you keep going and inspiring me and many others you come in contact with. Happy, happy birthday my Dear!

I am so thankful I took the time to tell her how I felt. I had bathed her as a child and as an adult. I had stood by her bed for so many days and nights, and I had gained so much faith by watching her example. I had given her to God and watched Him turn her into a mighty blessing to many people. What a privilege to be her mom.

Life didn't stop. By Christmas Wendy was still in chemo treatments. She had an infection under her arm and was on antibiotics. Despite it all, she and her family came to Minnesota for the holiday. We were all together. No words could ever describe how special that Christmas was. All my babies and all my grandbabies were there together. We were united. We were family! Trouble wasn't gone. It silently hid in the shadows. Our prayer warriors never gave up. One crisis after another, they fell to their knees and brought our family before the Throne. The year was coming to an end but not the troubles. Still, we were so very thankful for so many things God had done.

On New Year's Eve we decided to keep celebrating and had a "bunko" party. We had tables and dice, food, friends, and laughter. Wendy had a new dog just a year old. Breezy was a small beagle with the softest ears you could imagine. She was a cuddly one and loved Wendy completely. That night the dog began acting oddly, and she soon crawled under the bed and pushed herself up against the wall. She wouldn't come out with any coaching. She was shaking all over. Wendy became very emotional, and they took the pup to the emergency vet. Breezy was diagnosed with Addington Disease and pills would control it. An emotional Wendy and family left to return to Illinois with pup still recovering. This event reminded us that Wendy was able to allow herself to show her emotions to a dog more easily than with people. We learned to gauge her feelings from her reactions to her dogs. This was her reality. It was hard to understand when you don't think that way, but this was the reality we had to learn to live with.

As I put away the decorations, the house seemed naked. The festive colors were gone and so was the family. There had been a whirl of laughter, smiles, hugs, and basking in love, and now it was over, and there was silence all around. I was content as I sipped coffee and recalled the holiday. Now there were no deadlines awaiting me and I felt confused as to what to do with myself. Was this lack of crisis a new reality?

Reality is defined as the state of things as they actually exist, as opposed to an idealistic idea of them. Night is reality. Fear is reality. Pain is reality. Cancer is reality. Learning to wait and live with an unclear vision of tomorrow was reality for us. I felt suspended between the warm comfort of the holidays and family, and the veil of darkness that hovered around me. I didn't want this sense of joy and love to leave me, yet I feared it was false and seeping away. I wanted to look upon the beauty of God and let the dark reality around me dissipate. He walked with me. That reality I could live with. Each moment of life was a gift from Him, and I would live in that reality. I knew He would uphold me in His victorious right hand. Turning my face upward I said simply, "God, if you can't take away the dark reality then extend your victorious hand, and when I am afraid help me to choose Your Reality!"

Barely a breath away, the two-headed monster rose up to take over our family once again.

DECISIONS

CHAPTER 19

It is odd how quickly chaos sneaks up on a person. For us it started again January third when Teri had trouble breathing and we rushed her to the ER. Once again, she had pneumonia. She was hospitalized for five days and again the infection had gone septic on her. Sepsis changed everything. This extreme infection turned life-threatening quickly. As is flowed through her blood stream, her entire body became inflamed. We were desperate to keep it from attacking organs. In the past, each time her blood pressure dropped so low it scared the admitting doctors. Still, she had fought her way back, and once again she did just that. They released her, weak and pale after five days, but this time her body didn't bounce back. Six days later, we were back at the hospital where the tests showed her problem was not pneumonia but fluid "surrounding" her heart and lungs. Since the radiation as a child had prevented her heart from growing to an adult size, the strain of pumping off fluid was immense. It needed to be drained. They punctured her and withdrew a liter of fluid and her breathing improved immediately. Still, she had to remain in the hospital.

Now came time for making decisions. Decision is defined as reaching a conclusion or solution after consideration. It could involve others, gathering information and opinions and evaluating all input. We make major decision throughout our life that force us to live with them for years to come. Some are exciting like getting married or having a baby. Some are life- changing like accepting Christ as our personal Savior. Some are to ensure our future like getting training or an education or buying a home. Some are easy to make, and some may be heart-breaking. They all take resolve and deciding on a choice of action. The days in front of us would be filled with decision making.

The first decision Guy and Teri had to make concerned their daughter, Ashley. Ashley was a dancer and had an audition with Boston Conservatory in two days. The audition was to be in Chicago. Should she and her father, Guy, travel there for the audition or stay home? Teri demanded they go. Her reasoning was that Ashley was just embarking on the rest of her life and Boston Conservatory was a life-long dream and she shouldn't miss the opportunity. Although hard for them to go, father and daughter took off for Chicago leaving Karissa with us, her grandparents, and Teri in the hospital under excellent care.

Decision number two would involve Teri along with Gib. More tests revealed her Aorta valve was leaking substantially. The doctors wanted to transfer her to Mayo Clinic, in Rochester, Minnesota. After lots of consultations, it was determined she could not do a hospital-to-hospital transfer unless she needed an immediate procedure that only Mayo could provide. Since they couldn't replace the valve while she had an infection and Mayo had never previously examined her, she would have to enter as a normal outpatient. But how could we take her home with fluid returning daily? If draining her was to be a daily thing, Teri would need to move into our home where we could take care of her around the clock. Before leaving the hospital, they would put in a catheter and Gib would have to learn how to drain her at home each day as we awaited word from Mayo as to when they would schedule her. Gib was not a natural caregiver. However, through the years God had instilled abilities in him he didn't know he had, and Gib was ready for this new responsibility. Gib, Guy, and Teri decided the best plan included moving Teri into our home so he could monitor and drain her daily.

Gib now had the third decision to make. He was a co- team leader for a mission trip to India. With both girls struggling he knew he couldn't fulfill his obligations of leadership, so he went to talk to Pastor Todd and expressed his need to drop out of leadership for the trip. As he shared that we feared we might lose Wendy and possibly both girls, his tears began to flow. Todd quickly comforted Gib and told him that not only should he drop all leadership responsibilities. and he shouldn't even be going on the trip. Gib feared he was letting others down, but as they talked, he agreed that dropping out was the right decision. He felt a huge burden was lifted from his shoulders. God had prepared the way for him to be available to care for Teri. So, with these decisions made, Gib began draining her daily taking off 200-700 ml each day. He had to do it slowly as it was painful if they tried to hurry. Again, we tried to keep the girls and Guy's lives as normal as possible. It was a temporary fix that would take us through until Mayo called. Hope was hung on the hook of Mayo. When? How? What could they do? So, we waited, and waiting always seemed such a burden.

Wendy had decision number four to make. I had flown to Wendy's to go with her to get the second opinion her insurance had agreed to pay. The people there were helpful, thoughtful, and considerate, but it didn't appear they had any answers other than what Wendy's doctor was already doing. She made decision easily saying she wasn't willing to drive the extra miles, face the traffic etc. when they didn't have more to offer. So, she decided to stay with her original doctor. Actually, this was an easy decision for her. She knew that her doctor was connected to the University of Chicago, where he was already getting second opinion input from their top-rated cancer unit. The head doctor there followed Wendy's case closely, consulted with other cancer units, and they all contributed to Wendy's care. This was an acceptable way to get lots of other opinions working on her case without involving her insurance. So, with decision number four behind her, she began a new round of chemo.

Decision number five would also be Wendy's. How would she manage the open incision under her left arm that refused to close after three surgeries? That sounds so much better than it appeared. It was a large gaping hole that allowed us to look right into her body. We didn't measure it, gut it appeared to continue growing. Each day it had to be packed with gauze inside and covered on the outside. It oozed and the outside bandage needed to be changed about every three hours. The side-effects were a pungent, unpleasant odor, inability to raise her arm high, a chance of infection, and an overall mess. Wendy felt this had a simple solution. She would go into the bathroom at work and repack the hole as well as possible and change the outer bandage herself. She would continue with chemo and that all seemed normal to her. On days she had chemo, she went to treatment and then on to work or vice versa. She was determined to keep working. So, every three hours she slipped off alone to take care of herself. She had done this earlier, but now it was increasingly more difficult and painful. She acted like this was all normal and the fight in her astonished all who knew her. Tired, losing hair, neuropathy in her feet, headaches, disturbed sleep, and many other side effects never stopped her. Each morning she rose, prepared for the day, and went into battle. When questioned she simply said, "I'll do whatever I have to do."

This was a new year with new challenges, hopes, fears and decisions. What wasn't new was simply waiting. January closed with no word from Mayo, Teri was now living in our home, her family came for "visits." She endured daily draining, and we watched her shrink in size from the strain on her body. Wendy continued packing gauze into her own body and covering it with a pad and this was all "normal?" She kept up with chemo. Perhaps February will bring success. We continued to hope. Winter passed slowly in Minnesota. Either the snow covers the ground, or the sky is a deep grey, and it is so easy for your feelings to slip into the same dark grey. Waiting is like that sky. There are no bright lights to illuminate your mind and soul. Instead, time seems to sound each moment like it is a huge clock ticking loudly. Nothing speeds it along. You exist, you wait, you survive, you wait, you answer questions all your friends express, you wait, you try distraction, but you just wait.

For me, it had been five months since hurting my ankle in Mexico. I was still doing PT. I had torn two ligaments and some of the scar tissue had grown over the joint. I had to have an extremely painful shot into the ankle joint, and I was a walking wounded warrior. When home, I refreshed myself by homeschooling Karissa each morning. It is the only time of day that appeared normal to us. Guy dropped her off on his way to work and we had a set pattern of subjects, topics, and sequences we follow. This part of the day lent itself to a sense of peace in the center of the storm.

Karissa gave me instant feedback when something wasn't clear. She asked lots of questions, was quick to catch on, and it was a delight to see when she understood and took on a new concept. Although I was enjoying the academic time with Karissa, the bonding, praying, and growing we were doing together, I was well aware that Karissa's allegiance was shifting to me in the absence of Mom. Teri was upstairs, sleeping most of the time, and missing out on the fun of seeing Karissa master new ideas. I was surprised that Teri didn't seem to fall into a pity- party for herself, but I saw the pain in her eyes when she questioned me about Karissa's progress. On one hand, I was enjoying it. However, on the other hand I ached that Teri was missing so much, and the moments were slipping through her fingers forever.

There was a quiet time with no decisions to be made. We just "did what had to be done." Teri needed my help showering, shampooing, drying her hair and curling it. Those were special times when we talked. She was so open, and she had faced the possibility of death so often, she didn't find it morbid to discuss what the future would be like for her girls if she died. Her greatest fear was that she would die before they are "launched." From the depths of my being, I could honestly say to her they were both already "launched." Ashley had the privilege of having Teri through most of her teen years, and Teri's love of God, reading, and learning were deeply instilled on her being. Although Karissa hadn't had nearly as much time, Teri's imprint was stamped all over her. Whenever I told Karissa something that was presented in a different way than Teri had stated it, Karissa quickly said, "My Mom says . . ." Karissa was an eighth grader, a time when many kids begin to question the input from parents. However, Karissa was doing just the opposite. She was deeply entrenched with Teri's teachings, and she was solid.

I reassured Teri that if she were to die, both girls would go through different times in their lives when they felt cheated, angry, and frustrated that they didn't have her. Yet, both girls were strong, resilient, and deeply entrenched in the Bible. They would suffer, yes, but they would be so loved, prayed for, and surrounded by things and ideas of their mother that they would always have her with them. Teri nodded, knowing it was all true and that they both belonged to the Lord who loved them even more than she and Guy. She was not worried about Guy much as he was such a strong Christian. She was confident he would be okay. His desire to be a great dad would get him through the roughest parts.

We hoped this moment of physical strain on her body would pass like all others had before, and on that hope, we embarked on a "redo" of Teri's bedroom at home. Friends joined us in this endeavor. Pauline cleaned, sanitized the whirlpool and bathroom while others tore up carpet or painted. Leon and Shane cut and fitted the new flooring and we all worked together to make her and Guy's master bedroom one she would love. Teri's color purple was everywhere. Everyone involved felt proud when we were done. Sadly, she was only able to sleep there two nights, but she was so proud of her room and the love shown by family and friends to make this dream come true for her.

Teri continued to shrink in size and was now only 100 pounds. Even as she became weaker, her laughter still filled the room. When she needed to stand, she wanted Guy, Gib, or me to be beside her. Once on her feet, she moved slowly using a cane. The daily draining was becoming more painful. Although her strength was declining, her hope seemed strong as she waited and waited for Mayo to call.

The sixth decision rested with me, and I saw no clear answer. How could I coax Wendy into opening up and sharing with me her deepest fears? Wendy had always faced problems straight on and felt a lot of talk about them was useless. Wendy was a doer, not a philosopher. The rare exception was when she expressed her motherly concerns about her boys. Wendy was like a mother bear with her cubs when it came to her boys. She would fight for them with all she had in her. That's why she would continue chemo after chemo after chemo. She always kept her emotions in check. Even when Quinn and I told her and Brad that Quinn had already asked Jesus into his heart, tears came into her eyes, but she quickly straightened herself and controlled her reaction. Thrilled beyond words, she showed only a smile and quick comment of, "great" while Brad was bubbling over with enthusiasm. Somewhere along her growing up, Wendy had equated strength and lack of showing emotion as the same thing. She simply didn't show outwardly what was going on inside her. This caused all sorts of problems for all of us that loved her. Even hugging was to be done quickly if at all, and your deepest thoughts were to be that – just deep! Brad and I had many frustrated conversations trying to figure out her wishes, her thinking and her affections. Her life seemed unchanging. Treatments, a new chemo, balding, and then repeat. Although her stoic approach to life was frustrating to the rest of us, it certainly sustained her throughout this battle. She was in constant pain but wouldn't outwardly acknowledge it. When she rose to walk, she held her left arm close to her body to prevent any juggling of that wretched underarm hole. She still laughed, but not as easily or as energetically. Every attempt I made to get past the wall she had erected failed. I found no solution to my decision, and it remained unsolved.

Our lives seemed to only be one of existence until finally, Mayo called, and we went for them to examine Teri from head to toe. Teri and I stayed in the hotel in Rochester, Minnesota, for 4 days of exams until the final test was done and it was time to meet the team of doctors for results. Guy came and the three of us went from doctor to doctor. Each gave us no hope when they told us there was nothing, they could do for her. She needed an Aorta valve replacement, but she was too weak and wouldn't survive the surgery. We were all crushed. We had pinned all our hopes on Mayo, and they had nothing to offer. Teri was so tiny now, under 100 pounds. Yet, she still had fight left in her. Now, there was nowhere to turn. We only had one doctor left to see.

We forced ourselves to make that last appointment. Oddly, he sat and stared at us a while. Finally, he said, "I am going to do something we never do at Mayo. I am going to send you home without a plan. I am going to contact the valve manufacturer and see if they have a child's size that will fit your tiny heart. Then, I am going to try to talk the surgeon into trying this. I am not giving up yet. I will not tease you and say I have an answer. I just want more time to try. Are you willing to wait a few days while I check it all out?"

Teri's face gave away her emotions. Hope, surprise, and peace spread across her eyes as she replied, "A few days will be fine. You see, no one has given us a glimmer of hope. Even if the answer at the end of the tunnel is no, we would have a few days of hope. Of course, we will wait. Afterall, you are the only one willing to fight for me."

He sat back in his chair and rocked while he stared at her. Finally, he continued, "You have a great attitude."

She smiled and nodded. Filled with emotion she was afraid to say more. So, we traveled home with only a thread of hope, but it was a thread! Again, we must wait.

Teri faced the seventh decision with prayer, consultations, more prayer, deep compilation, and even more prayer. This would be the biggest decision of her lifetime. If Mayo agreed to do it, this would be a dangerous surgery. On the other hand, without it she had little time left. We searched the Bible for God's direction. We weighed out her desire to have more time with her daughters. She meditated on the Word. She asked our advice. She called Shane and Kelly, and they discussed the benefits verses the risks. They told her that doing whatever she could to stay alive would speak volumes to their daughters' ears. They would see their mom was doing all she could to keep fighting and trust God for the outcome whatever it was. They discussed how to tell the girls and the conversation that needed to include the possibility of her dying on the table. Ashley knew the severity of her mother's illness, but Karissa was only 13 and sheltered from much of the reality. Of course, the final decision had to be Teri's, and she found solace in remembering that Jeremiah had said God has plans for us, plans for our welfare and future. So, she waited and pondered what God's plans might be, and prayed she would be ready.

Ten days later the doctor called. He had found a child's valve used in trials that would work. They could partially inflate it and it should hold. He said, "It took a lot of talking, but I got the surgeon to agree to do the surgery. He would only do it if I would assist. Of course, I will. We have you on the surgery schedule in a month with the pre-op exams a week before that. How does that sound?"

With tears of joy spreading down her face she agreed. Once off the phone I asked, "So, you have decided to go ahead?"

Her answer was so perfect. "I've decided it is in God's hands. If He wants me to do this, it will continue as planned. If not, He will stop it however He chooses. I am at peace to wait and see what He does." So, we went about living the month to the fullest and waiting to see if this was truly God's direction.

Teri surprised us with decision number eight. She announced she wanted to go see her sister. So. Gib and I loaded her into our car and took off for Illinois leaving her family behind. It appeared we were moving with all the luggage, draining paraphernalia, blankets, pillows, meds etc. However, once we set out, Teri traveled well, stretched out in the backseat. We listened to an audio book to help pass the time. The suspense of Joel Rosenberg's book kept us moving along the 300+ miles. As we neared Illinois, we played a CD of our "extended family son," Will. As he sang and the words filled the car, Teri shot up from the back seat almost screaming. "That's my song! Will wrote that song for me!" Hoping not to deflate her too much I reminded her he had written it before he even met her.

"I don't care **when** he wrote it. Mom, God gave him the words so he would be ready for me. That song was written just for me." As she sunk back and closed her eyes, a huge smile spread across her face. I listened closely to the words, and she was right. It WAS WRITTEN for her.

Our God is Big Enough
By Will Lopes

Oceans roar, mountains tremble
Nature bows, people pray, because they know
Our God is big enough

As we fear, As we fight
There might be tears, but we still believe
We still believe that God, Our God is big enough

Bigger than our problems, Bigger than our pain,
This is my assurance, that's why I proclaim
He has all the answers, He is above all things
There's no situation, He cannot intervene
Our God is bigger . . . My God is big enough

I let go of fear and shame
Surrender all to the God who reigns
My God is able . . . He is enough
To do the things He promised
. . . And to do much more

I choose to trust You, I choose to rest,
I choose to praise you, To believe and to know that you want my best

Teri had her own personal song. Written by the little brother she always wanted. She sang it over and over and often hummed it quietly when others were around.

Once we arrived at Wendy's, the girls ensconced themselves side-by-side on the couch and reveled in their time together. They sat there, limp, and weak, yet strong and mighty. I stared in wonder at my heroes. They had totally different personalities, goals in life and ideas on how to raise children. Yet, they were so alike. Strong, stubborn, warriors, funny, teasers, and they both bore the mark of their Savior. They had faith beyond their years and depth brought on from trials. They had a sheen about their faces, and they talked, shared memories, and tried to outshine each other's last story or joke. It didn't seem possible it could get any better than this, but it did.

A couple of days later, Shane and Kelly drove down for Easter. The day before they arrived, Wendy announced we had to make Shane's favorite dessert, "Caramel Brownies" and that she had made a decision. (Decision #9 remains my favorite). We would all be going to church together Easter morning even if both she and Teri needed to be carried. We finally had all three of our children together again, and the deep, deep joy and peace that filled me came from my Father. The service was deeply moving for all of us. Then, it was time for us to return to Minnesota.

Abruptly, things changed, and our world spun out of control. A few days after Easter, Brad called with devastating news. Wendy's doctor stopped all chemo. Tumors were growing even while taking chemo and new spots appeared on the chest wall. Hours of frustration and disappointment passed before Brad called again to say the doctor had relented and wanted to try one more chemo. Wendy made decision number ten and announced she was ready to go for her eighth round of chemo.

There was heaviness everywhere, a feeling of inability to get air deep into your being. People all over the world were praying for us. Friends were begging for us to find something tangible they could do for us. Strangers sent cards, Facebook messages and prayers. Our prayer warriors spent hours on their knees, and we were strengthened through their devotion. I spent many moments on my Eagles' wings flying above the chaos. It was hard to believe that we were only three months into the new year. So many decisions already. Wendy was about to take on another battle. Were any of us strong enough? She wasn't the only one suffering physically.

A few years before, I had been diagnosed with Macular Degeneration. Macular Degeneration is a vision impairment disease with no cure. It is a deterioration of the macula in the back of the eye and distorts things you see. It can cause blurry vision and often requires brighter lights for reading. That stage is called "dry". With a certain type of vitamin, it can continue in that state for a long time. Unexpectedly, my macular degeneration went from dry to "wet" in my right eye. This meant there was abnormal bleeding and I had to begin monthly shots in my eye. Had stress caused the change? I had no way of knowing. I was still dealing with my ankle injury and was trying to wean myself from the walking boot. The physical toll on me was showing outwardly what was going on inside my body. Still, I found myself looking up instead of giving up. My hope in Jesus rested in what He did for me on the cross not on what He might do for the girls' or my physical needs. My belief in God was NOT hollow. God is too great! Teri awaited life-threatening surgery; Wendy awaited starting one last chemo; and I couldn't help wondering what God's plans were for the girls. Would He step in and perform two miracles? Only He knew what the final chapter would be. Either way, He and we would be victorious over or through death. Uncertain of so many things, I was certain of one. We were the **Daughters of the King.** and He would lead the way in the fight ahead.

MARCH INTO HELL

CHAPTER 20

In the famous song, "the Impossible Dream," there is a line that says we must be "willing to march into hell for a heavenly cause". What cause could be more "heavenly" than to battle for the lives of our children? We were no longer in a fracas or skirmish but in a full-blown war. Satan was battling us for our souls. Sure, we were safe for eternity in God's hands, but our daily existence was being tormented. Was our faith in God only for the future only or was it for today? For right now? We were living the ABCs of battle - Agony, Betrayal, and Ceaselessness. I had added a "D" to the acronym to stand for denial. Each day had brought and would continue to bring burdens, heartbreak, struggles and suffering. Did we still have hope for victory or dreams to be fulfilled? Could we endure and persevere? Did we have the grit and staying power to continue? With no clear path leading away from this dogfight, we had no choice but to continue to march into this inferno for a heavenly cause. I was determined to battle for my daughters. I alone, if necessary, would fight to the end for them.

Armed with determination, I packed my clothes to return to Wendy's when Teri entered my bedroom. She spoke quietly saying she wanted me to know something. Barely above a whisper she said, "Mom, if we both die, I will hold Wendy's hand as we go into Heaven. She won't be alone."

Overwhelmed with thoughts shooting through my brain, I stopped what I was doing and faced her. "Teri, I am telling you that you two cannot do that to me. You will not both die! Do you hear me?"

A gentle smile of understanding spread across her face as she said, "I know, Mom. It was just a thought."

She had voiced my deepest fear. Yet, within the hysteria in my brain and heart, I felt a comfort I couldn't explain. Teri still wanted to take care of her little sister. If that happened, they would be together. Quickly, I turned back to my task and pushed the horrendous thought from my mind. Like Scarlett O'Hara, I would think about this tomorrow. I knew Teri was living in reality, and I was in denial, but I was far from ready to accept what she was saying. My trip to Wendy's was short-lived as I had to return for Teri's pre-op.

Finally, we reached day for "pre-op." Mayo Clinic was fascinating and appeared to be a city within a city. It was the most efficiently run place I have ever seen. We had tests in the morning and met with the doctor in the afternoon to get the results. We followed colored arrows to find our way through the maze. The underground area was filled with shops and people coming and going like a busy hive. Once inside, you needn't exit into the cold as all is connected throughout the blocks with tunnels, walkways etc. All 32,000 employees from janitor to chief surgeon were informative and always thoughtful and aware of the "person" they were talking too. Everyone we met or crossed paths with never forgot the human in the middle of the problem. They prepared us, answered our questions, and educated us on the procedure. They planned to enter through the ribs to reach the heart. Since her heart was so small, they would only partially inflate the valve. She was reasonably weak and so tiny, so we prayed her strength would hold out until April 20th, the day of surgery. Only a week away, we had a short wait, but one filled with deep emotions. Mayo Clinic seemed to spew confidence even from the walls. Teri was ready, we all were, so I made a quick trip to see Wendy.

I found Wendy in constant pain. She tried to say little about it, but her face was drawn, and her eyes had no sparkle. Finally, she had quit working and the left side where the huge opening remained was hurting constantly. There was an enlarged tumor there and it pressed on the nerves. Wendy said she could see "stuff growing in there." How did she feel seeing that monster devour her? The chemo aggravated it, and the pain never let up. Now there was chest wall involvement and a lymph node in the right armpit. She was still determined to fight this. She still hung onto hope that there would be a "wonder drug" that would do the job. She held her left side when she walked. For the first time she admitted the pain was off the charts and she was unable to sleep. She wondered if this eighth round of chemo would help.

My dilemma: I couldn't be in two places at once. Which girl needed me the most? Both wanted their "Mommy" and both deserved their mommy but I am only one. Both relied deeply on their God and their husbands. Teri was outspoken about her trust and faith in God. Wendy was private and wanted her time with God alone. I felt one on each arm pulling although neither said a thing. I realized I needed to be with them even more than they needed me. I needed to touch them, stroke their hair or head, try to make their lives easier, and try to help their kids face an uncertain time. I am sure it was often harder on me than on them when I left one to go to the other. Teri caught on how poorly her sister was doing, and she so wanted to be with Wendy and encourage her. Yet, Teri's own health prevented her from traveling.

I called on my eagle often. I closed my eyes and mounted up to fly above the pain I felt as I saw my daughters deteriorating. My relationship with God began to change. I no longer needed to even call out to God. He was constantly with me. Sometimes He and I walked along together not saying anything, and other times I pleaded. Of course, I had begged to have the diseases myself and spare the girls, but His answer had been no. I kept my words unspoken so others wouldn't hear, but God would quickly shoot me a positive thought. When I was low or emotionally teetering, He would shoot me names of people praying for us. As their face popped into my mind, I felt their strength and was reinvigorated. Other times He let it rain. To others the rain was an annoyance or at best a washing of the earth. To me, rain had become God's visual of His presence with me. It lifted my spirit, and I didn't need the rainbow to be reminded of His promises. As the clouds darkened, I smiled. God was washing my soul. The patter of the drops against the window were music to me and I closed my eyes and danced to the rhythm. I danced with joy that He was right there with me. I danced with joy that my daughters were in His hands. I danced with joy that tomorrow, or one day soon, the sun would burst through again. All I needed to do was dance and wait.

Those ABCD's of battle kept rearing up. Both the girls experienced agony. Their bodies were betraying them, and it was ceaseless in its endeavor to destroy us. I wasn't sure if Wendy was in denial like me, but Teri was not. Still, the three of us were unwilling to give up the fight. How could we defeat those ABCD's and change them to something positive? I would keep marching for that heavenly cause. Today would be the mightiest test of all. Today, Teri would go into surgery knowing it was life threatening.

As Teri was whisked off to surgery, Gib, Guy, Shane, and I settled in the waiting room to pass the coming hours together. It is strange how five minutes can sometimes seem like hours and like you are holding your breath under water. We had been told surgery would be four hours and we tried many tactics to pass the time. Card games, visiting, walking, eating, sitting, sitting, and sitting. Suddenly, people in the waiting room began laughing and running to the windows. We quickly rose to our feet to see what the commotion was. There, on the outside of the window was Spiderman climbing up the outside of the building. He paused and waved at the children. He put one hand against the window and kids ran to put their hand against his on the inside. Then, Batman appeared, and the excitement and squeals started all over again. What a hoot! In the midst of deep concern and pressure, Spiderman and Batman broke into our world to lighten it. Then, they continued up the side of the building to the floors above. Later we learned these were college boys that do it often as their contribution to help lighten the pressure people at Mayo are going through. It was a joy and a moment of distraction!

After about three hours a nurse came to give us an update. "Your daughter has been taken off the heart by-pass machine."

"What?" I asked. "She was never supposed to be put on the by-pass"

Gently and patiently, she replied, "I don't know any more about it as that was all I was told to relay to you. It is a good thing she is safely off it."

"Of course," I replied. Gib or Guy thanked her, and she quickly turned and left. That certainly started an entire new conversation as we speculated why Teri would have been put on the machine. Now the time seemed to drag even slower. I felt I could hear the click as the second hand jumped from one second to another on the large wall clock at the end of the room. Families came and went, and we remained. My head told me that time was not slower, but my heart shouted it had almost stopped. It was a good two hours later before the same nurse returned to say that the surgery was over,

Teri was in recovery, and the doctor was coming to see us. We followed her into a small consultation room and awaited his arrival.

As the surgeon entered the room, he literally fell into the chair. He leaned his head back against the wall and breathed deeply. He looked at our apprehensive faces and quickly said, "She is stable and in recovery."

He began to relate the progress of the five hours of surgery. They had entered by the fifth rib removing a piece of it. Her blood pressure had dropped quickly, and they had cut into the groin and attempted to thread a catheter through her tiny veins. They couldn't do it fast enough and her heart stopped. He did CPR on her for two minutes while they placed her on the by-pass machine. Then, they let her body rest for 30 minutes before continuing. Placing the valve was easy as it went right in. Sometime during the surgery, they had removed a liter of fluid from around her lungs. He told us that the doctor that had promised to assist him had been called to New York for emergency surgery, and he had found a substitute assistant. I remembered his reluctance to do this surgery and that he agreed on the condition he would have that one assisting. Now, only his skill and the grace of God had allowed her to survive the surgery. Shane remembers him saying. "We lost her once on the table- maybe two times." No wonder he was so exhausted. With a quick closing statement that she would be transferred to the ICU, and, once stable, we could see her. With that said he rose to leave.

As I stared at this man that had held Teri's life in his hands, I was overcome with gratefulness that he had finally agreed to do this surgery even after he first said no. We all thanked him, shook his hand, and watched a weary man walk away. The last five hours had been long for us but extremely difficult for him. We thanked God for him, the staff, the success of the surgery, and prayed blessings on him and strength for Teri.

The first few hours of recovery were actually funny. Teri was full of anesthesia and her comments kept us laughing and grinning. She had a great male nurse that she kept begging for a drink of water. He tried to reason with her saying she could have ice chips but no water yet. He didn't want her throwing up, so she would just have to be content with ice chips. She motioned for me to bend down. Thinking she was whispering she said in a normal voice, "Mom, this mean man won't give me a drink. I am so thirsty. I know you will get me one because you are my mom. Don't let him see you get it though."

I looked up to see the huge smile on his face. When I refused, she looked up at him and inquired, "What is your full name?"

Perplexed, he told her.

"Good," she continued. She repeated his full name over and over three times. He asked her what she was doing, and her reply stunned us. "When I get out of here, I will find you and you will pay."

As we laughed, she closed her eyes and quietly said, "I can't see you!"

The next day Kelly brought Karissa down to see Teri. She was awake enough to visit a little and then they returned home. Within three days our laughter faded as we began facing one problem after another. Teri's kidneys weren't functioning, and she lost strength in her left arm and couldn't raise it. She couldn't take more than five steps. They reduced her pain meds to allow her body to start returning to normal, but that increased her pain level immensely. She needed to move around to prevent pneumonia and they continued to suction off fluid. The process was very painful. Our prayer warriors were once again on their knees. Fluid was being drained off her right side also. Her feet were quite swollen, and they pumped diuretics in her as she continued to fight to get better.

Meanwhile, Brad was filling us in on Wendy. She had lots of pain in her hips and back. Her left arm was swelling with lymphedema. She couldn't get comfortable in bed, so she was sleeping in the recliner now and suffered muscle spasms even as she attempted to remain independent. We needed to go back to Illinois. But was Teri going to be okay?

We moved to a hotel room across the street from the hospital with two large beds. It would be so much more convenient just to pop across the street and we could all take turns slipping over to the hotel for a nap. Five days passed from the surgery and Teri still couldn't stand or walk. Her left arm still dangled and fell useless to her side. Her kidneys were only slightly working. The next days were rugged. One tiny step forward and a leap backwards. Finally, after seven days she was moved from the ICU and placed in the PCU (progressive Care Unit) a sort of graduation. She was very slowly doing better but teetering on pneumonia.

Wendy was rapidly doing worse. We had to make a choice. Teri had Guy, Shane and Kelly, and multiple friends supporting her. Wendy had Brad and his parents, and they needed us as much as Wendy did. So, mid-week with Shane and Kelly settled in the hotel room and Guy went home to work and be with the girls, Gib and I decided we needed to go to Illinois, and we would leave Teri in the hands of loved ones. Just before leaving, into this chaos stepped Teri's favorite doctor from the Twin Cities. Dr. Thatcher had come to visit and even though she was in great pain, she was thrilled to see him. He encouraged her, they shared complaints and joys, and his visit raised her spirit a lot. She made him promise he would be at her funeral, and he answered that nothing could keep him away.

Upon arrival in Illinois, we found Wendy entrenched in her recliner, only leaving to go to the bathroom. When she returned to the recliner it took many minutes for the pain brought on by movement to subside. The tumor was resting on a nerve and the pain and tingling was terrible. She had pain shooting through her back. We eagerly awaited a CT scan on Friday as well as an ultrasound that we hoped would tell us exactly what was going on.

Friday arrived and I took Wendy for the scans. We waited for the nurse, and Wendy was quieter than normal. She wasn't hungry, didn't want to make small talk, and was obviously apprehensive. The nurse came and asked Wendy to follow her to the testing area. I watched my girl limp and struggle, leaning on her cane and stooped over like she was 90 years old. My heart broke as her pain washed over me. My little pink bunny was losing her battle and I was helpless to do anything about it. I followed behind and settled in a chair near the room and prayed the pain would be bearable as they moved her around on the table to adjust her for the scans. Suddenly, I heard a deep moan erupt that continued and continued, and I knew how desperate she must be to allow that noise to escape her. I had learned to turn off all tears in front of my daughters so they would not suffer more when they saw me, but I lost it. Tears flowed down my face and flooded my lap as my pain for Wendy overwhelmed me. I couldn't pray. I could only hang on. I knew I needed to stop crying before she came out of the room, but I wasn't sure I could. Suddenly, a picture of a dear friend popped into my mind, and I saw her on her knees. She didn't know we were having scans right now, yet I knew she was praying at that moment. Wings began to lift me up and peace flooded over me as I knew Wendy and I were not alone. My tears began to stop, and by the time they opened the door, Wendy looked up and smiled at me with genuine love in her face. Once again, I felt God's presence and it was such a joy to recognize His love.

Again, we waited. We wouldn't see the doctor until Tuesday, so we had the weekend to just be together. Shane called to say that Teri had the tubes removed and was feeling better. However, she was struggling with memory problems and muscles. Also, she was experiencing panic attacks when they get her up to walk. She was so afraid she would fall even though they had a tight belt around her, and they always had her safe. She was still struggling with controlling her left arm, neck, and hand, and Guy and Shane were taking turns being with her. Kelly was being mom back in the Cities. Gib and I discussed the need for Shane and Guy to be at work and decided that Gib would leave Sunday to drive back to Mayo. I would stay with Wendy. The hotel room in Rochester was always occupied, but between all of us, the receptionist never knew who was sleeping in that room. That would be funny if it weren't so pitiful.

As we awaited results of Wendy's scans, April closed, and May quietly snuck onto the calendar. The old saying crept into my mind. "April showers bring May flowers." I had missed most of the showers, being inside with the girls. I rarely slipped out. When I did run errands, I would skip, jump, and stomp in the puddles and look up into the rain and allow God to wash me. Some of the rains physically cleaned the dirty snow piles away while others seemed to reach down inside my heart to clean the dirty pain away. Even though rain had become a friend, I found I sought sunshine. I wanted to bask in the warmth of heaven so, surely, surely, surely May will bring flowers, spring, and sunshine.

The results were in. Wendy's tumor was deep inside. It had grown to 8.5 cm even while on chemo. There was also a tumor in the bicep, and new growth now in the opposite side, the right arm pit. There appeared there was nothing left to do. Still, Wendy was unwilling to give up, so the doctor decided to try a toxic oral chemo. The hope was that this would be different by giving her chemo daily instead of once a week. Perhaps, just perhaps, the dull bombardment could sneak up on this persistent cancer and force it to let go. The pills were so toxic no one could touch them with their hands. They had to wear gloves. Overall, Wendy was weak, nerve pain was constant and enormous, and muscle spasms in her back continued. She was still as independent as possible, and she was determined to fight on. Brad cleared his throat and spoke in a strong voice. "How long do we have?" The doctor stumbled around and mumbled, not wanting to answer.

Finally, he declared, "Let's see what the oral pills do," and he quickly left the room. Later, his assistant took Brad aside and whispered, "Three to four months." Wendy was back on a schedule of six pills for 14 days and then week of rest. There was nothing new I could do so I returned home.

We brought Teri home from Mayo only to rush her back to Mayo two days later as she struggled to breath. Confusion was everywhere. It appeared she has pneumonia, yet nothing shows up on an Xray. There was a parade of doctors of all specialties through her room including infectious disease specialists. They all heard something with their stethoscopes, but they are not sure what. The heart valve was working great, so what was going on? Each new battle was more tiring than the one before, and this war seems ceaseless. She was on antibiotics and began eating a little. Social workers came by and worked with Gib to prepare to take her home again. She appeared to be stronger and able to walk around the room with her walker. With all this talk of her doing better, I bought an Amtrak ticket to go back to Wendy's.

The day before I was to leave, I was walking through the lobby when something in the gift shop glittered and caught my eye. Upon inspection I found two colored glass angels. One was red and one was purple. They had crystal wings and hung from a thin thread. What a perfect way to have each girl feel my presence even when I was with the other. Quickly, I purchased them and shoved the red one in my pocket. I headed to Teri's room with the purple one dangling from my fingers. I hung it above her bed and said, "Now, Mom will always be with you even when I am at Wendy's." The angel spun and caught the sun as the reflection danced off the wall. Smiling, Teri said, "Look Mom, it even dances." We both laughed and she kept her eyes on it.

Shane and Kelly had come to Mayo to see her when suddenly Teri was having huge problems breathing. She was frightened. They thought she had pneumonia again. Her breathing was raspy, but a quick Xray showed clear lungs. How could this turn around so quickly? What was causing all of this? Teri asked if they could bring in a cot and I could sleep there. I said I would, and Shane quickly stepped up and intervened. "Mom, you need your rest if you are going to Wendy's tomorrow." Immediately, Kelly spoke up and volunteered to stay with Teri, and Teri was completely content with her being there. The decision was made; Kelly stayed, and after a tearful goodbye, Gib, Shane, and I started back to our hotel across the street. The three of us walked the long empty corridor of the hospital as it was late at night. In silence we held hands, and I was crying. I lamented as to why she had to take a turn for the worse just as I was going to leave. Neither man replied. There was nothing to say.

Early the next morning Shane wished me Happy Mother's Day. Stunned, I stared at him in unbelief. I didn't realize it was Mother's Day, but boy did I feel like a mother! With two of my three children in crisis, my only healthy child in pain watching his sisters deteriorate, I reached out to hug him. Ah, it felt wonderful to be held in his strong arms. Shane was the world's greatest hugger, and I didn't want to leave this cocoon he provided. I would see Teri in a few minutes and Wendy by tonight. I truly was blessed. I would get to see all three of my children on Mother's Day. After that respite, we smiled at each, took a deep breath, and walked across the street to see how Teri and Kelly were doing.

Teri was again not eating, and they were still concerned she had pneumonia. but she and Kelly had made it through the night together. and I would be leaving her with full support of Kelly, Shane, and Gib with Guy returning on the weekend. I knew it was time for me to go but it was tearing me to pieces. Gib had loaded my suitcase in the car. Looking back, I know it was harder on me to leave than it was on Teri. Again, the strength I drew from Gib's hand was just enough to get me into the car on the way to the train. We talked about the prayer warriors on their knees all over the world, and the blessings God was pouring out even in the midst of this horrible scenario. Then, we pulled up in front of the train station and a sense of panic swept over me. How desperately I needed my eagle, and I couldn't see or feel him anywhere. Gib helped me board the train and went back to the car. I stared straight out the window at his car. I knew he couldn't see me through the tinted windows of the train, but I put my hand on the window just in case.

This was my lowest moment. I was deserting Teri. Throughout her life, in every crisis, I had stood by her and now I was leaving. My brain said I had to go but my heart was breaking. I knew it was for me I was mourning, but what if she needed me? As the train began to slowly roll, I felt desperate. I had never walked away from any challenge, and I felt I was running away. This is all wrong. Oh, God, where are you? How can I do this? How can I be in two places? How can I leave my support (Gib) behind? I need his hand to hold on to. I need to be a part of this, yet Wendy needed me too. Deep inside a fear took hold that things would never be the same again. Would Teri just disappear while I was gone? The train began to speed up and I saw Gib raise his hand out the window and wave to me. Quickly, his car disappeared, and I was on my way to a different crisis. I fell back into my chair thankful the train was not full and I had my own little space. Deep sobs clamored to escape, and I felt I was made of glass and was shattering into tiny pieces. There was no one there to pick up the pieces. The more I cried, the deeper the desperation. Was I completely breaking down? Somewhere, somehow, someone was praying for me at that moment. I was totally unable to pray, yet I could feel the presence of God in my tiny space.

I had marched into this inferno for the heavenly cause of fighting for my girls. Was I losing the battle? I had marched into this inferno with eyes wide open. I wanted to fight this pestilence that controlled my daughters. I wanted to execute the Lord's vengeance on cancer, pain, affliction, and decay. Instead, I was met with pain everywhere. Their pain, my pain, their families' pain, the doctors' pain. There was defeat everywhere I turned. Wasn't saving my girls a heavenly enough cause for this agonizing trip?

Frustrated and disenchanted I remembered scripture that said vengeance belonged to the Lord. It was His battle, not mine. The only way I could be triumphant in this conquest was giving it back to the Lord. I struggled to release any control I thought I had. I had given my girls to Him years before. Now, I had to give their burdens and pain to Him. Humbled and hurting I repented of my self-righteous fight and turned the battle and the results over to the One they belonged to. I backed away from my "march into hell" I thought was so noble. I rested in His way, truth, guidance and will. I was giving up control; I was looking up as I had said, "The battle is Yours, Father. The outcome is Yours."

Slowly, very slowly, I began to approach the Throne. I began to plead for Him to touch me, give me strength I didn't have, renew my faith, walk with me, carry me, heal my broken heart, and change my panic into peace. Finally, in my mind, I saw my Savior with his hand outstretched for me to grasp. He was there, waiting for me to take His hand and walk with Him. Now, my tears changed to ones of joy instead of pain, hope instead of fear. and contentment instead of panic. Slowly, it became well with my soul. My Savior had met me where I was, picked me up, given me strength, and walked beside me hand in hand. As the hours passed and the train sped toward Wendy, peace grew in my heart as I allowed Him to touch me. The tears stopped and I began to feel stronger by the moment. I was walking with Him again and it felt so right, so good, so real. I looked out the window only to see small rain drops clinging to the glass. They slid gently to the bottom and disappeared. They washed away the dust on the window. They reminded me that even with Gib far away, I could do this because God had taught me that even as it rained, even as it poured, I could dance.

STRONGHOLDS AND QUICKSAND

CHAPTER 21

Once I reached Wendy, her first words startled me. "Happy Mother's Day, Mom." For a few hours I had forgotten it was Mother's Day. "Happy Mother's Day to you too," I replied. I pulled the red glass angel from my pocket and told her this was how she'd know I was always with her. Like Teri, she smiled and watched it twist as I hung it above her. Again, its refection danced on the wall. I told her Teri had commented that it danced, and she began giggling. "Sure, it dances, but Mom, it isn't even in the rain." We both enjoyed our joke and watched it sway as it found its resting spot. As I stared at her, the pain was clear in her eyes. I saw how she moved around carefully protecting her back and flinching when the pain stabbed her. I noticed her body trembled when the pain hit. Morphine helped some, but she limited herself on how much she took so she could communicate and be involved in family life.

I hadn't been gone all that long, yet I could see the deterioration that had taken place in my absence. The weekend was coming, and Brad would be travelling to Iowa to bring Casey home from college. If I saw a massive change in just a few days, how shocked will Casey be after five months of not seeing her? Once Brad left Wendy began to cry. She didn't want Casey to see her like this, frail and in pain. Quinn had been around to watch her downward spiral, but Casey had been in a protective shield at school. Brad warned him on the ride home. However, that first moment he saw her, the shock was obvious in his eyes. He attempted to cover his feelings, but Wendy saw it immediately. Still, her excitement at seeing her first-born outweighed the sadness, and she laughed with joy at seeing him. Finally, her family was back together in one house and the world was right.

Back at Mayo, Teri didn't get to go home as planned. Her recovery continued to be frustrating. Her lung problems were now attributed to aspirations of tiny bits of food. Gravity was pulling tiny particles of food to the bottom of her lung, and there they sat. She had to sit up perfectly straight to take pills or eat in order to keep things from going down the wrong pipe. She slowly began eating, very little at first, but at least eating. Her lungs were now attached to the chest wall so there is no place for the fluid to form. Nevertheless, the fluid searched out new places and found small pockets outside the upper chambers of her heart and set up home. To prevent this, she needed to have more protein to help control the level of fluid. She needed to move around more but still she was so weak. It seemed we were on a merry-go- round that kept speeding up. Up and down and round and round we go with no chance of escape. Guy was trying to be an integral part of her care while running interference with insurance, and Kelly was taking over the driving of the girls allowing Guy more time with Teri. Ashley and Karissa were anxious for their mom to return home (or at least our home a few blocks away) so they could see her more. Finally, Teri had a blood transfusion, and they sent her home to our house. She was using a walker full time, but she didn't have the drain tube. She felt free. Again, our pink bunny was fighting her way back.

Wendy's newest CAT scan explained the terrible back pain. The T12 vertebrae had been compressed and cracked under the pressure of the tumor pushing against it. She needed surgery. They would insert cement to secure it. I couldn't stay for the surgery as it was again time for my eye shot. I left planning to return in five days. Again, I boarded a plane and left a daughter in crisis. I felt like a yoyo. I kept dropping one girl behind, falling, and then being yanked up for only a split second before being dropped again.

Once home, Karissa and I met and worked on school, plans for the future, and just enjoyed our time together. It is fun to see her developing as a self-starting student. She was having to do most of her work on her own and she was rising to the occasion and preparing herself for a transition to public school in the fall. She had persisted in her studies, bringing herself up to grade level and she finally enjoyed learning. I loved seeing this success nestled between our problem.

A couple of days after my eye shot appointment, Ashley had a dance performance and Teri was unable to attend since she was back in the hospital. She had so hoped to be able to go, but it was just impossible. How I loved to watch Ashley float. Her body was so expressive and told a story as she moved. I sat in awe of her beauty and expression and for a moment forgot all about the problems outside. What a great God to place the timing so perfectly that I got a chance to see Ashley dance once more.

In the meantime, Wendy had the back- cementing procedure done. It was excruciating and much worse than anticipated. They started three hours late so the waiting in an uncomfortable position made it even worse. They believe the break was about two weeks old. No wonder she had been in so much pain. During the procedure they had used only local anesthesia and it was far from enough. She had moaned, screamed, held onto the table and was in deep distress until he finished. Later she said it was the worst pain she ever experienced, and the doctor said if he had to do this again, he would put her completely out. Wendy had already stated the same thing. Afterwards she had to lay on her back for two hours, and that pain was also terrible. She had endured and so had Brad. He had waited helplessly as she was in agony. Brad had become a most thoughtful caregiver, and she was in good hands. A few days after the procedure I returned to find her continuing to have back spasms. In spite of all that, she began round two of the toxic oral drug. Her audacious spirit kept her fighting. Her determination to beat this might not be realistic, but it was inspiring.

Finally, Teri was back in our home from the hospital. She was starting to eat and trying to walk. A physical therapist came to the home to get her moving. She was weak from so much time in a hospital bed and building her up would take time and effort. Guy came every day after work and was such an encourager to her. He cared for her needs, held her, watched TV with her, talked about the girls and decisions to be made, and worked hard at balancing his time between her and the girls. He and Gib sorted out all medical questions leaving me free to help her with daily personal needs. Her daughters were able to drop over, but their family remained fragmented because of necessity. Still, Teri kept the dream of getting better and returning home to a full family unit again

Gib oversaw this front and I needed to return to Wendy. So, two days later, I flew back to Wendy's. When I called Gib to tell him I was safely there, he said Teri was in the hospital once again. The fluid that found new places to settle around the top of her lungs was pushing on the lungs and making breathing difficult. The problem was that the fluid wasn't all in one place like before, so it couldn't be easily drained. Diuretics helped some but it was very taxing on her body. There were no simple answers.

Hanging up the phone, I wandered back into the room with Wendy. I found her smiling with closed eyes.

"What brings on that smile?" I asked?

"Blake Sheldon," she replied.

"What? THE Blake Sheldon? Explain."

"His song, 'Savior's Shadow' says it all. Mom, I am standing in my Savior's shadow. Listen."

She turned on the music and as the words were sung clearly, I watched her face relax and deep, deep joy fill her soul. She opened her mouth and began to sing with him. She was transported into the shadow of Jesus. She was walking with Blake in His shadow, and she knew it was where she belonged. All I could do was lift my praise to Jesus and thank Him for finding this song for her. The lyrics spoke of her Savior crying for her and never forsaking her. Now Wendy had her own song. Like Teri, I heard her singing or humming it often. Sometimes, she would sit with ear buds in place, and I would see her nodding and smiling. I knew she was in her Savior's Shadow. When the morphine didn't touch the pain, the song did. Thank you, God. Thank you, Blake Sheldon.

Ashley, Teri's oldest, was graduating from High school. In Minnesota, it is an expected rite of passage to have an open house for the graduate. But that would be impossible since I was living most of the time in Illinois. Yes, I did have to return monthly to Minnesota for my eye shot, but that was only for a few days and there was no way I could host an open house. Teri was still in the hospital, and they had started thickening everything she ate so that it couldn't go down the wrong pipe. They had changed antibiotics, but she still wasn't eating enough.

Again, I called on Kelly. We began communicating about the possibility of having an open house for Ashley when I came home for my shot. On the other hand, Wendy had a birthday coming and she had cried when she realized she would pass it without her Dad since he would be in Minnesota. Tiny seeds of ideas began to grow. Could Gib fly in and surprise Wendy for her birthday? If Teri was still in the hospital, then he wouldn't have to be there. Then, perhaps, just perhaps, we could drive back to MN for my eye shots and have the open house while there. From those tiny seeds of ideas grew a plan. I began ordering decorations online to be delivered in Minnesota. Kelly and I began planning the menu, and I mentioned our germinating idea to LeAnn who mentioned the need in our Sunday School class. George, the class leader, adopted the idea and ran with it. He contacted Kelly, and set up a work crew that trimmed bushes, planted flowers, and got the yard ready. Kelly just took over and I was astonished at the results. Besides our Sunday School class, neighbors, and friends all rallied. Suddenly, our friends had something tangible they could do. I lost all pride. Anyone who wanted to clean inside or out was welcome! I was in awe at how quickly things came together. Ashley was going to get a great open house!

Ashley had been accepted at multiple dance schools, but her interest was piqued at Belhaven University in Jackson, Mississippi. The school was not even on her initial list, but they contacted her. With Teri still in the hospital, Guy and Ashley drove to Mississippi to visit the school. Leaving Karissa with Kelly, Gib and I headed to Illinois. Kelly was so efficient in preparing for the open house and now arranged activities for Karissa. She had the older cousins take her to KTIS music fest, Como Zoo, Valley Fair amusement park, and even one day set aside for Karissa's best friend. Kelly was definitely in the running for Superwoman.

Meanwhile, Wendy continued to suffer in horrible pain. After a few days, Gib returned to Minnesota, so Brad and I were again working together. It was only a few days into June and a new word began surface. The dreaded word, hospice, was whispered by Brad and I nodded but remained in denial. Wendy sensed the next step and began to fight harder for independence. The doctor suggested stopping treatment, but she demanded another chemo. The doctor never said the word, but she sensed it. She was not ready for hospice, yet her relaxant was not easing the pain. Wendy was never a crier, but suddenly she began to cry at anything that frustrated or confused her. She became unable to make simple decisions and would cry in frustration if anyone demanded a reaction. Tough times were too simple a description.

Friends from her work descended on Wendy with a Dairy Queen Blizzard and balloons and she was thrilled. Brad took a much-needed night out with his buddies, and we each found our own way to get through each day. Brad would often walk up to me and say, "Tina, do you need a hug?" I smiled, knowing he needed one, and we'd hug each other. Our united strength would get us through another day. Friends constantly inquired how Gib and I were doing. My newest escape mechanism was to do as little thinking as possible. When Wendy couldn't stand up on her own even with a walker, I wanted to burst into tears. Instead, I played Scarlet O'Hara from Gone with the Wind and would say to myself, "I'll think about it tomorrow." Other times I'd close my eyes and call my eagle. He always came. I could recite information like a computer, but my heart was falling behind. I seemed to be fighting to stay in denial, but I was quickly losing. Wendy was fully disabled now and only left the house for doctors' appointments which became major problematic events since moving and transporting her was not only painful but traumatic to her body. Brad and I began using an office chair to roll her from the recliner to the bathroom. Her mind was still quick and that allowed us to have fun conversations. I slept hard as I was exhausted every night, but God continued to give me strength daily.

Each morning brought a new lesson in reality. Reality can be so ugly. Dreams are shattered, hope is destroyed, frustration reaches an unbearable level, and we try to pretend it is all fine. Denial battles with acceptance and we feel sucked down into a quicksand we can't escape. Quicksand appears solid but when you step on it, it liquefies and loses its strength and ability to support you. Slowly, slowly it sucks you in. You can escape it, but you need to lean back, not panic, and methodically work yourself toward the edge. You may not recognize quicksand when you first see it, yet suddenly you realize you are caught. Satan is just as deceptive. He makes your thoughts appear solid, yet when you fall for his deception, he pulls you in deeper and deeper. I realized he had me caught in the ABCD's of battle. I had been caught up in their agony. I was angry at the betrayal of their bodies. The ceaseless onslaught was overwhelming, and I easily slipped into denial. My heart couldn't catch up with my mind and logic. Satan had formed a stronghold in my life – a stronghold of lies. When anything negative happened, I slipped into discouragement. How could I get out of this pit? How can others go through their daily existence when my world was deteriorating daily? How could we keep the four grandkids lives anywhere near normal with their mothers on the edge of life every minute? Yet, that was what we had to do. I saw no rain. I saw no eagles. I saw no open palm. I only saw quicksand sucking me down. As Gib returned home to be with Teri, he too felt this pull in the quicksand. One day she was better, and he was hopeful. The next day she faced a new problem and crashed. She had come back from the brink of death so many times, we had come to expect that. One day Teri asked Gib if this was the way the rest of her life would be, one hospital stay after another, and not being part of her family. He had no answer.

One of the biggest problems for Gib and me was that we were unable to be together. I didn't have Gib's hand to hold, and I am not sure he was getting many hugs. Gib had two pastors walking with him, Bob, and Todd. He gained strength from them. Our time together was so very precious as we leaned on each other, prayed together, and cried together. We would fight for each girl until there was victory over or through death. Our lives were tough, but not without hope. We lived on Bible verses and songs. Often. I thought of the song, "Because He Lives, I can face tomorrow." It reminded me this is temporary. One day soon, there will be no pain, no tears, and no heartache.

In the midst of days of discouragement, we got emails from people telling us how this was affecting their lives. God was working, touching hearts, bringing others to Him through all of this. He was being glorified and that was beautiful. We knew we were not special. However, our God was. He reminded me daily the girls belonged to Him. He never promised life would be easy, but that He would walk hand-in-hand with us. Our circumstances stunk, but there was a lovely aroma I smelled when we walked together with Him! Satan was fighting to keep us discouraged, but I decided to change the ABCD's of battle to a positive thing. Why not instead of agony we saw Assurance; instead of betrayal we counted Blessings; instead of ceaselessness we saw Confidence; instead of denial we experienced Dependence. If we could keep those in our minds, even I could pass from denial into total dependence and not be sucked into Satan's quicksand. Teri was already there, and I was never sure where Wendy was in her thinking. I knew with a change in my attitude, God would destroy Satan's stronghold.

Memorial Day offered a break as Shane and his family came down for the extended weekend. It was a bittersweet time as we cooked out and shared laughter knowing all the time that Wendy was putting on a great front to cover her excruciating pain.

BOOM! BANG! CRASH! ROARING BLAST! REVERBERATIONS THAT SHOOK THE GROUND WE STOOD ON!

Our world crashed. Even though we had been walking this direction it is devastating to hear the doctor say, "Wendy, it is time for HOSPICE. I have no other chemicals in my arsenal. There is a new mass on your right side, and it has grown even while you received chemo. There is no reason to continue this toxic attack on your body. We have nothing left to do."

Wendy sat staring straight ahead. She didn't cry. She begged for one more chemo. He only shook his head and left the room. His assistant, a friend of Brad and Wendy's, quickly sat down and began explaining how hospice could provide many helpful things. She pointed out that if a new chemo got clearance, they could always remove her from hospice, and she could fight again. Suddenly Wendy looked up. There was one more possibility. In the meantime, she could have things to make her life easier. She would agree to it assuming there was always the ability to cancel out of hospice. Assured that was the case, the plans were set into motion. The assistant called and ordered equipment to be delivered that afternoon.

Earlier that week God had been preparing us for this meeting. Two times Wendy had fallen as her legs collapsed and she had fallen to the floor in horrific pain. The second fall had been the night before this meeting. It was a living nightmare. She had slipped forward out of the rolling chair as we took her to the bathroom. She was screaming in desperate pain with a leg turned backward and Brad was trapped between her and the door frame. Brad was strong but this looked impossible. He squatted in front of her, she put her arms around his neck as he prayed desperately. He knew his own strength would not be enough. I got behind and placed my arms under her armpits. As he rose, pulling her up, a deep guttural scream came from him as all three of us sobbed and fought to bring her up and straighten that leg and settle her on the rolling chair. Long moments passed as we all three cried and tried to regain our composure. Finally, Brad orally thanked God for doing what he, Brad, couldn't. "God, I could never have lifted her up without You. Thank you for Your strength." We sat in the hallway, until our breathing returned to normal. It was worse than brutal. Later that night we sat the boys down and told them what had happened and how we couldn't physically continue this path. They realized the gravity of the situation and between tears and silence, reality wormed its way into all our hearts. Denial disappeared and dependence took its place.

Oddly, the answer God sent to help us was hospice. It would supply the help we needed. Within hours, Wendy had a recliner that would raise her up to a standing position. She had a free-standing toilet we could place right by the side of the recliner, and she could transfer herself. No more rolling chair trips. No more falls. We didn't know what lie ahead, but a new chapter with Wendy began. After she was settled in her new recliner, she quickly slipped off to sleep. I looked out the window to see a gentle drizzle falling. I slipped out the door and stood in the light mist. I turned my face up toward my Father. As the rain washed over my face, I began to call out to him. "Please, God. Wash me clean. Chase Satan from my spirit. Fight for me to release the stronghold he has on me. Draw me close to you and chase away the fears and discouragement he has tried to replace You with. Totally replace the agony, betrayal, and ceaseless denial I have had with assurance, blessings, confidence, and complete dependence on You. Wash me now, Lord. Remind me how to dance in the rain."

Slowly, very slowly I began to sway. My feet didn't move, but my arms began to sway with my upper body. Slowly, I began to feel God's presence, He was drawing me to Him. I began to smile knowing my life and my girls' lives were in His hands. The assurance of His presence, my dependence on him, the confidence that He was with me allowed me to sense His blessings. Then, and only then could I once again dance in the rain. And dance I did!

Wendy was only five days into hospice and things seemed to change hourly. Helpers poured in and encouraged, but Wendy's mobility decreased. She had PT come to get her moving, nurse to check on her and adjust meds, a helper to bathe her, and a Chaplin to visit and pray with her. Despite all the help, her pain level went through the roof. Her leg hurt even when sitting but was impossible to stand on. Finally, in desperation it was decided we must take her to the hospital to see what was causing this new pain and her inability to stand. It was the day before her birthday. She was afraid to go to the hospital. I promised to stay overnight with her in her room and she relented. The ambulance came with four young body builders to lift her from the recliner to the gurney. Quinn had removed the dogs and held them outside so they wouldn't attack the men who would surely hurt Wendy. The four took the corners of the sheet beneath her and as they lifted her to the gurney a primal howl escaped from her that nearly brought everyone in the room to their knees. The four men broke out in sweat, not from the effort, but from the emotion. I have never heard before or after a howl of pain that came from so deep within a soul. As they loaded her in the back of the ambulance, I looked between the seats to see them inserting an IV for pain. I rode in the front of the ambulance with the driver. Brad came behind in the car. At first the siren was frightening. I texted Gib and Kelly and they instantly started praying. Oddly. I could sense their prayers and peace swept over me. As the cars along the route pulled to the side to stop, I silently thanked them for protecting my baby in the back. It was humbling to see their respect for the flashing lights and siren. Sure, they were obeying the law, but I saw it as God clearing the path before us.

Once they settled her on the examining table the ER doctor quietly asked Wendy what she wanted from this visit. She actually smiled as she replied, "Find out what is hurting so bad and fix me." He laughed and said that was his plan. Tests, transfer to a room (with a small cot-like sofa for me) and pain meds allowed us a bit of comfort while we waited for the orthopedic surgeon. Casually he described the culprit. Her femur was broken about two inches below the hip and the doctor said, "it is just flopping around in there and no wonder it hurts so much." Brad got a kick out of his casual description. Surgery was scheduled for the next day (her birthday) and they would insert a rod from hip to knee and that would stabilize her and stop the horrible pain. We didn't know the time yet, and she had no idea her Daddy was already planning to fly in and surprise her for her birthday.

Everyone left her room for the night. They doped Wendy, and she drifted off into a deep sleep. In the dark, I took a trip down memory lane. It was 45 years ago when Wendy came into this world struggling to survive. My blood had been destroying hers, so they had delivered her a month early. After a fitful week she had fought her way through two close calls at exchanging her entire blood and showed the world she was a fighter. Many years ago, I had been in a spiritual battle with God for control of my kids. They were my greatest treasures and finally I had relinquished them to Him. I am not sure how you give back someone that already and forever belongs to God, but I released my power over them to their Creator. My fear had been that He would send them across the world as missionaries, and I had struggled with letting them go. Instead, He had led me down the most beautiful path of parenthood and taught me unconditional love, and when I wavered, He had always been there. I remembered the red shoes, the shaking legs on gymnastic balance beams, the strong will, the laughter that erupted from her sometimes inappropriately but always contagious. I recalled watching her be baptized after she accepted Christ. I reminisced about the life-long friends and our memories with them as she wormed her way into their hearts. I thought of her search for a "group" to belong to in high school, and her finding solace in Brad and finally the battle of the last four years.

Although I would never wish the pain my girls experienced on anyone else, or the deep sobs I felt when one of them cried out in agony, I can say from the depth of my being, that He had brought me joy and peace throughout the journey. That so outweighed the fear and pain. I thanked Him from the very depths of my soul.

Tomorrow, I knew Wendy would undergo surgery to stabilize her, not to cure her. She faced weeks or months of the unknown ahead as this was all new territory for all of us. The cancer was in the bone, eating away at her strength. Yet, He was here giving us peace.

I thought about the heroes that lived right in front of me. I had heard the definition of a hero is an ordinary person doing extraordinary things. Each of my three kids fit that description. They had not done it alone. They had all relied on Jesus and lived with a personal and loving relationship with Him. My son was a strong man of God. Beside me, Gib had never wanted to be a caregiver but had risen to the occasion with strength and love. He was a rock and steady influence on all of us and he prayed many times a day for a miracle for each daughter. Their downward spiral never quieted his plea to God. I couldn't imagine life without his hand to hold. Yes, God had replaced the dreaded ABCD's with a new set. I was Assured, Blessed, Confident and Dependent on Him. I closed my eyes and drifted into sleep knowing He was in the room with us.

Wendy's birthday burst on the scene with balloons all around her hospital room. As we waited for the surgery, Brad and I knew Brad's father was at the airport picking up Gib. Time passed when they should have arrived, and they didn't show up. Frustrated, I called, and Gib admitted they were lost and would be there in 15 minutes. The orderlies came early to take Wendy to surgery, and I took them out into the hall and explained they couldn't have her yet. They agreed she needed her dad for her birthday. Finally, I spotted him walking down the hallway toward the room. I swept back into her room and announced, "I didn't know what to get you for your birthday so I ordered the only thing I could think of. Are you ready for your present?" She nodded and I stepped into the hall and ushered Gib inside. She began to cry, and they hugged and hugged.

As we took her down the elevator to surgery, Gib and Brad went into the holding area to wait with her while Brad's dad, Jerry, and I went to the waiting room. An emergency was ushered into the OR ahead of her, so they ended up having two hours to visit before she went into surgery. How she loved her surprise birthday gift!

Surgery went well, but afterwards Wendy was unwilling to try to stand. The therapist warned that if she didn't get up now, she might remain bedridden. Still, she refused to try. So, a couple of days later we had Wendy transferred home by ambulance. Hospice had replaced the recliner with a hospital bed and Wendy was set right in the center of the hubbub of the home. Everyone was thrilled to see her smiling and the horrible pain replaced with a bearable level of discomfort. Brad and I would take turns sleeping in their recliner next to her bed so she wouldn't be alone.

A day later, Brad felt confident that with his mom to help, and the hospice helpers, they could manage Wendy. So, Gib and I took off to return to Minnesota so I could have my eye shot, catch up with Karissa's home schooling, and have an open house for Ashley. Wendy was safe for now and we needed to turn our thoughts toward Teri and her family.

INDEPENDENCE DAY: FREEDOM

CHAPTER 22

A few days before we returned home, Teri had had a rough procedure where they put a tube into her lung and sucked stuff out. As she recovered, her dear friend, Debi, had flown in from California and visited her in the hospital. She had braided Teri's hair and lifted her spirit. Then, a few days later we finally got some good news. Teri went to Mayo for a heart check, and all was well. She was starting her long road to recovery. The tubes, IV's and interruptions were gone, and tiny as she was, she was ready to begin to rebuild. Again, hope reared a tiny head and we all wanted to cheer, "Go, Teri, Go!"

Mid-week Teri was back in the hospital to have a feeding tube inserted so they could get nutrition into her. They had used anesthesia to insert it. Soon, they had been unable to awaken her and had called a "code blue" and people had rushed in to work on her. Gib and Guy stood by and waited for the medicine to counteract the anesthesia. This was supposed to be an out-patient day surgery and it suddenly turned into an overnight stay to watch her closely. Gib and Guy needed to take lessons on how to feed her through the tube, cleanse it etc. A new chapter was beginning for Teri.

Meanwhile, my friend, Leann took me for my eye shot. Later that day I spent time with Karissa doing schoolwork. Then, I talked with Kelly and discovered the party was coming together for Saturday. An army had descended on the house, power washing, bush trimming, flower planting, and daily the mail came bearing gift cards to restaurants where we could bring home meals. I had eight appointments to cram into five days as I ran from one to another: dentist, doctor, hair, nails etc., and only lists and notes kept me aware of where I was to be. Teri remained in the hospital so visits there were shoved between other things. It took energy to even smile. As the day of the open house approached, it became obvious Teri wouldn't be able to attend the party. She was devastated and tried to act nonchalant to cover her disappointment.

Saturday dawned with bright sunlight and the army of workers showed up again with food, energy, and organization. With Kelly in charge, the decorations went up and I took pictures of everything and headed to the hospital to share it all with Teri. I climbed into her bed, and we scrolled through the pictures and discussed each decoration, display of Ashley's dance and artwork, and even the food being served. I included Teri the best I could even though she was unable to physically attend.

As I drove home, I kept thanking God for his army. He always provided. As I turned into my drive, I saw all the cars lining the street. People had turned out to show Ashley and all of us their support. Then, I spotted the out-of-state tag. Norm and Debi had made it. She would be inside waiting to give me the longest, strongest, and sweetest hug imaginable. What joy danced in my heart. I didn't need the rain today to remind me that God was here, and He had sent His angels. The workers chased me from my own kitchen, and I became a visitor to the party. The hugs, love, encouragement, joy, and concern were tangible in the air as I made rounds of so many friends. Some had driven long distances to be there, and we were so very thankful. Ashley felt like a queen as everyone showed their interest in her plans for the future and a close friend swept room to room taking pictures, we could share with Teri later. The open house was a huge success thanks to Kelly, dear friends, God's army in our Sunday School Class, and life-long friends that took over the kitchen. Finally, almost all were gone when Guy came to say the hospital called to say they had moved Teri to another room. Quickly, the five of us piled into the car to go see her and report the day's events.

We didn't find Teri in a regular room. Instead, she was back in the ICU. How could she make such a sudden turn? She had seemed fine when I left her before the party. The staff shared that she had been found unresponsive and they had done chest compressions. She responded, they stopped the feeding tube, inserted a breathing tube. and moved her to the ICU. Now she was on a ventilator. What a set-back! She had struggled so hard to start healing and building up her strength. It was deflating. I knew then there is no way I would be able to leave to go back to Wendy's tomorrow.

A quick call to Brad reassured me he and his parents were troopers and they could hold down the fort until I felt I could return. Odd how I felt peace. I sensed that God had sent His angels to be with Teri and with Wendy. I sensed angels were stroking their hair and crooning to them. God was not distant or ignoring any of us. He was responsive and touched us as we waited.

Two days passed and Teri gained a little strength. She sat in a chair with a nose tube, and our prayer was that she could get enough oxygen to sustain her. She was still in the ICU but doing better, so it was time for us to leave and drive to Wendy's. Teri took our exit well and reminded me she had her purple glass angel to remind her I was there in spirit.

Six hours later, we arrived in Illinois to find Wendy moving very little in the bed. The next day the physical therapist would come, and we would see the extent of her ability to move. Her pain level was better, but we didn't know what to expect from her. She had lost most feeling in her legs. However, the lower pelvic area and lower back were very painful. Her resting pain level was about a two, but when we moved her, it shot to a ten. Her mood was usually positive, and she loved having company. Yet again, we waited to see life played out before us.

Usually July means sunshine, but a gentle rain woke me as I heard it drain along the window. As I lay in the quiet basement bedroom at Wendy's, I began to pray and draw near my God. With Teri in ICU and Wendy in hospice, I thought about Teri's statement that if they would both die, she would hold Wendy's hand as they entered heaven. I had told Wendy a few days before what Teri had said and she had smiled and nodded. It was obvious that had brought comfort to her. However, I had still been hopeful one of them would survive. Now, was that even a remote possibility? I seemed unable to pray, just wait. In the silence I heard the patter of the raindrops against the window. As I listened, they seem to have a rhythm. Pat, pat, pause. Pat, pat. Pause. Pat, pat pause. They seemed to speak. "I am here, I am here, I am here."

Suddenly, I was transported back to that day in Nairobi, Kenya, when I watched Teri dance in the rain. I had feared gunshots only to discover God's blessing showering down on the kids and staff. That's when I saw Teri dancing and twirling in the rain. The joy, the cleansing, the deep contentment that I saw in Teri's face that day began to creep slowly into my being. If my two little pink bunnies could do this, I certainly could. Now, as the rain got louder, and my strength got stronger. I sucked in and inflated my chest and held my breath. Tears trickled down my face and fell on the pillow. "God, you are so Good. No matter what the circumstances You are here with me. Thank you for sending Jesus to redeem me and bring me back into a relationship with You. Thank you for having the Holy Spirit with me always. Thank you for the 40+ years with each girl. Thank you for all the memories. Oh, God you ARE so good." I turned my eyes to the window and saw the rain had suddenly stopped. Sunshine flooded the room. He had touched me. He was telling me no matter how hard it rained, I needed to get up and dance. Dance in the rain or dance in the sunshine, but dance.

I rolled over in bed and faced Gib. He sensed my presence and slowly opened his eyes, "What's up?" he asked.

"Our God is so good," I replied.

He reached out and pulled me into his safe arms and we had nothing more to say. We just hung onto each other and rested in God. It was the weekend, so Brad was sleeping in the recliner next to Wendy. Gib or I would take turns on weeknights when Brad was working the next day. It was comfortable, she felt our presence, and we were confident we would be near if she needed us. Upstairs Wendy wasn't alone. Teri was in constant care, and for a tiny moment all was okay. I felt free. I felt blessed.

July 4th was Independence Day for our great nation. It was always an opportunity to spend time with family and friends and think about the sacrifice others had made for our freedom. This 4th of July proved to be a little Independence Day for Teri. She was moved from Intensive Care to Critical care and gained a little weight on the feeding tube. She would have another swallowing test tomorrow to see how much food she was still aspirating. Hope reared up again as they tried to get her eating under control. We were able to talk to her on the phone and discovered the doctors were discussing sending her home again and Gib would have to leave to be there. When? How soon? I was taking such delight in having him with me.

Wendy, however, wasn't improving. It became more and more difficult to turn her in the bed. The tumor growing under the left arm was putting so much pressure on the open hole under her arm that Brad could hardly pack the gauze inside. If we turned her to the left, she screamed with pain and began trembling. The pain wasn't touched by the morphine and any other meds they tried. Meanwhile, the tumor on her right side pushed against the lungs and when we tried to turn her on her right side to bathe her back, she couldn't breathe and gasped for air and would begin to turn blue. We all knew if we didn't rotate her that bed sores would appear on her back so we would force a move, but she would beg us not to move her. If we started to turn her either way she would sob, and her blood pressure would skyrocket. It was a no-win situation.

A few days earlier we learned our dear friends, Pastor Bob's son was in dire situation. He had overdosed and was in a coma. We prayed for Bob, Donna, and Anthony over and over throughout the days. Teri, Wendy, Anthony; Teri, Wendy, Anthony. Then, we got the call. Anthony had passed on. We were heartbroken at the waste of this young and vital man.

That same day, our dear friend, Joan, was going to visit Teri in the hospital and we were so thankful she would have a visitor. Of course, Guy went every day after work, taking the girls sometimes, but Teri was spending countless hours alone in her hospital room.

Wednesday morning Wendy woke Brad at 5:30 AM struggling to breath. She didn't call for him. He sensed her struggle and came awake. At 6:15 he came downstairs and quickly said, "I can't wake her, and she is struggling to breathe." He turned and practically ran back up the stairs. I quickly threw clothes on and followed. Her catheter wasn't flowing and that was putting strain on her. Her pain was off- the- chart and it showed as she rocked her head back and forth. We called the nurse, and she was there by seven. The pain caused by the plugged catheter had taken an enormous toll on her body. Soon, the nurse told us to call Casey home from work. Was this the end? I was thankful Gib was there and we gathered, prayed, stroked her hair, cried, whispered encouragement and slowly, over hours, her heart slowed down, and her blood pressure began to drop. We had a parade of people through the house; nurses, social worker, and the chaplain all came, and each had a unique gift they brought to us as we waited. It was so obvious God was orchestrating their appearances. By afternoon they began to back off on the morphine and brought her to a higher level of consciousness. She opened her eyes and then smiled at all of us. "Welcome back," I managed. She smiled and looked from face to face that surrounded her bed. She appeared content and no worse for the crisis she had survived.

Later that day, Wendy and Brad's pastor came by and as he stepped up to the side of the bed he went right to the point. "Wendy, are you ready to meet God?" She nodded, then quickly changed and shook her head. "Wendy, when God is ready for you, you will be ready." He then began to describe heaven as best he could. She closed her eyes and listened intently. Then, a smile spread across her face and all pain left her brows. She was in complete peace. He prayed for her and left. A little while later the chaplain returned. Sitting by her head, he began to softly sing "Amazing Grace" and to our surprise Wendy began singing with him in a perfectly clear and astounding voice. They sounded like angels. God's grace spread through the room, and we all knew we had dodged the bullet.

Gib called Guy to check in and discovered that Teri was coming home from the hospital tomorrow. Gib went to the computer to make plane reservations. I followed. "No, you can't go. You must stay. She almost died. I need you. You can't leave. She might die tomorrow." He kept typing. "Are you listening to me?" I demanded.

Slowly he turned and quietly said, "I have no choice, Tina. I have to go. It is my responsibility to be there to take care of her. I don't want to leave you or Wendy, but I have to go."

Desperation overwhelmed me. How could he desert me now? How could he leave Wendy? Why was he doing this? No logic ruled me. For the first time I felt I couldn't, I just couldn't do this without him. Where could I run? Where could I get away from all of this? Where are you now, God?

Unable to think or handle what was before me, I ran upstairs and began cleaning. I was scrubbing areas already clean. I rubbed and rubbed hoping that would rub this all away. Surely, he would reconsider. Surely something else would happen to fix this. He came upstairs and quietly said I would have to take him to the airport tomorrow morning. How could I take a deserter away? How could he expect me to do that? My hysteria was just under the surface. I found Brad and asked him to call his dad to see if he could take Gib to the airport. I knew if I took him, I would become hysterical when he exited the car. It was set into motion. Gib would leave and Jerry would take him. Gib told Wendy matter-of-factly, and she had no problem with understanding he had to go. What was wrong with all these people? They all seemed accepting of Gib deserting. Never did it cross my mind that I was the one not thinking straight.

Wendy gained strength throughout the rest of that night and by morning was back to her new normal. Gib said goodbye and I behaved myself as he left with Jerry. I wasn't angry, just frustrated, and desperate for him to be at my side. They drove away and I prayed in desperation for God to give me strength. Once inside I busied myself with chores determined his departure wouldn't hurt so much. Later he called and said Guy was bringing Teri home and he was preparing supper. Once they arrived, Teri asked where the breathing equipment was that was supposed to delivered. A few phone calls showed the driver didn't have an order so couldn't bring anything. Since it was after working hours, nothing could be done. Gib and Guy told Teri they had to take her back to the hospital and she defiantly shouted, "No, I am not going back to the hospital no matter what." All the encouraging, cajoling, and demanding didn't move her. She was NOT going back to the hospital. So, Guy went home to get his necessities and took up residence in the adjoining bedroom. He would set his alarm and check on her every hour. She was hooked to her oxygen and was comfortable.

I was sleeping in the recliner by Wendy before dawn when my phone rang in the dark of the night.

"Where are you right now?" Gib asked.

"In the recliner by Wendy. Why?"

"Get up and get out of where she is," he whispered.

I looked up to see her steady breathing. She had not awakened at the phone call.

As I pushed the button on the electric recliner and waited for it to descend, I kept asking what was going on. He remained silent. Settled in the other room, I listened as he continued. "Teri is unconscious and unresponsive. We are in the Emergency room at the hospital, and, Tina, it doesn't look good."

My mind couldn't wrap around what he was saying. He continued, "Every hour Guy got up to check on her. At 2 o'clock she appeared fine and as he stepped into the hallway; she called his name. He heard a thud and ran back into the room to find her on the floor, unconscious. He called for me and I called 911 and started CPR while the operator prompted me. Guy watched and waited for the medics and directed them in. They arrived, took over, and worked on her quite a while before transferring her here to this hospital. Now, the doctors are running tests and we have called Shane and Kelly to pick up the girls and bring them to the hospital. Tina, it doesn't look good. She is hooked to machines now, and we are waiting to see what they find."

"I don't understand. She just came home from the hospital. They don't send you home unless you are ready to come home. I don't understand." A fog engulfed me.

He related the story of the no-show equipment and her insistence to stay home and still I was unable to grasp all that was happening. Finally, he said he would call as soon as the doctor came out and I hung up. Stunned, I sat still and began to cry. Suddenly, Brad burst in the room like a madman on his way to see Wendy. "Brad," I called" Wendy is okay. It's Teri."

He sat down beside me, and I related all I knew. He pulled me into his arms as I cried. When I leaned back, I saw Casey sitting in the chair silently watching. "What and how do we tell Wendy?" I asked.

Brad quickly called his pastor who was there in a matter of minutes. After hearing everything he offered his advice. "Let me get this straight," he said. "Teri is still alive at the moment and hooked to machines. Is that correct?" I only nodded. "Then, we tell Wendy one thing at a time. Wait a while and tell her more. You are not lying to her but giving her time to absorb what you are saying. Step- by- step will be easier than all of a sudden."

That made so much sense as Wendy was drifting in and out of sleep anyway with the high morphine level. Still, it was excruciating to tell her Teri was not responding. Tears slipped out of her eyes, and she went back to sleep. Did she understand or was she escaping?

Soon, Gib called again. The doctor had come out and told them that Teri was brain dead. He said he never told people things were 100 percent sure, but he had never seen anyone come back from where she was. Even if she continued to be "alive", she would not rise above this level. He suggested they turn off the machines. By then, three pastors, Gib, Guy, Shane, Kelly, Ashley, Karissa and Ashley's best friend were waiting. Gib had called to tell me they were taking her off the machines.

As soon as I could control myself, I went to tell Wendy they were going to remove Teri from machines. Again, tears flowed down her face, and she went to sleep. Oh, how I wished I could go to sleep. How I wanted to close my eyes and this all to disappear.

My phone pinged. Pastor Todd had simply written, "She gently slipped away to Heaven with no pain."

I experienced a strong release. Teri now had full independence. No more pain, no more lonely days and hours in the hospital alone, no more battles. She was free. No more tubes, no more struggles to breath, no more panic attacks, no shots, no surgeries. She was home - her real home with Jesus. Teri had her Independence Day. TERI WAS FREE!

Again, Brad allowed me to cry and cry until finally it was time to tell Wendy. This was the most difficult thing I had ever done. She was facing death herself; she couldn't travel with me to attend any service for Teri, she wouldn't be encouraged and loved on by others, and she would face this without her extended family and friends.

The next time she awoke I stood by her bed. I cleared my throat in preparation and she whispered, "She's gone, isn't she?" I nodded. No gentle tears crept out. Instead, a series of deep. deep sobs escaped her. I held her as best I could, and we cried together as Brad stood helpless on the other side of her bed. Once she finally quieted and slipped off to sleep, I sat down to make a plane reservation. Now, I was going to leave her.

Gib called again to relate the final moments and then asked if I wanted anything done before I got there. "Yes, oh yes. I want that room emptied of all the equipment and her meds and everything. I need it to look like a guest room or it will always be Teri's sick room to me." He agreed, and I gave him my time of arrival and we hung up. Once again by Wendy's bedside I told her I had to leave. "I know, Mom. I sure wish I could go with you." Her voice was quiet but unwavering.

"I know sweetheart. But you will be with me all the time, and I will be with you. Look at your glass angel and remember we are together in spirit all the time."

"I know, I just wish we could be bodily together." She barely whispered as she drifted into sleep.

After packing I made the rounds of the family for last hugs, reassuring each one I would be back as soon as I could. Ronnie and Jerry had come to be with Brad and Wendy. Jerry would take me to the airport. I went into Casey's room to say goodbye and as he wrapped his arms around me, we hung on to each other. I knew he was thinking his time was coming soon, and he hurt for me and for himself. We hung onto each other for a long time. Finally, we whispered encouraging words to each other, and I rose and left.

Lastly, I came to say goodbye to Wendy. Oddly, she seemed strong and vibrant. "I will be okay, Mom. Brad and Ronnie will take care of me. Hurry back as soon as you can." I couldn't stop the tears and leaned down and watched as my tears fell onto her face. She didn't wipe them away. Instead, she touched my face, and we said nothing. There was nothing to say. Words were useless. Only love passed between us.

Brad carried my suitcase out to his dad's car and reminded me that he and his mom could take care of Wendy. "Take as long as you need, Tina. We aren't going anywhere." Brad hugged his wonderful, big bear hug, and I climbed into the car to begin a dreaded trip home. On the way to the airport, I suddenly remembered that Wendy's best friend, Charie was arriving for the weekend. Wow! Had God ever orchestrated that! He knew the timing all along. Her trip had been planned for a while, yet now she was arriving just as I was leaving. Wendy would have support! Charie got into the car with Jerry, and I went inside to check in.

Once on the plane I thought about all the times I had stood by Teri's bed thinking she would die. I had known in my heart she would die before me, but never, never in my wildest thoughts did I think she would die without me at her side. After all we had been through together, and I wasn't even there! My pink bunny can no longer keep going. I finally understood why God had Gib leave me and go home the day before. He was supposed to be there. Now, for sure, I was going to lose both girls. Now, my nightmare was true. I was going home to bury daughter number one. Soon, how soon would I do this again? Ideas exploded in my brain faster than I could process them. How were Teri's girls? Was Wendy okay? Exhausted, I fell back in the seat and prayed. "God, I don't know why, but

I know you do, and I trust you. You are holy and sovereign, and you have been glorified in Teri's life. Now, may you be glorified in her death. She is in paradise with Jesus and in no pain. She can breathe without struggling. Thank you for giving her to us. Now, take my pain and pull me into your mighty arms."

As I entered our home, I approached her room. There was no sign of Teri there. A gentle presence hovered but no medicines, no machines, no objects that didn't belong. "How did you manage to get it clean so fast?" I asked as I turned to face Gib.

"God did it again," he replied. "The equipment company was here within an hour. and then the doorbell rang and there stood Joan and Mary. They had gone to the hospital to see Teri and were told she had died, so they came to see what they could do. I turned them loose on the bedroom and they tore the place apart and put it back together in a short time. They were fantastic. They worked hard and fast in love and were happy to have something they could do to help. God had sent them at the right time." It was so obvious in Gib's voice and demeanor that he had come to accept God's intervention as natural and expected.

My best friend, Debi drove down from Grand Forks to take over the household. She did grocery shopping, laundry, cooking, encouraging, taking me wherever I needed to go and stood beside me as I viewed Teri's dead body and said goodbye. Gib, Debi, and I held each other and cried, and I stroked Teri's hair. The pain was gone from her face. Teri was celebrating her Day of Independence with her Savior, and I rejoiced for her even though I hurt so deeply for myself.

Later, a group of us sat around the dining room table to plan her celebration of life. God raised up Ashley as a confident and knowledgeable lady. She knew songs and Bible verses her mother wanted included. Ashley wanted to design the program, and she suggested we all wear purple in Teri's honor. Then, she even volunteered to speak. It was decided that Pastor Bob would speak even though he had only buried his own son a few days before. Ashley and I would speak, Guy and Karissa would read scripture, we would ask Teri's college friend flying in and her heart doctor, Dr. Thatcher, to speak. Of course, Will had to come and do the music including her song, "Our God is Big Enough." Details were addressed and the program was pretty well set. As it all was coming together, I got an email from Joan telling of her visit with Teri in the hospital just three days earlier. As Teri had related to Joan three things God had taught her, I read in astonishment at what Teri had shared with her. We quickly decided to include a bookmark in the program telling of Joan's encounter with her.

Meanwhile, Wendy was doing okay physically, but being so far from her family was taking its toll on her. I got a text saying simply "I need my Mommy." Broken, I called Brad. He reassured me she was fine just at a low moment. He was constantly with her and although she desperately wanted to be in Minnesota she was doing okay. "Don't worry about her, Tina. Just let this be Teri's time," All I could do was press on.

The service was on a Saturday. Relatives and friends flew in, drove, or got there however they could. We set up a table for guests to write memories and everyone was including something into a future book. Teri's impact on so many people was evident. The church was filled, the love overflowed, and memories were shared. It seems odd to say a funeral was beautiful, but this was truly a celebration of her life. You could feel the love in the air, the pain was there, but the love was stronger. The hope and assurance that we would see her again soon was the foundation of everything. We all mourned and rejoiced together.

After the ceremony and all had gone, the family and closest friends gathered in Shane and Kelly's backyard. We opened the cards, told stories, laughed at Teri's antics, and encouraged one another. There were few tears. Teri's death was expected. We just had no idea of the timing. No matter, it was too soon. She left a gaping hole in the family, but each person there was a better person because of Teri's influence on their lives. We truly celebrated her life.

The next morning, as suddenly as it all it started, it was suddenly over. People began leaving, planes took loved ones away, cars left, and we were left to face reality. Teri was gone. Those years of fighting were over. She had true victory over death, and we were left behind to hurt. Now, each of us had to come to terms with her departure.

Now, my thoughts turned to Illinois. I must return. Wendy needs me. I began packing my clothes and I noticed Gib got a suitcase and started packing also. Confused, I asked, "Where are you going?" Without even pausing he replied, "With you. There is nothing holding me here now."

I was stunned. We had been apart so much I didn't realize he could go with me now. It seemed so surreal. "How long can you go for?" I asked uncomprehending. "As long as you can." He replied. Wow! That changed everything. Wow! He could be with me, with Wendy, with the boys and Brad. We were ready to make our next journey. All attention was now focused on Wendy and her family.

Teri Coleman Glirbas

Teri's Memorial Picture

IN LOVING MEMORY

Teri Coleman
Glirbas

"Heaven is close today."

"DIVINE SUFFERING" BY ASHLEY GLIRBAS

Teri's Memorial cover by her daughter Ashley

Artist's Reflection

No one can deny that my mama lived her life on earth deeply connected to her Savior, Jesus Christ. Reflecting on her life, I just had to draw a golden tear drop aflame, to represent the power and eternal blaze of the Holy Spirit in her life. She was flooded with Godly providence, grace, joy, and gratitude. She clung to this beauty even in the midst of her constant physical, emotional, and spiritual suffering, as portrayed by the purple puddles and the purple area encompassing the tear drop. Still, in every season and circumstance, Mama could see beyond a "little yellow blob" perspective, or an earthly perspective. At the same time, she understood how God was working at the present time.

For my eighteenth birthday, Mama gave me a beautiful card. On the front, there was a purple flower, an orchid . . . an exotic, rare, and delicate orchid, to be specific. She wrote this beautiful analogy about my being this flower, in need of special care in the Green House, or the Holy Spirit's care. Mama had watched me strive to be strong, but she had experienced that Godly strength was found in weakness and dependence on God's grace (2 Corinthians 12:9-10). I am sure she felt like an orchid too. She was fragile for sure, at least on the outside . . . but she was by no means weak on the inside.

Mama's death held a strange aura. There was peace, hope, joy, and gratitude. The Holy Spirit's presence was tangible. Our family likes to say that she entered Heaven with "a sonic boom." I can not really put it accurately in words. However, my dear sister in Christ, Karly, summed up those last few events at the hospital with "Heaven is close today." I cannot begin to explain all that God has accomplished through her life and death, but I do know that her playful smile, thoughtful gifts, encouraging words, and affectionate hugs will be remembered with awe and delight.

Ashley Glirbas

Ashley's reflections on the cover she drew

TERI'S EULOGY

TINA COLEMAN, MOTHER, AND FRIEND

Greetings, I am Teri's mom, Tina. I thank you for being here.

November 1967, Gib and I took out a loan from God in the form of a tiny baby. July 8, 2016, that loan came due, and Teri slipped from our presence into the presence of God. During those 48 years, we experienced some of the greatest joy and deepest valleys of our life. Through the years, people have asked me what it was like to parent a child with an acute and then chronic illness. Although I would never wish Teri's trials on any person or parent, my answer is simply one word- <u>Blessed</u>. Allow me to take you on our journey.

Teri taught me that the most important thing in life was <u>relationships.</u> Teri was physically beautifully. Many thought she looked like the baby on the Gerber baby food bottles. She was full of life, and from the moment her brother, Shane, got her to laugh, till the end of her life, she was filled with laughter just searching for an appropriate (or inappropriate) way to escape. But it didn't take long for me to realize that she was the teacher, and I was the student. Early on, I saw how spiritually beautiful she was. Quickly, she began a life-long knack of worming her way into people's hearts as is evident with all of you in this room. I watched with fascination as she forced a response from everyone she came in contact with. Whether it was a childhood friend, school chum, doctor, or adult relationship, she treasured everyone God put into her life. She demanded much from all of us, but never more than what she gave back.

The second major lesson she taught me was a <u>deep, unshakeable faith.</u> When she was diagnosed with cancer at 7, she had the faith of a child. As we began our daily trips to the U of MN for radiation, she stopped at a bench and beckoned me to join her. "I want to pray, Mommy." As I sat next to her, she asked God to do her a favor. "Please don't let in snow until I finish my radiation." Now, she had me nervous. We wouldn't finish until the first part of November and in MN that is "iffy" for snow. Suddenly, one day, she began throwing up and the doctor cut her treatments in half. That would extend us to at least mid-December. How was God going to honor the prayer of a little girl? One Saturday in early December it began to snow. Fearfully, I woke her and showed her the snow. Her reaction? "That's okay, Mommy. I don't have treatment today. God won't let it snow on my treatment days." No matter what I offered as "maybe", she wasn't buying any of it. You've guessed by now. Treatment day- no snow. On the final day of treatment, she again beckoned me to the bench to pray. In utter faith she prayed, "Thank you God for keeping the snow away from us on treatment days. You can let it snow now." We opened our eyes to see big, beautiful snowflakes landing on our hair. "See, Mommy. Isn't God good?" As I thanked God for honoring the prayer of a child, tears rolled down my cheeks and I had my initiation into complete faith. Through the years incident after incident repeated the lesson learned that day.

The third thing Teri taught me was never to assume where the other person was coming from. When she was 10 and shooting her insulin into her teddy bear, I assumed she was trying to kill herself. My assumptions were wrong. Actually, she only wanted to be "normal," and normal people didn't take shots every day. Now don't get me wrong Teri was "normal". She slammed doors when angry. She demanded so much of a person's time and energy. She turned everything into a competition. She was hurt deeply by betrayals, and she was stubborn. Boy was she stubborn!! Yet, I often was reminded to ask why she was angry or why she was hurt and not to make assumptions.

The last and most important thing I learned from Teri was living out Psalm 37:4 "Delight yourself in the Lord, and He will give you the desires of your heart." In spite of her health, Teri got the desires of her heart. Teri married the "Guy" of her dreams, raised two fantastic daughters, went to Africa 5 times, made memories with all of us, and taught us all about deep love of laughter. Her greatest desire was to impact others, especially her daughters. I'd say she accomplished that.

Some define Teri by her medical problems which were many. From cancer twice to diabetes, congestive heart failure, 2 by-pass surgeries, difficulty in breathing and processing food she suffered. But don't make the mistake of feeling sorry for her. Those medical problems only drove her <u>right into the arms of her Savior,</u> and she found shelter there. As you see on the bookmark in your program, her life-long surrogate Aunt Joan shares that in her last days of suffering she was still soaking up the joy of the Lord. In the words of Galen Call, one pastor who influenced her immensely, "Teri is free from the weakness, pain, and decline that have 'shadowed' her life. I say 'shadowed' because the light in her was so strong, and now it has burst out in all its glory."

Teri trusted, believed, and lived out her faith. I can't wait to see her again in glory.

TERI'S EULOGY

ASHLEY GLIRBAS, 19 YEAR OLD DAUGHTER

Last week on July eight at 9:52 AM, Mama's worldly heart beat for the last time. Here is what I have to say about her.

People always wonder, "Why does God let bad things happen to good people?" but my mama taught me to ask the question, "Why does God let good things happen to bad people?" Throughout her entire time on earth, my mama strove to show me the grace of God. It was really hard for her to be in bed most of the time, and to not be able to go places with us, cook, or clean. But she was always ready to pray with us and battle the demons plaguing our lives. She talked with us about the Bible and theme from the various books. She desperately wanted us to be close and educated with an understanding of who God is and how to effectively love the world or how to be missionaries. She laughed with us till we cried, but at the end of the day, everything was about Jesus. Although she loved to have fun, Godliness superseded happiness and comfort.

My Mom continually chose courage, and her spiritual gift was faith. She was willing to go to Kenya when she did not know what to expect and was worried about her health . . . but she went 5 times. She fought to stay alive for my family when she longed to be rid of suffering and see the face of Jesus. During her last months on earth, she kept talking about how excited she was over what God had been doing in my life and my approaching adventures in college. She may have jokingly complained about silly little details sometimes, as we all have done. But I never heard her once blame God about her pain and limitations. She could not walk, stand, or sit well for more than about five minutes towards the end of her time with us.

That was on top of all the other issues she faced. She was never bitter, even though she faced two rounds of Hodgkin's, type one diabetes, two heart by-pass surgeries, other minor surgeries, countless bouts with pneumonia, and constant pain all over her body. She appreciated certain types of pain, which distracted her from other kinds of pain. Still, she knew she was in a battle, and Satan was the real enemy, not her health issues. Without her, I do not think I would have had the courage to pursue the arts, especially dance.

I do not have any reason to be angry and bitter towards God, concerning her death. When her physical heart was failing her, she prayed to be able to watch me grow up, and God granted her that grace. Mama always saw me as God's child and not hers and lived out that commitment through how she raised me. Her death is only a reminder to me that God heeded her prayer, and that He has hated to see her suffer . . . and He feels the same way about me! I can only start to imagine how vigorously she is sprinting, leaping, dancing, and singing with Jesus right now! I hope that I will be faithful to pass on the legacy that she has left for younger generations to see . . . a legacy drenched in the light of God's grace and majesty.

I have felt a lot of strange, puzzling emotions piercing through me during this season. Mainly joy and grief. Why am I joyful? Simply because God was always bigger than the failing of her flesh, both physically and spiritually. I rejoice because my mama is stronger than she has ever been before, being totally immersed in the essence of love. I remember a woman of God who, unlike me, worshipped with all her might and was not preoccupied with whether or not she looked like a fool; this affected the little decisions of her everyday life, but especially her worship of God Almighty. Her story had radically impacted lives, and I know it will continue to show people the wonders of Jehovah Rapha (the Lord that heals) and how He has neither left my mom nor the rest of my family alone.

I ache inside with a chasm left behind, but it is the shape of my mom, which casts a powerful silhouette of love! She served me as one of my best friends, and one of the few people who truly understood my heart, thought process, and personality. She taught me that I was not a foolish "cry baby", but a passionate disciple designed for God's perfect plan. Jesus is faithful, and I know He is taking such good care of her! Thank you, Blessed Trinity, for loving my mother! Now help us to celebrate her with the same joy and gratitude by which she had run to You in the shadow and reflections of Your grace . . .even in the storms.

TERI'S EULOGY

DR. JACKSON THATCHER, TERI'S CARDIOLOGIST, AND FRIEND

Teri is someone important to everyone here. Mother, wife, daughter family and friend.

Though for me Teri was first and foremost a patient. In sharing her life adventure with me, Teri and I became friends. So, I am here today like all of you, because I love Teri, and she is so much more than a patient and friend. She had the faith of Daniel as I walked with her so many times, through the Vallely of the Shadow. No One spoke as loud as Teri when she got that quiet, deliberate, yet so gentle speech of hers revved up. From the get- go she wanted me to be objective and completely honest with her about her care. She would present her objectives and then provide me with direction we would go. So, I would help her get through a few little things.

Like her Mission Work in Africa, which was such a great part of her life, or having daughter, and the adopting a second wonderful baby girl. And somehow, through God's Grace it all turned out more than OK, Again, and again.

But, when I visited Teri in the hospital this January, I knew her condition was so much worse than anything she had faced over the years. We spoke about her limited options, and her choice of attempting valve replacement to marshal on a bit longer, even while the rest of her heart was failing from the very radiation therapy which had cured her cancer a second time and bought her the rest of her wonderful life.

Of course, Teri hoped for just a little more time, but not for herself. Rather for her family, Guy and especially the girls. We spoke about our gratitude for each other's friendship over so many years and then very quietly she asked me if I would come here, today, to be with her at her funeral. And in her heart, she knew I would. So, yes, my dear friend, Teri . . .I am here . . .We are all here with you today In love And at least a little faith Made so much greater by knowing you.

TERI'S EULOGY

JOY BURKE, TERI'S COLLEGE FRIEND

I started penning these on the plane, addressing Teri, as I made my way here.

So, I have been to Minnesota 4 times before, all for happy reasons. The year before you were married, you and Guy showed me all around Minneapolis/St Paul. The year you were married, for your fortieth birthday celebration, and for our girls' weekend at your parents' home in 2012. This is my fifth time here, the first without you. You are here in spirit, loving on through Guy and your girls' lives, as well as your families' memories.

Kelly said there will be a memory book, to write out memories of you. How do I sum up a lifetime of memories? For 30 years we have been part of each other's lives. There were time and seasons where we went a few months without talking, but we always counted on each other as a true lifelong friend. Someone we could call at any time and when life got rough. We shared our greatest joys with each other. Your two greatest joys are your daughters. You are a tough, loving, level- headed Mama Bear who fiercely loves her cubs.

A unique bond we had was our childhood cancers and our families. Both were families of faith that believed God would heal their children. When I was in the hospital, my mom read these words as they leapt off the page from John 11:4 ". . .This illness does not lead to death, it is for the glory of God, so that the Son of God may be glorified through it."

Teri, even in your death, your life is testament to these words. Through your life, your illness, your triumphs, and setbacks, God has been glorified. And as believers we know you are fully healed.

TERI'S LEGACY

JOAN MURPHY, FOREVER FRIEND

Last Tuesday, I knew I was going to Methodist Hospital to see Teri. I knew it the day before. It was decided and I knew nothing was going to get in the way of this appointment. I'm not usually that decisive but this time there was not a question where I would be on Tuesday morning, July 5, 2016.

When I entered the room, Teri was lying curled on the bed wearing sweats and there were fuzzy socks on her feet. I remember thinking how dark she was around her eyes, how frail she looked, and how beautiful her hair was! All this I took in my first few seconds after entering the room.

Teri took her pillow, tossed it at the foot of the bed, laid her head on it, and looked straight at me. We began a conversation I will never forget. She explained how she was feeling a little stronger since the feeding tube was introduced and how Guy, Ashley, and Karissa had brought her a strawberry shake for Fourth of July. This memory made her smile. With a soft, sometimes raspy voice, she talked about the possibility of being released from the hospital either Thursday or Friday and I could tell she was counting on that.

After a discussion on her daughter Ashley's open house, we wandered into my asking Teri how she passes the many hours in the hospital – did she read? watch TV? etc. She said reading takes too much energy and she usually just falls asleep. What came next really got my attention.

"Mostly," she said, "I have done a lot of thinking in the last seven months in the hospital and God has been teaching me." I was intrigued by this and so I asked, "Teri, what has God been teaching you?" I somehow knew the answer was going to be very important. At this, she paused and said, "Wait a minute- I want to get this right." She was deep in thought, and I wondered if Teri was still on track with my question.

Just then her pointer finger went up and she said in that raspy halting little voice; "Number one- Every Day is a Gift." I knew this was important because this was a person who had learned the true value of a "day". (I am listening hard because I have no paper to write on and must remember this.) She paused, gathering thoughts and strength.

"Number two - It is a Privilege to Suffer With Him." At this point I knew I had been taken to a place I had never been before. Suffering is something I run from. But I listened to more because I could see there was more, and I was amazed at what came next.

"Number three – We must Thank Him for the Privilege of Suffering With Him." My only thought was, "This is super-natural wisdom." I felt so very honored to be there. These three concepts are likely in the Bible somewhere, but it was the way Teri succinctly said it without frills or commentary that pierced my soul. But these were not "concepts" to her. This was life to her, lived, experienced, real.

I was reeling with this encounter with God through Teri and wanted more, but just then the Physical Therapist Assistant came to take her for PT, though I wondered what on earth he could do with this tiny, frail woman with the lovely hair – so frail.

I hugged Teri, told her I loved her and left (my 15 minutes were up and that's enough when visiting a very sick person) but as I walked away, I knew something wonderful had just happened to me. God was teaching me through Teri, and I needed to remember every word. To the best of my ability, I have tried to preserve those 15 minutes, word for word for you.

Teri has been somewhere I have not been; the School of Suffering. How I wish I had a great talent for writing! I want so much to give away what Teri gave to me. But I have not been there. She has!

But praise the Almighty God of Love - no more!! No more suffering, pain, longing to be home with family. Teri, you are free, and you are HOME!

MY HEARTFELT ETERNAL THANKS, TERI!
Your Forever Friend, Joan

CERTAINTY AND THE UNKNOWN
CHAPTER 23

Your mind and your heart don't always stay in sync. One often rushes ahead of the other and chaos results. Emotions can capture your heart and your mind and lead you to the threshold of uncertainty. Suddenly, we were in the car driving back to Wendy's on our way to another conclusion. I had the odd sensation I could reach out into space and capture emotions. They seemed so tangible. I felt like I was looking through a kaleidoscope of emotions; ever changing, coming forward and disappearing, altering when you least expected it. Grief - demanded my attention but had to be delayed. In its place was an anticipatory grief, as I knew what lie ahead. Relief - that some pain was over for one daughter, only brought anguish over what we would find when we arrived. Comfort - that Gib and I were finally together. Gratefulness - crowded in as I thought of all the love, support, and warmth that God had showered on us through so many people. Sadness - swept through the car as I felt I had deserted Guy, Ashley, and Karissa. Tension - always tension kept draining my strength to face the future. Peace - knowing God was there in the car and embarking on the rest of the journey with us. We played an audio book to distract, but I have no idea what it was about. The six hours passed with no talking, just listening, and thinking.

Once we arrived, we woke Wendy just long enough for her to see we had returned. She smiled, eased the tension from her forehead, and slipped back into sleep for the night. Brad slept on the recliner while Gib and I fell silently into our bed in the basement bedroom.

Morning came and I anticipated describing events of the past week to Wendy. She quietly said she didn't want to hear any of it. However, I insisted sharing some things about the funeral. Slowly, it began to comfort her as she felt a part of the family. I explained that Teri was cremated and wanted her ashes spread over the ocean especially toward Africa. I shared the program, pictures, songs, and verses with her, until she quietly said she needed to sleep and slipped away for a few hours.

Brad brought us up to date on Wendy and how she was sleeping around the clock. We shared all the news from the funeral. A few hours later Wendy awoke, and I felt I needed to ask some hard questions. Was she ready to talk about her own future service? I began by asking what color of fabric she wanted in her coffin. Her answer surprised me. "I don't want a coffin. I want to be cremated and my ashes sprinkled over your lake where we spent so many vacations with the boys." She had never expressed this before, so I instantly went to find Brad. After hearing this, he went to inquire if that was really what she wanted. I left them alone and they talked quite a while, and Brad returned to say the decision was reached that she would be cremated as she asked. After that, the rest of the questions were easy. Over the next few days, we discussed Bible verses. Like many people, she found great comfort in the 23rd Psalm. Then, she said, "Mom, there's a series of verses somewhere about the trumpet sounding and the dead arising and Death not having victory. I want that one." I quickly found the passage in I Corinthians and read it to her and she nodded her head and smiled. "That's it," she said. "Death won't have victory over me because I will be with Jesus." Then, barely above a whisper she spoke "Teri will be waiting for me. She will hold my hand." She closed her eyes, smiled, and drifted into sleep while I wept beside her. Yes, Teri would be waiting. They would be together. That was so comforting to her. Yet it meant I would be without both of them. I longed to make the journey with her.

Days slipped by, and she spent more time asleep than awake. She struggled to stay awake long enough to eat a little. Her resting heart rate was climbing and would skyrocket when we moved her. Her systems appeared to be slowing down to a crawl. Her dear friend, Megan and her mom, Mary Ann, flew down from Minnesota to spend a day. Wendy tried to stay awake, but the meeting was short as she slipped in and out of naps. Time had no meaning for her. She had "her" song recorded and listened to it whenever awake. She was definitely where she belonged, "in His Shadow."

Toward the end of the month, while she slept, I began gathering pictures and putting them on a display board for the funeral. I worked in another room, and she never asked what I did when she was sleeping. Other times I began removing her clothes from the closet and putting them in bags in the basement. I didn't want this task left to Brad.

One day, when the closet was mostly empty, he sat on the edge of the bed shaking his head. "It seems like she is disappearing a little each day."

"I know. But her clothes are all in the basement. They have not left here. I will not remove anything."

"It's okay, just a weird feeling. It's so hard to think she will be gone soon." My only answer was a long hug.

Shane and Kelly came for the weekend, and I remember sitting with Shane and asking how he was really doing. With tears brimming his eyes he related how Teri would often stop by his house and ring his doorbell. When he answered she simply said, "I need my bro -hug.". He would scoop her into his arms and give her a bear hug, and after a while she would push back and say, "That's what I needed. Thanks." With no more explanation she would get into her car and drive away. Barely above a whisper he continued, "I really miss that." I ached that I could do nothing to ease his pain. One sister had died, and the other was on the brink. There were no words or actions that could ease that.

As we turned the calendar to August, I thought it was so surreal that Wendy had only been in hospice for two months. It seemed a lifetime. I had to return to Minnesota for an eye shot and again, Brad's mom, Ronnie stepped up to help. Once back in Minnesota, we were swept up into a busy week with appointments. Ashley was having wisdom teeth removed, dinner with friends, and spending time with Karissa and Guy. Soon, very soon, Guy would be taking Ashley off to Mississippi to start her college career. Soon, Karissa would be starting at an Arts High school, and life was moving on for them. It felt like we were floating between worlds. Chaos, excitement, anticipation on one side and pain, waiting, and confusion on the other. I planned to fly to Mississippi to help move Ashley as Guy drove her and her belongings down there. With plans in place, we returned to Illinois.

Daily caring for Wendy was difficult but would have been near impossible without hospice. The most wonderful crew showed up to do so many things for her and us, even advising and encouraging us. These people were a lifeline to us. Gib helped when he could, but her personal care was left to Brad and me.

One day Wendy's pastor came to visit. He stood by her bed and came directly to the point. "Wendy, we need to talk about what you want at your service."

"Mom and I have talked about the music and verses," she replied.

"What message do you want me to give those attending?" he inquired.

"I want you to present the plan of salvation for them." She said without pausing.

Carefully choosing his words he continued. "Since this is a strong, staunch, traditional area, I will share it gently, so I don't offend them."

Suddenly, Wendy's voice was as strong as ever. "OFFEND THEM!" She paused for effect. "I don't want anyone leaving that service without a chance to know Jesus."

A huge smiled passed over the lips of the pastor. "Consider it done! They will hear!"

Content, she smiled and slipped off into sleep.

Each person deals with death or impending death in a different way. That was completely evident in those last days. The summer Olympics began, and Wendy became more alert. She and Quinn watched hours of gymnastics and track events and shouted and lamented over each victory and failure. It was a wonderful bonding time for her with her youngest son. In spite of her condition, she savored every moment.

Casey was having a much greater difficulty handling her condition. He sought to escape the house whenever he could, as he just couldn't handle seeing her frail and in pain. His insides were on fire, and his pain was visible. He tried not to look at her in fear that was the way he would remember her, and he was short with his answers so as not to be caught up in a long conversation. I often heard him taking deep breaths to control his emotions.

Brad continued to care for Wendy with a gentle touch. She wanted him to pack the underarm as he did a better job than the nurse. He never backed away from the smell, the blood, the gross job, and the only time I ever saw it really get him down was one day when she cried from pain as he did it. As soon as he was finished, he headed to his bedroom where I found him on the bed, head in his hands, crying. "I hurt her." He mumbled. "I hurt her."

I reminded him how the job had to be done and how careful he was, but he was broken hearted he had caused her pain. Still, the next day he went right back to doing it again. He tended to all her physical needs no matter how gross, disgusting, or basic they were. I have never before or since seen such a beautiful example of love played out. I was again reminded of the heroes all around me.

Of course, life doesn't exist on just one level. Wendy wasn't the only concern. Brad was struggling, trying to balance work, caring for Wendy's and his own emotions only to get a phone call from his mom that would normally have taken him to the ground. His beloved father, Jerry, had just been told his prostate cancer had metastasized and there was a tumor on his spine. Jerry would soon meet with a specialist and begin radiation treatments. Brad was struggling to focus. But where should he focus? He and Gib made an appointment to meet with the funeral home, and he ordered a beautiful red urn for her ashes. He was trying so hard to face what was coming. Meanwhile, Wendy's body systems appeared to be in transition. Things seemed to be working in slow motion. I was to leave the next day for Mississippi.

However, it wasn't to be. I cancelled my plane trip. Hospice told us Wendy could pass in hours or days, but more likely days. She was young, her body was strong in many ways, and she may linger. I had promised Wendy I would be here at the end, so I couldn't leave. She might pass while I was gone, and I could never face that. I had already missed ushering Teri into eternity. I was determined not to miss that with Wendy. She was alert some in the morning and barely eating. Brad hovered and her sense of humor erupted when she said, "Give me some space." We all laughed that even though she was only awake in short spurts, she was vibrant and alive inside a failing body.

We learned that even as she appeared unconscious, Wendy could still hear us. So, we sang, whispered words of love, and played "her" song. Her resting heartbeat hovered at 130 and shot to over 200 if we moved her. Knowing we couldn't leave her propped on either side, the bedsores developed, and broke the skin into horrible open and seeping abscesses. I could only rejoice that she no longer has feeling so there is no pain. We never told her about them. Once again, the pain was Brad's and mine as we see her body deteriorate. She had no interest in eating, so we watched, loved, and waited. Since school was about to begin, Brad alerted the high school, so they knew what was going on with Quinn.

Brad began compartmentalizing like Gib and I were doing. He had to put his dad on the back burner to be handled later. Ronnie and Jerry met with the specialist, and they were setting up a plan of treatment. There was pain everywhere we looked. Deep in the mire, even there, I could feel strength. God was not pounding on me like a mighty wave, He was not shaking me or demanding I listen. Yet, I knew God's army was praying for all of us. Oddly, it felt tangible. His power surrounded every space in the room. He was there.

Kelly continued to provide good times for Karissa as she stayed with them while Guy made the four-day trip to Mississippi. There was one bright shining star in all of this. Shane's oldest daughter was very, very pregnant. As we were ushering family members into Heaven, we would be ushering a tiny new life into the family. I was eager. I have loved babies since I was tiny, and I looked so forward to a new vibrant life in the midst of this chaos. Shane's kids continued in their normal activities, and I loved hearing about them as it kept me aware that the entire world wasn't in chaos. Guy got back to Minnesota after settling Ashley and spending two days on the road alone. When I asked him if he listened to music or a book to pass the time alone, His answer surprised me. "I listened and talked to God. We had a lot to settle, and it was a great time with Him alone for two days." I understood. What a precious time for him.

One evening both Wendy's dogs began acting strange. The black lab kept pacing and pawing Wendy's bed and the small beagle crawled under the bed and stayed against the wall all evening. Neither would come when we called them. I said, "I wonder if they know something we don't." I had always heard that dogs sense impending death but I said no more. No one responded so we all went to bed leaving Brad in the recliner.

Early morning, Brad stood at our bedroom door speaking in a breathless voice. As I awoke from a fretful sleep, I grasped he was talking to us. He kept saying, "I've been up since 6:15. It is 8:15 and Wendy is still unresponsive. I can't get her awake." As the words sunk in, I rose to say, "We'll be right up." He took off to return and I jumped up to throw clothes on and follow him. Gib wasn't far behind.

We tried to awaken Wendy, but she didn't respond. We could see her chest gently move up and down, but each breath seemed labored and far between. Her hospice care- angel came in the back door planning to bathe her. Casey had left for work and the house was eerily quiet. The dear lady stepped up and began talking to Wendy and gently washing, drying, and massaging her. Brad, Gib, and I slipped into the next room and discussed this new level of nonawareness. Soon, our angel stepped in and asked, "Do you want to turn her so I can bathe her back?"

We rose and went to her bedside. Again, we called to her, touched her, and watched her chest. "Is it still moving?" I asked as I was unable to tell myself.

"Do you have a stethoscope?" Brad asked our helper.

"Yes, in the car," she said as she exited.

Once he had it in his hands, he struggled to find a place where he could hear through the tumor. Finally, he said, "There is a very faint heartbeat, but it is very slow and very weak."

Unknown to us, our angel called the nurse, and she was on the way. Upon her arrival she examined Wendy and asked, "Are both the boys here?"

"No, Casey is at work."

"It is time to call him home, Brad. Now!"

Realizing what she was saying, he grabbed his phone and called Casey telling him he had to come home immediately. I went into the bedroom and got Quinn. Then, we all stood around the bed and watched as the nurse continued checking vitals. Then, Wendy quickly sucked in some air, and all stopped. No movement of her chest. The nurse listened and announced, "**She is gone.**"

Brad and I rushed to the end of the bed and fell into each other's arms. Tears flowed and although we knew this was coming it seemed so unreal. After a minute, I heard a car in the driveway, and I stepped into the garage to face Casey. "She's gone." was all I could manage. Soon he was inside, and he, Brad and Quinn held each other and sobbed.

So, this is what it is like? One moment she is here and the next she is gone? Was she aware? Was she scared? Did an angel or Jesus meet her? Was Teri waiting? I have no idea what I was expecting, but it was so simple, so quiet, so "normal." I picked up Brad's phone and hit the pastor's number. He answered immediately. "Brad?"

"No, it is Tina. She is gone."

"I will be right there." And he was. Before I could even think he was beside Brad and putting his arm around his shoulders, whispering to him. The nurse had noted the time of death and Gib, Casey, Quinn, and I went to sit down in the next room. I had no idea what we were to do now. So, we waited for someone to tell us. Ronnie and Jerry arrived. Finally, I heard the pastor tell Brad they had to notify the funeral home so they could come. Brad nodded and the call was made. The funeral home arrived and only one man entered the home. He approached the pastor and they quietly talked. Then, the pastor turned to Brad and asked, "Are you ready?" Bewildered, Brad only nodded. The other men entered with a gurney and began to start preparing to move her. Pastor made the rounds of everyone in the room speaking to each one and appraising how they were doing. The men pushed the filled gurney through to the front door and Brad followed them with Quinn close behind. Once outside, the Pastor looked up from the others and spotted Brad outside on the driveway. Immediately, he turned and went out also.

"Brad, you know she is no longer there, don't you?" he inquired.

"Yes, but I promised her I would be with her till the end, so I needed to walk her out."

Pastor and Brad stood by the hearse, with Quinn a little behind, as they loaded her in and they watched as it drove down the street. She was gone, truly gone. Both my babies were with the Lord. They had left together. Neither one suffered anymore, but there was a valley so deep and empty inside me it felt like it led to the gates of Evil. Life would never be the same. I had no daughters. Who would I share my dreams and disappointments with? Who would talk to me about makeup, clothes, kids, recipes, etc.? Who would I pass my jewelry too? No holiday would be the same without their laughter. No plans would be easy to make without their input. The reality of the loss of both of them sunk deep inside me. I hadn't lost one daughter; I had lost both. I had the strangest feeling I had been embalmed. I wasn't sure I could stand up and walk. There were quiet voices all around me, but I couldn't comprehend anything they were saying. Where are you now God? Why can't I feel you now? Where is my escape plan now? I waited. I waited. I waited.

I turned to hear Gib speaking to me. "Tina, did you hear me?" I shook my head.

"You need to see if the boys are okay."

I scanned the room. They weren't in sight. I saw Quinn outside with Brad. Again, he was staying near his dad, and I knew he was in his caregiving mode. He would always be there for Brad. But where was Casey? My questioning expression forced Gib to say, "I think he went into his room."

I quietly knocked before entering and found Casey stretched out on his bed with his arm across his face. I simply said. "I have no words. I am just here for you." He nodded and kept his arm across his face. I started to rise, and he touched my arm and pulled me down. So, I sat on his bed for a long time. Neither of us spoke. We just touched and tried to keep breathing. At last, he released my arm, and I got up and left. I knew we would all survive even if things had changed forever. I knew each person would have to face their own demons alone, but we could stand alongside each other. Wendy was gone, but never would she be gone forever. She lived in the hearts of each of us, and the boys were her legacy to the rest of us. There would be a time for grieving and a time of healing, but we would make it!

The next few days were spent making plans, seeing to details, and the many things that had to be done. There were many scheduling conflicts between the church availability, the Pastor's schedule, etc. so her funeral was set for Labor Day Weekend, 11 days away. I needed to return to Minnesota for eye shots. So, five days after she died, after meeting with the pastor to plan the service, Gib and I traveled home for a couple of days. Once back in Illinois, people started arriving. Some driving, flying, and arriving any way they could to be with us, and their love was sustaining us. God had reappeared in many details and my moments of frustrated doubts slipped away.

There was no rain. I missed the rain. I needed the rain. Instead, God poured out his sunshine on us and the warmth sunk deep inside. The day of the funeral arrived, and we had a visitation before the service. So many people came to encourage, share stories, and love. I was so impressed that the hospice team showed up, and they were a joy to my heart. Casey had a surprise visit from many of his friends from college. They had driven from Iowa and even Minnesota to be there. Lifelong friends had driven the six hours to surround us. Our family had flown in from far away, and everyone wished they could lift the burden from us. Friends from both Brad and Wendy's work came to tell us the impact these two had made on their lives. The program turned out beautiful and the service matched. The music was superb. I spoke, then Jerry spoke, and then the Pastor presented Jesus in a beautiful way.

He told the story of a famous tight-rope walker that stretched his rope across Niagara Falls. First, he asked the crowd if they thought he could cross. As they cheered, he crossed and returned. Next, he placed a wheelbarrow on the rope and again asked the crowd if they thought he could push it over and back. Again, the cheers rose, and he crossed and returned. Then, with help from his assistant, he placed a 200-pound rock in the wheelbarrow and questioned the crowd as to what they thought. The crowd crowed, clamored, and cheered until he struggled his way over and back. Finally, he removed the rock and asked simply, "Now, who will get in the wheelbarrow and trust me to take them over and back?" Abruptly, the cheering stopped as the crowd looked from one to another waiting for a volunteer. No one came forward. Finally, the rope walker spoke again. "You believe in your head I can do it, but you don't trust me with your life. So, do you really believe in your heart?"

Pastor continued. "That is what Jesus asks us. We believe He is the Son of God in our head, but do we believe Him in our heart? Are we willing to trust Him with our life enough to get into the wheelbarrow with Him? Do we trust Him completely?"

He closed the service by relating that Wendy trusted Jesus that much. She had given her life to Him and entrusted her eternity to Him. Now, she was in heaven with Him. Finally, he asked us all to bow our heads. He said, "If this is the first time you have had Jesus explained to you in this way and you now understand what He did for you, and you trust Him, would you raise your head and look at me." Later he took me aside and told me he stopped counting at 35. Wendy's life and death had touched so many.

There was a meal at the church following the service and so many took the time to share with us, her parents, the impact Wendy had on them through her life, as well as her process of dying. It was encouraging and thoughtful of them to seek us out and share. Later that evening our out-of-town relatives and Norm and Deb gathered at Brad's parents for a cookout. We shared stories that made us laugh. We shared memories, and it was a positive day as it came to a close. Almost everyone was there.

Except, Elyse- Shane's daughter, was home with a newborn. She was always especially close to Brad, and she wasn't there to hug and support him. Also, she was not there to receive the love and hugs she needed. What a joy when two days after Wendy passed, little Addie burst on the scene reminding us of the circle of life. Now, with a week-old baby she had to stay behind in Minnesota. We missed her!

A day or two after the celebration of Wendy's life, we packed up and headed home. It was such an odd feeling. There was no crisis to return to. We weren't rushing. With little fanfare, we loaded the car and felt empty as we headed home. Now I could cry, but no tears came. We still had a memorial service for friends in Minnesota to prepare, and Brad and the boys would come up for that.

As we drove home, the same emotions that hovered around the car on the way there, were again demanding attention. Grief - was no longer anticipated or needed to be delayed. Now it was reality. Relief - that the girls were together and pain-free and that crisis after crisis was over. Now they both had their Independence Day. They were free of the shackles of this world. No more tears, fears, pain, concerns, or having to be strong. No more self-doubts, ceaseless agony, and bodies that betrayed them. God had shown His love daily in so many ways and I thanked Him. Gratefulness - abounded inside me as I realized we had a God that was so mighty He created the universe but wanted a personal relationship with me. Comfort- flooded over me as I knew He would lead us through the unknown and uncharted days of the future.

We barely caught our breath, been home a couple of days when a high school friend of Gib's was passing through town and we met for breakfast. As we related our saga and he prayed with us, my phone rang. It was Brad and I could barely understand him. "Tina, my dad is unresponsive. He is on the way to the hospital. Please pray." I didn't ask for details, they could come later, but the three of us earnestly prayed for Jerry and the family. It wasn't long when Brad called again with devastating news. Jerry hadn't ever regained consciousness. He had had a massive heart attack and slipped away. Stunned and overwhelmed with sadness for Brad and Ronnie we cried, prayed, and waited for details. Later, we were told Ronnie was driving Jerry and suddenly he was in trouble. She pulled the car to the side of the road and a trucker helped her pull him out. The rest was history. The cancer in his body had put such a strain on it and he just couldn't come back. Seventeen days after Wendy left for Heaven, Jerry had joined her.

The morning of Wendy's memorial in Minnesota came the same morning Brad and his mom held a wake for Jerry. Therefore, Brad and the boys were unable to attend. It was a relatively small group that gathered, and we were able to spend time with dear friends and neighbors. We shared with them Brad's newest tragedy, and we prayed for their family. As it closed, it felt like a door slammed shut. We had been preparing ourselves for the death of Teri for years. For less than three months we had Wendy in hospice and mourned her daily even while she was still alive. Suddenly, we realized we had been in mourning for a very long time. The chasm left in the family would never close, but the girls would live on in our hearts and lives forever. We would share their story and our pathway and our journey and rejoice that they had both been victorious over death. They had passed through it and were with their Savior.

We all face the certainty of death sometime. We also face the unknown future that is constantly changing. Now, we had to learn how to move forward and that would be hard but not impossible since we had our Savior at our side. Our girls had shown such courage and Teri's "God is Big Enough" and Wendy walked in the "Savior's Shadow" and their strength was still flowing through us.

We would go on.

We would remember.

We would hurt.

We were sons and daughters of the King.

We would dance in the rain with our Savior.

We would see them again in the twinkling of an eye.

Wendy Janine Landl

June 15, 1971 - August 23, 2016

Wendy's Memorial Picture

WENDY'S EULOGY

TINA COLEMAN, WENDY'S MOM

First, I want to thank you for taking the time out of your holiday weekend to help us celebrate Wendy's life. We so appreciated your support. I am Tina Coleman, Wendy's mom, and I want to reflect on the life of my youngest child.

Our life with Wendy was amazing. She entered our lives with a bang. We lived in a small French border-town and Wendy was born in Geneva, Switzerland. From the beginning she had to fight to survive. Twice they called a team together to do a complete blood replacement in her body and both times, at the last minute, she fought her way back. We took home a tiny, jaundiced baby that was a fighter. That was the beginning of our lessons in amazement that would last a lifetime.

As a little girl she loved the color red. We would go to buy new shoes and she would only try on red ones. Once in a while, I could convince her to wear black shiny ones I had bought. However, she would put them on and sneak into her bedroom, remove them, and come out with the red ones on, smiling her impish grin as if I wouldn't notice.

She excelled in gymnastics. As a little girl she would stand on the balance beam and her legs were shaking so hard I feared she would shake herself right off the beam. But, by high school she had fought her way onto a top regional team and her performances showed so much confidence on the floor and apparatuses that once again she amazed us.

Wendy had a natural feel for the piano. She didn't love it so she never applied herself in practice. She would be in state contests and make it to the finals without ever knowing the song completely. She was small, her little legs dangling from the bench, and when she made a mistake, she would drop her head, giggle, and then continue. The judge, captivated, would send her on to the next level. Then, the little scamp would do it all over again. Each level, same mistake in the same place, same giggle, same promotion. For her piano teacher and those of us that knew it was no simple mistake, she amazed us.

Wendy was a deeply caring and loving person that usually hid her deepest feeling behind a stoic veneer. She loved laughter and smiled most of the time but avoided deep conversations. Even as a child she would keep her feelings hidden, and one day I told Gib that she wasn't mischievous enough to fit into this family. That same day, I pushed aside the hanging clothes in her closet to discover the back wall covered in crayon pictures. When confronted she simply said, "It must have been Shane, Mommy," (she often tried to blame her older brother)

Wendy rarely wanted to talk aloud about her spiritual walk with her Savior, but she loved the Lord and looked forward to being with Him soon. She accepted Christ as a young girl and Pastor Galen Call baptized her. From that moment on, he was HER pastor. She often asked for prayer not only for herself but for the three men in her life, Brad, Casey, and Quinn. She allowed only a few people to see those "inner" feelings and then only to see small parts of her at a time. She could frustrate her family and friends when she wouldn't open up and tell her thoughts. Still, the depth of love she had for people would be shown in her intense loyalty and concern for others. She was a "mother bear" when it came to her boys. If you made a comment about something they had done, she was so quick to "set you straight" about her boys.

Her best friend since childhood, Charissa, was one of the few that she opened up to. That friendship forged as a child withstood the passage of time and distance and was a comfort to Wendy even until the end. As she began to fight cancer, she slowly allowed certain others to enter that inner circle. One of those was a nurse advocate and friend from church who was always ready to answer questions, explain what was happening, or go to bat when she need help. However, she frustrated her doctors by always being carefree and never admitting side effect until the end days when they were evident in her appearance. She cried very little, but when she did, you knew she was either in great pain or deeply touched. I will always remember

Shane's surprise visit to her and her resting in his arms crying for joy. Her Dad's surprise appearance on her birthday this past June brought tears and strength she needed as she entered surgery. Again, she amazed us.

But the most amazing thing of all was the way she faced the monster, Cancer. A little over 4 ½ years ago we got the call no one wants to receive. "It is Cancer." At first, she was devastated and afraid, but it didn't take long for her to shift into battle readiness, pull up her armor, and take on the "the big C". We all thought she could beat this. But the type of breast cancer Wendy had was so aggressive; it kept reconfiguring itself to fight off the chemo. During those four and a half years she fought through eight chemo rounds, two radiation rounds, six surgeries, a gaping hole under her left arm, indignities to her body, and horrible bed sores. Yet, she fought on, still going to work throughout it all until she could no longer walk. She had attended every event her boys were in whether it was cold, windy, or raining. Her strength seemed endless, and her determination was unfailing. Each time she was knocked down, she got up with more determinations. She told me she often prayed when alone, and that was the source of her strength.

Wendy and her sister, Teri, were completely different personalities. They could laugh together till tears rolled down their faces. Each admired the way the other fought through their problems. They were both saddened by the fact that their own illness prevented them from traveling to be with each other in their darkest days. The hardest day in all this for me was when I had to tell Wendy just six weeks before her death that her sister, Teri, had died. She was broken hearted. However, a few days later she said. "Mom, Teri is waiting for me." Her strength was amazing.

These last few months were so difficult for her and all of us. She had her turn to be amazed at the love of others. Wendy's work family, Brad's work family, and their church supported them with love and concern though tangible gifts, food, visits, texts, and hugs. Wendy was amazed at those examples of love.

One of the most amazing things through all of this was Brad. His display of caring was the most beautiful example of love I have ever seen put into action. Even though it broke his heart to do things to her that hurt her, he pushed on, enduring, and lovingly tending to her needs. She amazed him by looking up into his face and smiling with deep love in her eyes. Until the very end she wanted to stay involved in her boys' lives. She wanted to know what they were doing, who they were with, and how they would do when she left this world. Her three men, Brad, Casey, and Quinn were all she concerned herself with. Slowly, with prompting from Brad, us, and the Holy Spirit, she gained comfort in the fact that Jesus would take care of her men. Then, and only then, she had the peace to let go. She was amazing.

So, as we go through the coming weeks and months and attempt to face our lives without her physical presence, my hope is that each of us remember her with amazement and accept the challenge she set before us. She taught us so much. She taught us to be amazed. She lived each day like it was a gift she wanted to enjoy. Still, her smile will always be only a thought away for us. I take solace in the fact that now, she is with her sister, Teri, in Paradise, feeling no pain and soaking in the light of her Savior. We are confident that our amazing gal awaits us and soon, very soon, we will see her again.

WENDY'S EULOGY

JERRY LANDL, FATHER-IN-LAW

Hello, I'm Jerry Landl, Brad's dad and half of Wendy's in-law parents that have shared Brad and Wendy's life here in Antioch. My wife Ronnie and I have experienced many interesting moments during that time, and it is perfectly fitting to share some of those special Wendy episodes with you.

Wendy was in our family for 22 1/2 years. She and Brad moved here after their marriage in January of 1994. During the next few years, we helped them move into their first apartment in Lake Villa, and two subsequent houses in Antioch. We learned quickly that Wendy was <u>a girl</u> of few words, but you could always <u>tell</u> her mood by the look on her face. We can remember the big smile she had when she brought home her first pet, Sambuca the cat. That cat was the first of several animals that came to join the Landl family over the years. **Wendy loved her pets.** Every time the family would go near a pet store they had to stop and see all the puppies.

When house one came along, it required some redecorating, and naturally it needed a dog to keep Sambuca company. Welcome to Carmel, a cute little Cocker Spaniel that Wendy thought was the <u>only</u> dog breed that could be considered. He now became a playful and fluffy creature in their house. As the next house came along, so did Middy, a large black lab. About a year later came Breezy, a little beagle. These two animals were a constant comfort to Wendy during the last few years and especially these last few months. As much as she loved them, it was obvious they loved her just as much. An annual family experience was watching the Westminster Dog Show. It didn't matter who won, all the dogs were winners in Wendy's eyes.

The lights of her life were her three boys. Her husband Brad, Casey who was born in 1997 and Quinn in 1999. The animals took a bit of a back seat to the boys, but Wendy knew how to include them as they all had fun together. As the boys grew, they started to participate in many sports. They played baseball, iceless hockey and eventually football and track. Even during her treatments with Chemo and radiation, even if it was raining, cold. or windy she and Brad would sit in the bleachers to cheer their boys on. No matter what, she would be there. Even though she was very athletic in high school, once she was married, she would rather watch sports than participate in them. Aside from watching the boys, the Blackhawks were her favorite team, and she had a thing for Duncan Keith. We never told Brad though.

We were all able to enjoy Sunday dinners on a weekly basis, and as the boys grew, we thought it best to include some games around the table and have some family fun. We would pick games like Scattegories, Catch Phrase, and Trivial Pursuit.

Wendy wasn't much of a game player, but if Apples to Apples was the choice, she was all in. Laughter filled the house on many of those days.

Wendy loved the flowers that she and Brad planted outside their home and couldn't wait for Spring to come every year so they could get started. We're sure that planting tradition will continue next year and many thereafter.

She is now with God and enjoying the company of her sister Teri, Aunt Jinkers, and many others that have been waiting patiently to meet and welcome her. For all of us, the fact that we had the opportunity to know her and love her, see her determination and strength, just made us all better people.

EPILOGUE

I have heard the old saying that life is for the living. I wasn't sure if we were even living except, we could feel pain. What was our new normal to be? We were in new territory and there was no game plan laid out. When I thought about the past eight months, I couldn't remember them as individual days. Instead of days, they were one medical event after another. Yet, oddly, most of those events weren't remembered as painful, but as rays of hope in the darkness. Most of all I remember being held in the upturned hand of God and riding out the storm or being lifted above it all on prayers of others. We had loved and that love had brought pain. The moment each girl had been placed in our arms, Gib and I chose to love no matter the outcome. We had almost half a century to bask in that love. So, we could definitely say it was worth it.

One day my life-long friend, Joan, handed me a large envelope. It was heavy with paper, and I asked her what it was. She simply said, "All the emails you sent since the girls got sick." Astonished, I had trouble speaking. She continued, "I thought you might want them when you write a book."

It took a minute before I could respond. "What makes you think I am going to write a book?"

"I know you started one years ago when Teri was little. Now you have the ending. The story is one that just needs to be told."

She was right. The story needed to be shared. God had sustained us through so much, showed His love and direction through so many people, and others needed to see His glory. Yes, years before I had started a book about Teri, so I had all the conversations from then already written. Now I had the documented ending. I only needed to document the middle. But I wasn't ready yet. Time needed to heal the open sores. I needed time to put it all in perspective.

Meanwhile, I was struggling with grieving two loses at once. I wanted to grieve one at a time. It was overwhelming me that I couldn't show each girl honor alone. Finally, a friend gave me an idea that worked. On even days of the month, I would ponder Teri's life, mourn her and rejoice she was with Jesus. The odd days of the month would be "Wendy" days and I did the same for her. That allowed me to honor each daughter as I felt she deserved. After the first few months, I no longer needed them separated, and I could switch my thoughts between them rapidly. But, at the beginning, this relieved my frustration.

Next, I found I had turned my tears off so much that when I wanted to cry now, I couldn't. I had been repressing emotions for so long that it had become automatic. I knew in my head that tears have a real purpose from simply cleaning the eyes to releasing built up toxins and reducing physical and mental discomfort. Yet, I only seemed able to cry at a television show or a movie. I actually sat in my bedroom and tried to make myself sad enough to cry. Finally, after struggling for weeks with guilt that I wasn't crying for my daughters, I came to realize that I had spilt the tears as I watched them suffer and was helpless to do anything for them. Now, they were fine. Now I was fine because I had released them into the arms of their Savior. I no longer needed to cry, I needed to live. My journey wasn't over. I had to embark on a new season of life. There would be other deaths I would have to face, others I would have to let go. But God was leading my journey and I loved having Him in the driver's seat. There was a bit of mystery about tomorrow. I was learning to live with anticipation of new lessons I had to learn.

We embarked on some much-needed trips. First, we went to Illinois to celebrate Brad's father's life, and spend time with Brad and the boys. Next, to Iowa to see Will inducted into the Hall of Fame at the college he attended in Iowa. He is so gifted in music, singing, playing, composing, and arranging. We thought we could use a little getting "puffed" up over his accomplishments. It was such a joyful weekend, and I again thanked him for his love of Teri and his gift of "her" song. I needed time with my sister, so we flew to California to spend time with my sister, Patricia, and Newell. It was much needed as we hadn't had time to really visit at either funeral. Finally, in November we chose to go to Jackson, Mississippi, to spend Thanksgiving with Ashley. The three of us traveled to New Orleans and spent the long weekend investigating that vibrant city. We loved the music, the museums, and the history that engulfs that city.

We joined a grief-share group, but quickly realized we were already far down the steps of grief. With Teri's constant decline over the last 15 years and Wendy's 3 months in hospice, God had been allowing us to mourn them even before their departure. He prepared us as best He could, so when the final event came, we were leaning on Him. Still, sometimes pain "hit" like a pounding or beating, yet other times it seemed surreal. I often felt numb and did only what was required of me. There were occasional "panic attacks" when we would realize we would never see the girls in their physical bodies again. Almost as quickly, the assurance that we would be reunited soon would replace the panic. We closed out the year with Brad and the boys coming for Christmas. When it got overwhelming, we would just hug whoever was nearby and go on.

Time appeared to be passing in a normal pattern until the next summer. My brother, Carl, called on Wendy's birthday. Following greetings, he simply asked, "How can I learn to live with leukemia?" I tried not to show the emotion that was pounding in my heart and brain. Once off the phone I ran through the house yelling at God. "NO! Not another one. NO! God, I am not strong enough to do this again. Stop it now, please!" Once I became quiet, God reminded me that He was my sovereign God and that meant nothing happened without His knowledge and allowance. I knew I didn't have the answers for Carl, but I did know the One who did. I flew to Oklahoma to be with him and Cheryl multiple times, and while he fought valiantly, we made memories of being together. He could be a rascal, a clown, a solid supporter, and he was always able to make me laugh. He had a gentle and caring side he usually tried to hide, but it began showing up often. Sometimes he would do the unexpected, but I always knew he would be there if I needed him. In the end, he lost the battle and he too, left us behind to miss him. Now, Gib and I had both lost our brothers. Carl had no children but at least he left me his wife, Cheryl, whom I love like a sister. We had so many loved ones awaiting us in heaven, it seemed closer than ever.

One day late in Carl's battle, I was visiting him in the hospital when my phone rang. Surprisingly it was Quinn. "Granny have you heard about Casey?" That brought me to full attention. He related that Casey had been in a serious car wreck, and at least had a broken leg and a concussion and he was awaiting surgery. I immediately called Brad for more details. As the story was revealed to me I found a corner of the hospital and sank to the floor to listen. The paramedics had found both occupants of the car unresponsive. They performed CPR on both. The young people recovered quickly and the other one asked the paramedics where the lady was that stood beside the car and kept telling them to hang on. The police searched the crowd and discovered no one had neared the car for fear it would explode. No one had stood by the window. At the same time other paramedics were questioning Casey if he knew where he was. He related to them that he had been high in the sky, going up when he had to come back down.

Brad asked a simple question. "Tina, do you think they were surrounded by angels."

I responded quickly, "Oh yes, I definitely do! They have been given a second chance at life."

I think their encounter affected all the rest of us more than Casey. He wasn't ready yet to acknowledge God's hand on his life. Both young people endured surgeries and rehab and we watched them shortly return to life as usual. I wondered what God would have to do to get Casey's attention.

Along about that time, I was asked if I was angry with God for taking my girls. I replied to them, that on the contrary, I had been allowed to see the true sovereignty of my Father. They asked for an explanation.

I told them that I have walked through the valleys and climbed the mountain tops with God. He has shared His presence, love, and comfort with me. However, I didn't grasp the complete sovereignty of God until I watched the last breath leave Wendy's body. At that moment I remembered Teri was waiting for her sister. Wendy was not afraid to be dead, only the process of dying. She wondered what those first seconds or minutes would be like. Would Jesus meet her, or an angel? Once she heard Teri's promise, all that changed. Wendy would not be alone even for a split second. She needed that reassurance and God had given it to her. Teri, on the other hand, was more than ready to pass into Heaven and only wanted to ease her little sister. Therefore, God had allowed her to go first. His supreme authority, his sovereignty, was most evident to me at that moment. He had prepared each girl with what they needed. Sure, they were too young, they would miss major events in their kids' lives, and we would miss them. I didn't know why He allowed them to go, but I submitted and trusted my personal God. I spent my entire life watching Him do extraordinary things in my life. He had met my every need when I allowed Him too, and now He met my daughters' needs. I saw His Lordship and authority in creation, in highs and lows of my life and I discovered He was worthy of my trust, my life, and my worship. Death is a part of this fallen world. Yet, His plan wasn't that originally. Each daughter had a deeply personal relationship with the God of the Universe. I don't understand the mysteries of the Almighty. I believe He was in control and even in my confusion, frustration, and pain, I saw how He had proven His love and direction for me over and over again. I trust Him and Teri and Wendy did too. I don't need the answers. He holds them as well as holding my daughters. Simply put, we are the **Daughters of the King** and trust Him to lead.

I have no idea if my answer satisfied the questioner. However, I felt privileged to have seen the presence of God. Now, I eagerly await a face-to-face meeting when He calls me to Heaven too.

One beautiful thing God did for us was allow us to see the impact Teri and Wendy had on others. We were inundated with emails, letters, and phone calls as people reached out to share their own journeys. We heard of failing marriages that were strengthened as they reappraised their lives. We heard of things the girls had said that challenged and strengthened others. We heard of difficult discussions that took place and healed relationships because of what they had seen in one of the girls. However, the most precious result started with a surprise phone call from my niece, Lindy, asking if she could come spend the weekend with us. Thrilled, we met her plane, and the conversations quickly became serious. She wanted us to tell her about our faith. She said she saw something in us she didn't have. and she wanted us to tell her about it. For two days the three of us talked, cried, shared, and many seeds were planted in her heart. We placed her on the plane home in the hands of the Holy Spirit.

Within a few days she had joined a Bible Study on the basics. A few weeks into it, she called perplexed. "I don't think I can wait until January."

Confused, I asked, "What happens in January?"

"We cover what we believe about Jesus. I already know what I believe.

I know He is the Son of God and died for me. I know I want Him as my Savior, and I don't want to wait until January."

Before I could take a deep breath, Gib responded. "Lindy, you don't have to wait until the Bible Study gets there. You can accept Christ right now."

I jumped in with, "You can do it right now on the phone. Do you want me to pray a prayer and you repeat after me?"

"No, I want to try it myself."

Immediately she began to pray with earnestness from the depths of her heart. She repented of her sinful life, acknowledged she need reconciliation with Him, praised Jesus for sacrificing His life for her, and she wanted Him to be her Lord and Savior. She invited Him to come into her heart.

Silence followed except for sobs from all three of us.

Quietly she continued, "Was that, okay?"

Gib and I responded almost in unison. "Not only was it okay, but it was also beautiful. Welcome to the family of God!" We all three laughed, rejoiced, and I told her she was to tell someone right away.

"Tell someone? I want to run down the street shouting it."

What joy. The angels were dancing in Heaven. Teri's and Wendy's lives had impacted their cousin, and we had been allowed to share this eternal moment with her. Now, not only were we related in human blood, but in the precious blood of Jesus. Thank you, Lord for allowing us to experience this moment. God is so good. He is good all the time.

Since then, time continues marching as we hurry to keep up. The girls' families have grown and stretched their horizons. Teri's daughter, Ashley graduated with her bachelor's degree and is now completing her master's degree again in Mississippi. She loves classical literature and is a wonderful writer. Karissa is completing college this spring. Her major is business with a marketing emphasis. She loves people and will be a great manager. The future looks bright for both of them as they try to decide what direction God is leading in their lives.

Wendy's oldest son, Casey, tattooed his mother's birthdate on his chest so she would always be with him. A couple of years after his car accident, he faced another trauma that forced him to reappraise his life. Since then, he had found his niche as a salesman and is successfully enjoying that career. He had been top salesman many months. Quinn is completing his college education this spring. His business major focuses on finance. He has applied himself and is a top student. Both boys are joys, teasers, and maturing into great men.

Each of the four kids have passed through multiple emotions from grief, anger, and acceptance, to living with memories. They have unique personalities, yet I see the stamp of their mothers clearly displayed on the lives of each of them. The girls left fantastic legacies in their children.

Brad has remarried a lovely lady, Shana, and we are thrilled to see him happy. They are a good match and she got herself a good man! We do not love her as a replacement for Wendy. Instead, we love her for herself, her positive approach to life, the happiness she brings Brad, the down-to -earth advise she offers him and her love and concern of the boys. It's extra special since she loves us too.

Guy's first commitment is his girls. His outside interests include Bible studies and pickleball, and it is hard to get him off the pickleball court. We pray for a woman to enter his world with a bang. We don't want him going through life alone. He is deeply committed to God, and we have faith God will direct his paths. Both sons-in-law seem more like sons. The "in-law" term doesn't convey the love and respect we have for both of them. They were perfect spouses for our daughters and fantastic dads. They will forever belong to us.

Most of Shane's family live nearby and we see them often. The Coleman Clan expanded when their son, Shane Vincent, married Krista. She is a bundle of giggles, intelligence, and fun to spend the evening with. Shane Vincent's mathematical head has led him to study to become a CPA and I have no doubt he will accomplish this immediately. Elyse is a writer and has a good job and she and Addie (who is six now) are lovers of the outdoors, and hike and take "adventures" weekly. Destiny and Josiah have moved to Oregon and are loving the West. I only wish they were closer in distance as they are a delight to be around. All the kids are chasing their own dreams and we watch their adventures with anticipation and delight. Shane and Kelly continue to flourish. We are careful to not make too many demands on them as now he is an only child. Kelly has proven her grit, love, and perseverance in everything she does, and they are happy and content. She is truly a daughter that we love deeply. Like all families, not everyone is walking with the Lord. Our prayers are continual, and our Lord is listening.

They say time heals all wounds. I guess I would agree with that to a certain extent. The landscape of our family is forever changed. We miss the girls daily.

As time passes, the pain is lessening, and most memories now bring joy instead of pain. Gib and I have learned so many lessons from trials. We cannot imagine life without each other, yet we know one of us will experience that. Someone recently said that they couldn't imagine how I could have made it through all this without a wonderful husband. Gib was a rock, supporter, lover, and friend. He is a very special man and a gift to me from God. He has supported me physically, emotionally, and spiritually. I lean on him for so much and can't imagine a day without him. However, the one person I could never have made this journey without is Jesus. He was and is the most important gift from God. My Father saw to it that I had a piece of Him at all times with the Holy Spirit to live in me. That is why I came through this standing up. Every person has their own journey, doubts, reassurances, and decisions. I pray my journey of faith will remind you that you don't have to travel this journey alone. Our Triune God is there with you. The Father, the Savior, and the Spirit walk with you and angels surround you. Be encouraged! Know that nothing is too difficult with this army on your side. Peace awaits you even in the midst of terrible pain and agony. There are surprise blessings God wants to pour out on you if you will only allow Him to.

Recently, it began to rain. Previous to all this, I would have been annoyed at the inconvenience it caused. Instead, I found myself sitting and staring out the window and smiling. The rain was gentle, washing the earth, and cleansing my soul. There was some thunder and lightning as God showed off His power, but the rain danced on the deck outside the sliding glass door. I remembered Wendy saying the popping rain looked like frogs jumping. Then, I thought of that day in Kenya when I watched Teri dance in the rain. I know water can be destructive and floods destroy lives. This too, is a part of life. While others may experience the trauma of violent and rushing water, I pray they will come out downstream with an appreciation of our powerful Lord and seek Him as they rebuild. I have learned to not wait for the storm to pass but to dance in the rain. God had shown me firsthand His mighty power, strength, and sustaining love. Never again would I dislike the rain. Instead, I would dance.

I don't want you to just learn to dance in the rain. I want you to see what extraordinary things our God can do with and for a very ordinary person. He can do the same for you if you let Him. He is Almighty and I am so thankful He taught me to dance in the rain. The harder it pours, the harder I dance.

I will forever dance in the rain for my Abba, Father.

Dancing in the Rain

HELPFUL BIBLE VERSES FOR EACH CHAPTER

Chapter 1: Genesis 22; Psalm 94:22, 150:1-6; Proverbs 19:20; Isaiah 45:8; Matthew 6:19-24,33

Chapter 2: Psalm 8:2; Isaiah 11:6, 54:13; Matthew 18:10; Luke 18:16, I Thessalonians 5:23-24

Chapter 3: Psalm 95:1-4, 121:1-2; Proverbs 2:6, 3:12, 13:24, 21:15; Philippians 4:6

Chapter 4: Genesis 15; Joshua 1:9; Psalm 46:10; Jeremiah 17:7-8; I Corinthians 10:12; James 1:2-4

Chapter 5: Psalm 51:2, 54:4, 91:1-2; Proverbs 20:11; John 15:7; Romans 8:31; Hebrews 10:23

Chapter 6: Joshua 1:9; Psalm 13:1-2; Isaiah 41:10; Matthew 6:34; John 14:27

Chapter 7: Psalm 27:3; Proverbs 15:13; Romans 7:19, 8:37-39; Philippians 4:6-7, 11-13

Chapter 8: Job 5:20; Ecclesiastes 3:1-5; Joel 2:23; Philippians 4:6-7,11-12

Chapter 9: Jeremiah 29:11; 2 Corinthians 12:9-10; Hebrews 11:1; James 1:17; I John 1:8

Chapter 10: Psalm 34:7, 91: 94;22, 127:3; Romans 8:26-28; Hebrews 1:14

Chapter 11: I Samuel 1:27; Proverbs 11:2; Matthew 18:3; John 1:12-13; Romans 8:28-29; 2 Corinthians 11:30; Galatians 3:3, 6:4; Ephesians 2:8-9; Hebrews 11:6

Chapter 12: Psalm 91:1-16; 136:1-26; 149:3; Matthew 10:7; Mark 16:15; Romans 10:15

Chapter 13: Psalm 55:22; Romans 8:28; 2 Corinthians 12:9; Philippians 3:8. 4:13,19

Chapter 14: Psalm 73:23,139:9-10; Isaiah 32:2, 40:31,41:10-13, 49:16; Lamentations 3:25

Chapter 15: Psalm 71:14; Proverbs 12:15, 15:22; Isaiah 40:31; Hosea 12:6; James 1:12, 5:7,37:7

Chapter 16: Deuteronomy 2:7, 32:6; Psalm 91:11-12; Proverbs 3:23; Galatians6:2

Chapter 17: Numbers 15:38-41; Isaiah 43:2; Romans 8:18; 2 Corinthians 4:16-18; Philippians 3:13

Chapter 18: Exodus 17:8-15; Matthew 6:3; I Corinthians2:14, 13:12; Philippians 4:8-9; Hebrews 11:1; James 1:2, 12; Psalm 27

Chapter 19: Proverbs 3:5-6; Isaiah 41:10; Jeremiah 29:11, Philippians 4:6-7; James 1: 5; I Peter 5:7

Chapter 20: Psalm 94:1-3, 121:1-2; 2 Chronicles 20:15; Matthew 19:26; Revelation 6:10

Chapter 21: 2 Samuel 22:3; Psalm 9:9; John 8:32; Romans 12:2; 2 Corinthians 10:3-5; Ephesians 6:12-13; Hebrews 11:1; James 4:7; I Peter 5:8

Chapter 22: Psalm 119:71; Luke 14:27; Romans 8:18; 2 Corinthians 4:17; James 1:2-4, 12; I Peter 5:10; Isaiah 25:8; I Corinthians 15: 55-58

Chapter 23: John 11:25; Romans 5:3, 8:38-39; I Corinthians 15:50-57; I Thessalonians 4:16-17; 2 Corinthians 5:1; Revelation 21:4

Epilogue: Joshua 24:15; Psalms 18:2; Isaiah 40:29-31; Romans 15:13; I Thessalonians 5:16-18

Daughter and Heir: John 1:12; Romans 8:14-17; 2 Corinthians 6:18; Galatians 4:5; Colossians 1:2; John 3:1

Dance: Psalm 149:3; 150:1-6

Rain: Job 5:10; Psalm 68:8, 72:6; 147:8; Isaiah 45:8, 55:10; Jeremiah 10:13, 51:16; Joel 2:23; Zechariah 10:1

Printed in the United States
by Baker & Taylor Publisher Services